Business and Legal Forms

for

Authors

and Self-Publishers

Tad Crawford

Third Edition

Allworth Press, New York

04 03 02 01 00 99   8 7 6 5 4 3

Published by Allworth Press, an imprint of Allworth Communications, Inc., 10 East 23rd Street, New York, NY 10010.

Book design by Douglas Design Associates, New York, NY.

Library of Congress Cataloging-in-Publication Data

Crawford, Tad, 1946–
Business and legal forms for authors and self-publishers/Tad Crawford.—3rd ed.
    p.   cm.
Includes index.
ISBN 1-58115-395-3 (pbk.)
   1. Authors and publishers—United States—Forms. I. Title.

KF3084.A65C73 2004
343.73'07807052—dc22   2004022586

Printed in Canada

Table of Contents

The Success Kit

Attaining the knowledge of good business practices and implementing their use is an important step toward success for any professional, including the professional author. The forms contained in this book deal with the most important business transactions that an author is likely to undertake. The forms on a CD-ROM are also included to make customization easier. The fact that the forms are designed for use and that they favor the author give them a unique value.

Understanding the business concepts behind the forms is as important as using them. By knowing why a certain provision has been included and what it accomplishes, the author is able to negotiate when faced with someone else's business form. The author knows what is and is not desirable. The negotiation checklists offer a map for the negotiation of any form.

All forms, whether the author's or someone else's, can be changed. Before using these forms, the author should consider reviewing them with his or her attorney. This provides the opportunity to learn whether local or state laws may make it worthwhile to modify any of the provisions. For example, would it be wise to include a provision for arbitration of disputes, or are the local courts speedy and inexpensive, making an arbitration provision unnecessary?

The forms must be filled out, which means that the blanks in each form must be completed. Beyond this, however, the author can always delete or add provisions on any form. Deletions or additions to a form are usually initialed in the margin by both parties. It is also a good practice to have each party initial each page of the contract, except the page on which the parties sign.

The author must ascertain that the person signing the contract has authority to do so. If the author is dealing with a company, the company's name should be included, as well as the name of the individual authorized to sign the contract and the title of that individual. If it isn't clear who will sign or if that person has no title, the words "Authorized Signatory" can be used instead of a title.

If the author will not be meeting with the other party to sign the contract, it would be wise to have that party sign the forms first. After the author gets back the two copies of the form, they can be signed and one copy returned to the other party. As discussed in more detail under letter contracts, this has the advantage of not leaving it up to the other party to decide whether to sign and thus make a binding contract.

If additional provisions that won't fit on the contract forms should be added, simply include a provision stating, "This contract is subject to the provisions of the rider attached hereto and made a part hereof." The rider is simply another piece of paper, which would be headed "Rider to the contract between _____ and _____, dated the ____ day of _____, 20____." The additional provisions are put on this sheet and both parties sign it.

Contracts and Negotiation

Most of the forms in this book are contracts. A contract is an agreement that creates legally enforceable obligations between two or more parties. In making a contract, each party gives something of value to the other party. This is called the exchange of consideration. Consideration can take many forms, including the giving of money or writing or the promise to create writing or pay for writing in the future.

Contracts require negotiation. The forms in this book are favorable to the author, so changes may be requested. This book's explanation of the use of each form should help the author evaluate changes either party may want to make in any of the forms. The negotiation checklists should also clarify what changes would be desirable in forms presented to the author.

Keep in mind that negotiation need not be adversarial. Certainly the author and the other party may disagree on some points, but the basic transaction is something that both want. This larger framework of agreement must be kept in mind at all times when negotiating. Of course, the author must also know which points are nonnegotiable and be prepared to walk away from a deal if satisfaction cannot be had on these points.

When both parties have something valuable to offer each other, it should be possible for each side to come away from the negotiation feeling that they have won. Win–win negotiation requires each side to make certain that the basic needs of both are met so that the result is fair. The author cannot negotiate for the other side, but a wise negotiation strategy must allow the other side to meet their vital needs within a larger context that also allows the author to obtain what he or she must have.

It is a necessity to evaluate negotiating goals and strategy before conducting any negotiations. The author should write down what must be achieved and what can be conceded or modified. The author should try to imagine how the shape of the contract will affect the future business relationship with the other party. Will it probably lead to success for both sides and more business or will it fail to achieve what one side or the other desires?

When negotiating, the author should keep written notes close at hand concerning goals and strategy. Notes should be kept on the negotiations, too, since many conversations may be necessary before final agreement is reached. At certain points the author should compare what the negotiations are achieving with the original goals. This will help evaluate whether the author is conducting the negotiations according to plan.

Most negotiations are done over the telephone. This makes the telephone a tool to be used wisely. The author should decide when to speak with the other party. Before calling, it is important to review the notes and be familiar with the points to be negotiated. If the author wants the other party to call, the file should be kept close at hand so that there is no question as to where the negotiations stand when the call comes. If the author is unprepared to negotiate

when the other side calls, the best course is to call back. Negotiation demands the fullest attention and complete readiness.

Oral Contracts

Although all the forms in this book are written, the question of oral contracts should be addressed. There are certain contracts that must be written, such as a contract for services that will take more than one year to perform or a contract to transfer an exclusive right of copyright (an exclusive right means that no one else can do what the person receiving that right of copyright can do). So—without delving into the full complexity of this subject—certain contracts can be oral. If the author is faced with a breached oral contract, an attorney should certainly be consulted for advice. The author should not give up simply because the contract was oral.

However, while some oral contracts are valid, a written contract is always best. Even people with the most scrupulous intentions do not always remember exactly what was said or whether a particular point was covered. Disputes, and litigation, are far more likely when a contract is oral rather than written. That likelihood is another reason to make the use of written forms, like those in this book, an integral part of the business practices of any author.

Letter Contracts

If the author feels that sending a well-drafted form will be daunting to the other party, the more informal approach of a letter, signed by both parties, may be adopted. In this case, the forms in this book will serve as valuable checklists for the content and negotiation of the letter contract. The last paragraph of the letter would read, "If the foregoing meets with your approval, please sign both copies of this letter beneath the words AGREED TO to make this a binding contract between us." At the bottom of the letter would be the words AGREED TO with the name of the other party so he or she can sign. Again, if the other party is a company, the company name, as well as the name of the authorized signatory and that individual's title, would be placed beneath the words AGREED TO. This would appear as follows:

AGREED TO:
XYZ Corporation

By_____
Alice Hall, Vice President

Two copies of this letter are sent to the other party, who is instructed to sign both copies and return one copy for the author to keep. To be cautious, the author can send the letters unsigned and ask the other party to sign and return both copies, at which time the author will sign and return one copy to the other party. This gives the other party an opportunity to review the final draft, but avoids a situation in which the other party may choose to delay signing, thereby preventing the author from offering a similar contract to anyone else because the first contract still may be signed.

For example, if an investment group wanted to wait and see if they could license rights they were contracting to buy in a book, they might hold the contract and only sign it after they knew they could sell the license. If the sale of the license did not come through, they might not sign the contract and the deal would be off. The author can avoid this by being the final signatory, by insisting that both parties meet to sign, or by stating in the letter a deadline by which the other party must sign. If such a situation ever arises, it should be remembered that any offer to enter into a contract can always be revoked up until the time that the contract is actually entered into.

Standard Provisions

The contracts in this book contain a number of standard provisions, called "boilerplate" by lawyers. These provisions are important, although they will not seem as exciting as the provisions that relate more directly to the author and the writing. Since these provisions can be used in almost every contract and appear in a number of the contracts in this book, an explanation of each of the provisions is given here.

Amendment. Any amendment of this Agreement must be in writing and signed by both parties.

This guarantees that any changes the parties want will be made in writing. It avoids the possibility of one party relying on oral changes to the agreement. Courts will rarely change a written contract based on testimony that there was an oral amendment of the contract.

Arbitration. All disputes arising under this Agreement shall be submitted to binding arbitration before _____ in the following location _____ and shall be settled in accordance with the rules of the American Arbitration Association. Judgment upon the arbitration award may be entered in any court having jurisdiction thereof. Notwithstanding the foregoing, either party may refuse to arbitrate when the dispute is for a sum of less than $_____.

Arbitration can offer a quicker and less expensive way to settle disputes than litigation. However, the author would be wise to consult a local attorney and make sure that this is advisable in the jurisdiction where the lawsuit would be likely to take place. The arbitrator could be the American Arbitration Association or some other person or group that both parties trust. The author would also want the arbitration to take place where he or she is located. If small claims court is easy to use in the jurisdiction where the author would have to sue, it might be best to have the right not to arbitrate if the disputed amount is small enough to be brought into the small claims court. In this case, the author would put the maximum amount that can be sued for in small claims court in the space at the end of the paragraph.

Assignment. This Agreement shall not be assigned by either party hereto, provided that the Author shall have the right to assign monies due to the Author hereunder.

By not allowing the assignment of a contract, both parties can have greater confidence that the stated transactions will be between the original parties. Of course, a company may be purchased by new owners. If the author only wanted to do business with the people who owned the company when the contract was entered into, change of ownership might be stated as a ground for termination in the contract. On the other hand, money is impersonal and there is no reason why the author should not be able to assign the right to receive money.

Bankruptcy or Insolvency. If the Publisher should become insolvent or if a petition in bankruptcy is filed against the Publisher or a Receiver or Trustee is appointed for any of the Publisher's assets or property, or if a lien or attachment is obtained against any of the Publisher's assets, this Agreement shall immediately terminate and the Publisher shall transfer to the Author all rights in the Author's writing, including but not limited to all rights of copyright therein.

This provision seeks to protect the author against the publisher's business failure. However, the bankruptcy laws can tie up books with publishers that have failed. The author must carefully review the financial strength of any potential publisher.

Complete Understanding. This Agreement constitutes the entire and complete understanding between the parties hereto, and no obligation, undertaking, warranty, representation, or covenant of any kind or nature has been made by either party to the other to induce the making of this Agreement, except as is expressly set forth herein.

This provision is intended to prevent either party from later claiming that any promises or obligations exist except those shown in the written contract. A shorter way to say this is, "This Agreement constitutes the entire understanding between the parties hereto."

Cumulative Rights. All rights, remedies, obligations, undertakings, warranties, representations, and covenants contained herein shall be cumulative and none of them shall be in limitation of any other right, remedy, obligation, undertaking, warranty, representation, or covenant of either party.

This means that a benefit or obligation under one provision will not be made less because of a different benefit or obligation under another provision.

Death or Disability. In the event of the Author's death, or an incapacity of the Author making completion of the Work impossible, this Agreement shall terminate.

A provision of this kind leaves a great deal to be determined. Will payments already made be kept by the author or the author's estate? And who will own the work at whatever stage of completion has been reached? These issues should be resolved when the contract is negotiated.

Force Majeure. If either party hereto is unable to perform any of its obligations hereunder by reason of fire or other casualty, strike, act or order of a public authority, act of God, or other cause beyond the control of such party, then such party shall be excused from such performance during the pendancy of such cause. In the event such inability to perform shall continue longer than ____ days, either party may terminate this Agreement by giving written notice to the other party.

This provision covers events beyond the control of the parties, such as a tidal wave or a war. Certainly the time to perform the contract should be extended in such an event. There may be an issue as to how long an extension should be allowed. Also, if work has commenced and some payments have been made, the contract should cover what happens in the event of termination. Must the payments be returned? And who owns the partially completed work?

Governing Law. This Agreement shall be governed by the laws of the State of_____.

Usually the author would want the laws of his or her own state to govern the agreement, unless a particular state had enacted laws favoring authors.

Liquidated Damages. In the event of a failure to deliver by the due date, the agreed upon damages shall be $ _____ for each day after the due date until delivery takes place, provided the amount of damages shall not exceed $_____.

Liquidated damages are an attempt to anticipate in the contract what damages will be caused by a breach of the contract. Such liquidated damages must be reasonable. If they are not, they will be considered a penalty and held to be unenforceable.

Modification. This Agreement cannot be changed, modified, or discharged, in whole or in part, except by an instrument in writing, signed by the party against whom enforcement of any change, modification, or discharge is sought.

This requires that a change in the contract must be written and signed by the party against whom the change will be enforced. It should be compared with the provision for amendments that requires any modification to be in writing and signed by both parties. At the least, however, this provision explicitly avoids the claim that an oral modification has been made of a written contract. Almost invariably, courts will give greater weight to a written document than to testimony about oral agreements.

Notices and Changes of Address. All notices shall be sent to the Author at the following address:_____ and to the Publisher at the following address: _____. Each party shall be given written notification of any change of address prior to the date of said change.

Contracts often require the giving of notice. This provision facilitates giving notice by providing correct addresses and requiring notification of any change of address.

Successors and Assigns. This Agreement shall be binding upon and inure to the benefit of the parties hereto and their respective heirs, executors, administrators, successors, and assigns.

This makes the contract binding on anyone who takes the place of one of the parties, whether due to death or simply to an assignment of the contract. Note that the standard provision on assignment in fact does not allow assignment, but that provision could always be modified in the original contract or by a later written, signed amendment to the contract.

Time. Time is of the essence.

This requires both parties to perform to the exact time commitments they have made or be in breach of the contract. It is not a wise provision for the author to agree to, since being a few days late in performance could cause the loss of benefits under the contract.

Waivers. No waiver by either party of any of the terms or conditions of this Agreement shall be deemed or construed to be a waiver of such term or condition for the future, or of any subsequent breach thereof.

This means that if one party waives a right under the contract, such as the right to receive an accounting from a publisher, that party has not waived the right forever and can demand that the other party perform at the next opportunity. And if the publisher breached the contract in some other way, such as not paying money due, the fact that the author allowed this once would not prevent the author from suing for such a breach in the future.

Warranty and Indemnity. The Author hereby warrants that he or she is the sole creator of the Work and owns all rights granted under this Agreement. The Author agrees to indemnify the Publisher against any final judgment for damages (after all appeals have been exhausted), as well as for reasonable attorney's fees and court costs, in any lawsuit based on an actual breach of the foregoing warranties.

A warranty is something the other party can rely on to be true. If the author states a fact that is a basic reason for the other party's entry into the contract, then that fact is a warranty and must be true. For example, the author might state that he or she is the sole creator of certain writing, owns the copyright therein, and has not infringed anyone else's copyright in creating the work. If this were not true, the author would be liable for damages caused to the other party under the indemnity clause of the contract. The checklist for Form 5, Book Publishing Contract, shows how to negotiate these provisions.

Volunteer Lawyers for the Arts

There are now volunteer lawyers for the arts across the nation. These groups provide free assistance to authors below certain income levels and can be a valuable source of information. To find the location of the closest group, one of the groups listed here can be contacted:

California: California Lawyers for the Arts, Fort Mason Center, Building C, Room 255, San Francisco, California 94123, (415) 775-7200; and 1641 18th Street, Santa Monica, California 90404, (310) 998-5590.

Illinois: Lawyers for the Creative Arts, 213 West Institute Place, Suite 401, Chicago, Illinois 60610, (312) 649-4111.

New York: Volunteer Lawyers for the Arts, 1 East 53rd Street, New York, New York 10022, (212) 319-2787.

A helpful handbook covering all the legal issues that authors face is *The Writer's Legal Guide* by Tad Crawford and Kay Murray (Allworth Press and the Authors Guild).

Having reviewed the basics of dealing with business and legal forms, the next step is to move on to the forms themselves and the negotiation checklists that will make the forms most useful.

Using the Negotiation Checklists

These checklists focus on the key points for negotiation. When a point is covered in the contract already, the appropriate paragraph is indicated in the checklist. These checklists are also valuable to use when reviewing a form given to the author by someone else.

If the author will provide the form, the boxes can be checked to be certain all important points are covered. If the author is reviewing someone else's form, checking the boxes will show which points are covered and which points may have to be added. By using the paragraph numbers in the checklist, the other party's provision can be quickly compared with a provision that would favor the author. Each checklist for a contract concludes with the suggestion that the standard provisions be reviewed to see if any should be added to those the form provides.

Of course, the author does not have to include every point on the checklist in a contract, but being aware of these points will be helpful. After the checklists, the exact wording is provided for some of the more important provisions that might be added to the form. Starting with Form 1, the explanations go through each form in sequence.

Estimate

Form 1 (Estimate), Form 2 (Confirmation of Assignment), and Form 3 (Invoice) are closely related. In a perfect world, the client and author would discuss the assignment and the client would then receive the estimate from the author. After agreeing to the terms of the estimate, both parties would sign the confirmation of assignment, which repeats the nearly identical terms. When the assignment has been completed, the invoice would be given to the client. It, too, would conform to the terms of the estimate and the confirmation of assignment.

As we know, writing is frequently sold without proper documentation. If the client calls for a rush job, the author wants to meet the deadline and may skip the paperwork. If the client has sent a letter or purchase order, the author may feel that the purchase order is sufficient documentation or may be concerned about contradicting its terms in the confirmation of assignment.

The truth is that inadequate documentation is a disservice to the client as well as the author. There are a number of issues that the parties must resolve. The client as well as the author wants to know the rights being transferred. The rights must be adequate for the client's intended use of the writing. The nature of the writing to be done, the due date, and the fee to be paid are important to have in writing, since a talk on the phone can more easily be given different interpretations by the parties. The client as well as the author wants to know if there will be reimbursement for expenses, how payment will be made, what happens in the event of cancellation, and how revisions will be handled. Some of the other provisions in the estimate include authorship credit, copyright notice, releases, and arbitration.

The estimate, confirmation of assignment, and invoice exist for different reasons. If the author knew that a confirmation of assignment would be signed for every job, the estimate and invoice could be far briefer. The estimate would merely describe the assignment, give a fee, and state that the assignment will be governed by a confirmation of assignment which must be signed by both parties before work commences. If there were a confirmation of assignment signed by both parties, the invoice would show an amount due and state that it was being issued in conformity with the terms of the confirmation of assignment.

In fact, the author cannot be certain that a confirmation of assignment will be signed by the client or, if it is signed, when it will be signed. For that reason, and the possibility that the client may pay by a check with a restrictive legend, it is wise to have the specifications and terms on each document that the author provides to the client.

The author should resolve conflicts between his or her forms and those of the client immediately. If the estimate is given, work commences, and no other forms are exchanged until the invoice is sent, the estimate will probably be found either to be a contract or, at least, to be evidence of an oral contract. On the other hand, if the estimate conflicts with the client's letter or purchase order, it will be very difficult to know in retrospect which terms the parties agreed to or those points where they differ. So, the author should point out and resolve such issues without delay. Or if the author has not given an estimate or confirmation of assignment, but disagrees with the terms of a letter or purchase order, reliance on the invoice to resolve these issues would not be wise. It is unlikely, for example, that an invoice alone can govern the terms of a transaction, simply because it is given to the client after the transaction has been concluded.

The estimate, like any of the forms in this book, could be simplified as either a form or a letter including only the terms which the author feels are most important. Form 1 seeks to resolve issues which frequently arise and to protect the author. Certainly, it is better to raise such issues at the outset of the assignment, rather than disagree later. Such disagreements are far more likely to cause the loss of clients than is a frank discussion of the terms before any work has been done. Form 1 is not intended as a proposal, although it could serve that purpose. The proposal would usually be a letter or an outline describing a project. The estimate would come after the client has shown an interest in the proposal and wants to move ahead with the project.

With slight modifications in Forms 1, 2, and 3, the author may choose to develop an estimate/confirmation-of-assignment/invoice form. A box would be checked to indicate for which purpose the form is to be used and be filled in appropriately. In this book, however, the forms are separate, since each has a different purpose and is intended for use at a different time in the relationship with the client.

Because the estimate, confirmation of assignment, and invoice are closely related, the negotiation checklists are very similar. For that reason, the negotiation checklist for Form 1 covers the points which should appear in a short-form estimate and assumes that Form 2 will be signed before work commences. If Form 1 is to be used, and especially if Form 1 is likely to be the only form used, then the negotiation checklist for Form 2 must be reviewed by the author. The negotiation checklist for Form 2 should also be used to review the purchase order, letter of agreement, or contract form offered by a client.

Filling in the Form

The author should provide his or her letterhead, then fill in the date, the client's name and address, and the author's number for the job. In Paragraph 1 the work should be described in detail. In Paragraph 2, specify how many days it will take to go from starting work to delivery. In Paragraph 3 give the limitations on the rights granted. In Paragraph 5 state the fee and any reuse percentage. In Paragraph 7 specify the types of expenses to be reimbursed by the client and the amount of any advance to be paid against expenses. In Paragraph 8 give a monthly interest rate. Fill in Paragraph 9 if an advance on the fee is to be paid. Check the boxes in Paragraphs 11 and 12 to indicate whether copyright notice or authorship credit will be given in the name of the author. State in Paragraph 13 the percentages of the total fee that will be paid for cancellation. In Paragraph 15 specify who will arbitrate disputes, where this will be done, and the maximum amount which can be sued for in small claims court. In Paragraph 16 give the state whose laws will govern the contract. The author can then sign the estimate. If the client agrees to the estimate and it will not be possible to obtain a signed confirmation of assignment before work begins, the words "AGREED TO" can be added and the client can sign the estimate.

Negotiation Checklist

❏ State that a confirmation of assignment form is to be signed before the commencement of work. (Preamble)

❏ Describe the assignment in as much detail as possible, attaching another sheet to the contract if necessary (in which case the line for Subject Matter would refer to the attached sheet). (Paragraph 1)

❏ Give a due date, which can be expressed as a number of days after client's approval for author to start work. (Paragraph 2)

❏ If the client is to provide reference materials, the due date should be expressed as a number of days after the author's receipt of these materials. (Paragraph 2)

❏ Limit the grant of rights and state that the transfer of rights takes place when the author is paid in full. (Paragraph 3)

❏ Specify whether the client's rights are exclusive or nonexclusive. (Paragraph 3)

❏ If electronic rights are not entirely reserved by the author, specify the nature of the electronic rights granted. (Paragraph 3)

❏ All rights not granted to the client should be reserved to the author, including rights in preliminary materials. (Paragraph 4)

❏ The fee must be specified. (Paragraph 5)

❏ Any expenses which the client will reimburse to the author should be specified to avoid misunderstandings. (Paragraph 7)

❏ If expenses will be significant, provide for an advance against expenses. (Paragraph 7)

❏ Require payment within thirty days of delivery. (Paragraph 8)

❏ Specify any advance to be paid against the fee on signing the contract. A schedule of payments is especially important for an extensive job. (Paragraph 9)

❏ State whether the author's copyright notice will appear with the work. (Paragraph 11)

❏ State whether the author will receive name credit with the work. (Paragraph 12)

❏ Fees for cancellation at different stages of the assignment must be specified, plus payment of any expenses incurred. (Paragraph 13)

❏ State that the author owns all rights in the work in the event of cancellation for any reason. (Paragraph 13)

❏ Specify a time to pay cancellation fees, such as within thirty days of client's stopping work or the delivery of the work. (Paragraph 13)

❏ If any valuable materials accompany the manuscript, such as original photographic transparencies, require that these be insured and returned within thirty days of use.

❏ Review the standard provisions in the introductory pages and compare to Paragraph 16.

❏ Review the negotiation checklist for Form 2, especially if Form 1 is going to be used without Form 2 or if the author is reviewing a purchase order or contract provided by the client.

< Author's Letterhead >

Estimate

Client _____ Date _____

Address _____ Job Number _____

This Estimate is based on the specifications and terms which follow. If the Client confirms that the Author should proceed with the assignment based on this Estimate, it is understood that the assignment shall be subject to the terms shown on this Estimate and that Client shall sign a Confirmation of Assignment form incorporating the same specifications and terms. If the assignment proceeds without a Confirmation of Assignment being signed by both parties, the assignment shall be governed by the terms and conditions contained in this Estimate.

1. Description. The Author shall create the Work in accordance with the following specifications:

Title _____ Number of words_____

Subject matter _____

_____

Other materials to be provided _____

Form of Work ❑ double-spaced manuscript ❑ computer file (specify format)_____

2. Due Date. The Work shall be delivered within _____ days after either the Client's authorization to commence work or, if the Client is to provide reference materials, after the Client has provided same to the Author, whichever occurs later.

3. Grant of Rights. Upon receipt of full payment, the Author shall grant to the Client the following rights in the Work:

For use as _____ in the _____ language

For the product or publication named _____

In the following territory _____

For the following time period _____

Other limitations _____

With respect to the usage shown above, the Client shall have ❑ exclusive ❑ nonexclusive rights.

If the work is for use as a contribution to a magazine, the grant of rights shall be first North American serial rights only unless specified to the contrary above.

This grant of rights does not include electronic rights, unless specified to the contrary here_____ in which event the usage restrictions shown above shall be applicable. For purposes of this agreement, electronic rights are defined as rights in the digitized form of works that can be encoded, stored, and retrieved from such media as computer disks, CD-ROM, computer databases, and network servers.

4. Reservation of Rights. All rights not expressly granted shall be reserved to the Author, including but not limited to all rights in preliminary materials.

5. Fee. Client shall pay the following purchase price: $_____ for the usage rights granted. A reuse fee of_____ percent of the initial fee shall be paid in the following circumstances_____

6. Additional Usage. If Client wishes to make any additional uses of the Work, Client shall seek permission from the Author and pay an additional fee to be agreed upon.

7. Expenses. Client shall reimburse the Author for the following expenses: ❑ Messenger ❑ Travel ❑ Telephone ❑ Other _____ At the time of signing the Confirmation of Assignment or the commencement of work, whichever is first, Client shall pay Author $_____ as a nonrefundable advance against expenses. If the advance exceeds expenses incurred, the credit balance shall be used to reduce the fee payable, or, if the fee has been fully paid, shall be reimbursed to Client.

8. Payment. Client shall pay the Author within thirty days of the date of Author's billing, which shall be dated as of the date of delivery of the Work. In the event that work is postponed at the request of the Client, the Author shall have the right to bill pro rata for work completed through the date of that request, while reserving all other rights. Overdue payments shall be subject to interest charges of _____ percent monthly.

9. Advances. At the time of signing the Confirmation of Assignment or the commencement of work, whichever is first, Client shall pay Author _____ percent of the fee as an advance against the total fee.

10. Revisions. The Author shall be given the first opportunity to make any revisions requested by the Client. If the revisions are not due to any fault on the part of the Author, an additional fee shall be charged. If the Author objects to any revisions to be made by the Client, the Author shall have the right to have his or her name removed from the published Work.

11. Copyright Notice. Copyright notice in the name of the Author ❑ shall ❑ shall not accompany the Work when it is published.

12. Authorship Credit. Authorship credit in the name of the Author ❑ shall ❑ shall not accompany the Work when it is published. If the Work is used as a contribution to a magazine or for a book, authorship credit shall be given unless specified to the contrary in the preceding sentence.

13. Cancellation. In the event of cancellation by the Client, the following cancellation payment shall be paid by the Client: **(A)** Cancellation prior to the Work being turned in: _____ percent of fee; **(B)** Cancellation due to the Work being unsatisfactory: _____ percent of fee; and **(C)** Cancellation for any other reason after the Work is turned in: _____ percent of fee. In the event of cancellation, the Client shall also pay any expenses incurred by the Author and the Author shall own all rights in the Work. The billing upon cancellation shall be payable within thirty days of the Client's notification to stop work or the delivery of the work, whichever occurs sooner.

14. Permissions and Releases. The Client shall indemnify and hold harmless the Author against any and all claims, costs, and expenses, including attorney's fees, due to materials included in the work at the request of the Client for which no copyright permission or privacy release was requested or uses which exceed the uses allowed pursuant to a permission or release.

15. Arbitration. All disputes shall be submitted to binding arbitration before _____ in the following location _____ and settled in accordance with the rules of the American Arbitration Association. Judgment upon the arbitration award may be entered in any court having jurisdiction thereof. Disputes in which the amount at issue is less than $_____ shall not be subject to this arbitration provision.

16. Miscellany. If the Client authorizes the Author to commence work, the terms of this Estimate Form shall be binding upon the parties, their heirs, successors, assigns, and personal representatives; the Estimate Form constitutes the entire understanding between the parties; its terms can be modified only by an instrument in writing signed by both parties, except that the Client may authorize expenses and revisions orally; a waiver of a breach of any of its provisions shall not be construed as a continuing waiver of other breaches of the same or other provisions hereof; and the relationship between the Client and Author shall be governed by the laws of the State of _____.

Author _____

Confirmation of Assignment

Form 2, the Confirmation of Assignment, follows Form 1, the Estimate, almost exactly. Ideally, the client will review the estimate and request whatever changes are necessary. Then both client and author will sign Form 2 to make a binding contract. If Form 1 has not been given to the client, or if an estimate has been used that only gives limited information such as a project description and a price, then it is even more important to use Form 2. By signing Form 2 before the commencement of the assignment, the parties resolve many of the issues likely to cause disputes. Since the goal with any client is to create a long-term relationship, the avoidance of needless disputes is a very positive step. If the client requests changes in Form 2, the author can certainly make revisions. Nonetheless, the agreement between the parties will be clear, which promotes creating the best writing and a long-term business relationship.

Filling in the Form

Fill in the date and the names and addresses for the client and the author. In Paragraph 1 describe the assignment in detail, attaching an additional sheet to the form if needed. In Paragraph 2, specify how many days it will take to go from starting to delivery of the work. In Paragraph 3 give the limitations on the rights granted and specify whether the client's rights are exclusive or nonexclusive. In Paragraph 5 state the fee and any reuse percentage. In Paragraph 7 specify the types of expenses to be reimbursed by the client and the amount of any advance to be paid against expenses. In Paragraph 8 give a monthly interest rate for late payments. Fill in Paragraph 9 if advances on the fee are to be paid. Check the boxes in Paragraphs 11 and 12 to indicate whether copyright notice or authorship credit will be given in the name of the author. In Paragraph 13 state the percentages of the total fee that will be paid for cancellation. In Paragraph 15 specify who will arbitrate disputes, where this will be done, and give the maximum amount that can be sued for in small claims court. In Paragraph 16 give the state whose laws will govern the contract. Both parties should then sign the contract.

Negotiation Checklist

❏ Describe the assignment in as much detail as possible, attaching another sheet to the contract if necessary (in which case the line for Subject Matter would refer to the attached sheet). (Paragraph 1)

❏ Give a due date, which can be expressed as a number of days after client's approval for author to start work. (Paragraph 2)

❏ If the client is to provide reference materials, the due date should be expressed as a number of days after the author's receipt of these materials. (Paragraph 2)

❏ Time should not be of the essence.

❏ State that illness or other delays beyond the control of the author will extend the due date, but only up to a limited number of days.

❏ State that the grant of rights takes place when the author is paid in full. (Paragraph 3)

❏ Limit the grant of rights to the final form of the work, so that rights in research or earlier drafts are not transferred. (Paragraph 3)

❏ Specify whether the client's rights will be exclusive or nonexclusive. (Paragraph 3)

❏ Limit the exclusivity to the particular use the client will make of the work, such as for a contribution to an anthology, a magazine ad, or a direct mail brochure. This lets the author benefit from other future uses, which the client must pay for, and leaves the author free to resell the work for other uses if possible. (Paragraph 3)

❏ Name the product or publication for which the work is being prepared. (Paragraph 3)

❏ State the language in which usage is permitted. (Paragraph 3)

❏ Give a geographic limitation, such as local, regional, the United States, North America, and so on. (Paragraph 3)

❏ Limit the time period of use. (Paragraph 3)

❏ Other limitations might include the number of uses. One-time use, for example, means that the work cannot be given other uses. Or the use might be restricted to one form of a book, such as hardcover, which would mean that the author would receive reuse fees for subsequent use in paperback. This same approach might be used to restrict the use to one printing of a book, so a second printing would require a reuse fee. The concept behind such limitations is that fees are based on the type and number of usages. (Paragraph 3)

❏ For contributions to magazines, the sale of first North American serial rights is common. This gives the magazine the right to be the first magazine to make a one-time use of the work in North America. This could be limited to first United States serial rights. If no agreement about rights is made for a magazine contribution, the copyright law provides that the magazine has a nonexclusive right to use the work as many times as it wishes in issues of the magazine but can make no other uses. (Paragraph 3)

❏ If the grant of electronic rights is included, consider whether an additional fee should be paid. This might take the form of a reuse fee and be a percentage, such as 25 or 50 percent, of the initial fee. If the electronic usage is the first and only use, of course, no reuse fee would be payable. If the electronic and non-electronic uses occur at the same time, the negotiation to set the initial fee might settle on an amount adequate to cover both types of usage. However, if one usage comes before the other (most likely nonelectronic before electronic), a reuse fee might be appropriate.

❏ Make any grant of electronic rights subject to all the limitations as to type of use, language, product or publication, territory, time period, exclusivity or nonexclusivity, and other limitations. (Paragraph 3)

❏ Do not allow electronic usages to involve abridgements, expansions, or combinations with other works unless specified in the contract. This can be set forth under "Other Limitations." (Paragraph 3)

❏ If possible when electronic rights are given, limit the form of the electronic usage to known systems such as CD-ROM, online, database, etc.

❏ For electronic rights, seek to avoid a situation in which the party acquiring the rights will make them freely available to the public (for example, by allowing downloading from a Web site) unless that is intended by the author. The restriction might take the form of a grant of "display rights only," so that the party acquiring the rights would not allow users to make digital copies.

❏ All rights not granted to the client should be reserved to the author, including rights in preliminary materials. (Paragraph 4)

❏ If the client insists on all rights or work for hire, offer instead a provision stating, "Author shall not permit any uses of the work which compete with or impair the use of the art by the Client." If necessary to reassure the Client, this might also state, "The Author shall submit any proposed uses to the Client for approval, which shall not be unreasonably withheld."

❏ Many authors refuse to do work for hire, since the client becomes the author under the copyright law. The author can point out to the client that work for hire devalues and can damage the creative process.

❏ In the face of a demand for all rights or work for hire, advise the client that fees are based on rights of usage. The fee for all rights or work for hire should be substantially higher than for limited usage.

❏ If the work is highly specific to one client, selling all rights for a higher fee would be more acceptable than for a work likely to have resale value for the author.

❏ Do not allow the client to assign usage rights without the consent of the author, since the client may benefit from reuse fees that more appropriately belong to the author.

❏ The fee must be specified. (Paragraph 5)

❏ Consider requiring a reuse payment computed as a percentage of the initial fee, especially for electronic reuses. (Paragraph 5)

❏ If additional usage rights are sought by the client, additional fees should be agreed upon and paid. (Paragraph 6)

❏ If it is likely that a certain type of additional usage will be made, the amount of the reuse fee can be specified. Or the reuse fee can be expressed as a percentage of the original fee, including for electronic uses.

❏ Any expenses which the client will reimburse to the author should be specified to avoid misunderstandings. (Paragraph 7)

❏ If expenses will be significant, provide for an advance against expenses. (Paragraph 7)

❏ Specify that any advance against expenses is nonrefundable unless, of course, the expenses are not incurred. (Paragraph 7)

❏ If the client insists on a binding budget for expenses, provide for some flexibility, such as a 10 percent variance, or for client's approval of expense items which exceed the variance.

❏ Require payment within thirty days of delivery. Make certain the interest rate for overdue payments does not violate the usury laws. (Paragraph 8)

❏ Deal with the issue of payment for work-in-progress that is postponed but not cancelled. A pro rata billing might be appropriate. (Paragraph 8)

❏ Specify any advance to be paid against the fee on signing the contract. A schedule of payments is especially important for an extensive job. (Paragraph 9)

❏ State that any advances against the fee are nonrefundable. This is not included in Paragraph 9 because of the interplay with the cancellation provision in Paragraph 13.

❏ Revisions can be a problem. Certainly the author should be given the first opportunity to make revisions. (Paragraph 10)

❏ If revisions are the fault of the author, no additional fee should be charged. However, if the client changes the nature of the assignment, additional fees must be charged for revisions. (Paragraph 10)

❏ Consider limiting the amount of time the author must spend on revisions, whether or not the revisions are the author's fault.

❏ If the client ultimately has revisions done by someone else, the author should reserve the right to have his or her name removed from the work. (Paragraph 10)

❑ With respect to revisions or the assignment itself, additional charges might be specified for work which must be rushed and requires unusual hours or other stresses.

❑ Any revisions or changes in the assignment should be documented in writing, if possible, since there may be a question later as to whether the changes were approved and whether they came within the initial description of the project. (Paragraphs 10 and 16)

❑ State whether copyright notice in the author's name will be required to appear with the work. (Paragraph 11)

❑ State whether the author will receive name credit with the work. (Paragraph 12)

❑ For editorial work, require authorship credit as the general rule. One of the values of editorial work is its promotional impact, so name credit is important.

❑ If necessary, specify the type size for authorship credit and placement of the credit.

❑ If authorship credit should be given but is omitted, require payment of an additional fee.

❑ Fees for cancellation of the assignment must be specified. (Paragraph 13)

❑ State that the author owns all rights in the event of cancellation. (Paragraph 13)

❑ Specify a time for payment of cancellation fees, such as within thirty days of client's stopping work or of the delivery of the work, whichever comes first. (Paragraph 13)

❑ Never work on speculation (a situation in which no fees will be paid in the event of cancellation or a failure to use the work).

❑ Specify that if the work is not published within a certain time period, the rights shall revert to the author. This would avoid, for example, a situation in which a magazine purchases first North American serial rights but never uses the work. Since the author cannot make use of the work until after publication, the failure to publish would be damaging to the author.

❑ State that the author owns the manuscript and any preliminary materials. This is especially important if either the manuscript or the materials are valuable, in which case the responsibility of the parties for risk of loss and insurance should be determined.

❑ Try not to give a warranty and indemnity provision, in which the author states the work is not a copyright infringement and not libelous and agrees to pay for the client's damages and attorney's fees if this is not true.

❑ If there is a warranty and indemnity provision, try to be covered under any publisher's liability insurance policy owned by the client and ask the client to cover the deductible.

❑ If the client insists on a warranty and indemnity provision, seek to limit the author's liability to a specified amount. For example, liability might be limited to the amount of the fee for the assignment.

❑ Require the client to indemnify the author if the client does not request that the author obtain needed copyright permissions or privacy releases (such as for models), or uses the work in a way that exceeds the use allowed by the permissions or releases.

❑ Specify that the author will receive samples of the work when published.

❑ Provide for arbitration, except for amounts which can be sued for in small claims court. (Paragraph 15)

❑ Review the standard provisions in the introductory pages and compare to Paragraph 16.

Confirmation of Assignment

AGREEMENT, entered into as of the _____ day of _____, 20 _____, between _____,
(hereinafter referred to as the "Client"), located at _____,
and _____ (hereinafter referred to as the "Author"),
located at _____,
with respect to the creation of certain writing (hereinafter referred to as the "Work").

WHEREAS, Author is a professional author of good standing;

WHEREAS, Client wishes the Author to create certain Work described more fully herein; and

WHEREAS, Author wishes to create such Work;

NOW, THEREFORE, in consideration of the foregoing premises and the mutual covenants hereinafter set forth and other valuable considerations, the parties hereto agree as follows:

1. Description. The Author agrees to create the Work in accordance with the following specifications:

Title_____ Number of Words _____

Subject matter_____

_____

Other materials to be provided _____

_____ Job number _____

Form of Work ❏ double-spaced manuscript ❏ computer file (specify format_____)

2. Due Date. The Author agrees to deliver the Work within _____ days after the later of the signing of this Agreement or, if the Client is to provide reference materials, after the Client has provided same to the Author.

3. Grant of Rights. Upon receipt of full payment, Author grants to the Client the following rights in the Work:

For use as _____ in the _____ language

For the product or publication named _____

In the following territory _____

For the following time period _____

Other limitations _____

With respect to the usage shown above, the Client shall have ❏ exclusive ❏ nonexclusive rights.

If the Work is for use as a contribution to a magazine, the grant of rights shall be for first North American serial rights only unless specified to the contrary above.

This grant of rights does not include electronic rights, unless specified to the contrary here_____ in which event the usage restrictions shown above shall be applicable. For purposes of this agreement, electronic rights are defined as rights in the digitized form of works that can be encoded, stored, and retrieved from such media as computer disks, CD-ROM, computer databases, and network servers.

4. Reservation of Rights. All rights not expressly granted hereunder are reserved to the Author, including but not limited to all rights in preliminary materials.

5. Fee. Client agrees to pay the following purchase price: $_____ for the usage rights granted. A reuse fee of ____ percent of the initial fee shall be paid in the following circumstances_____

6. Additional Usage. If Client wishes to make any additional uses of the Work, Client agrees to seek permission from the Author and make such payments as are agreed to between the parties at that time.

7. Expenses. Client agrees to reimburse the Author for the following expenses: ❏ Messengers ❏ Travel ❏ Telephone ❏ Other _____

At the time of signing this Agreement, Client shall pay Author $_____ as a nonrefundable advance against expenses. If the advance exceeds expenses incurred, the credit balance shall be used to reduce the fee payable or, if the fee has been fully paid, shall be reimbursed to Client.

8. Payment. Client agrees to pay the Author within thirty days of the date of Author's billing, which shall be dated as of the date of delivery of the Work. In the event that work is postponed at the request of the Client, the Author shall have the right to bill pro rata for work completed through the date of that request, while reserving all other rights under this Agreement. Overdue payments shall be subject to interest charges of _____ percent monthly.

9. Advances. At the time of signing this Agreement, Client shall pay Author ____ percent of the fee as an advance against the total fee.

10. Revisions. The Author shall be given the first opportunity to make any revisions requested by the Client. If the revisions are not due to any fault on the part of the Author, an additional fee shall be charged. If the Author objects to any revisions to be made by the Client, the Author shall have the right to have his or her name removed from the published Work.

11. Copyright Notice. Copyright notice in the Author's name ❏ shall ❏ shall not be published with the Work when it is published.

12. Authorship Credit. Authorship credit in the name of the Author ❏ shall ❏ shall not accompany the Work when it is published. If the Work is used as a contribution to a magazine or for a book, authorship credit shall be given unless specified to the contrary in the preceding sentence.

13. Cancellation. In the event of cancellation by the Client, the following cancellation payment shall be paid by the Client: **(A)** Cancellation prior to the Work being turned in: ____ percent of fee; **(B)** Cancellation due to the Work being unsatisfactory: ____ percent of fee; and **(C)** Cancellation for any other reason after the Work is turned in: ____ percent of fee. In the event of cancellation, the Client shall also pay any expenses incurred by the Author and the Author shall own all rights in the Work. The billing upon cancellation shall be payable within thirty days of the Client's notification to stop work or the delivery of the Work, whichever occurs sooner.

14. Permissions and Releases. The Client agrees to indemnify and hold harmless the Author against any and all claims, costs, and expenses, including attorney's fees, due to materials included in the Work at the request of the Client for which no copyright permission or privacy release was requested or uses which exceed the uses allowed pursuant to a permission or release.

15. Arbitration. All disputes arising under this Agreement shall be submitted to binding arbitration before _____ in the following location _____ and settled in accordance with the rules of the American Arbitration Association. Judgment upon the arbitration award may be entered in any court having jurisdiction thereof. Disputes in which the amount at issue is less than $_____ shall not be subject to this arbitration provision.

16. Miscellany. This Agreement shall be binding upon the parties hereto, their heirs, successors, assigns, and personal representatives. This Agreement constitutes the entire understanding between the parties. Its terms can be modified only by an instrument in writing signed by both parties, except that the Client may authorize expenses or revisions orally. A waiver of a breach of any of the provisions of this Agreement shall not be construed as a continuing waiver of other breaches of the same or other provisions hereof. This Agreement shall be governed by the laws of the State of _____.

IN WITNESS WHEREOF, the parties hereto have signed this Agreement as of the date first set forth above.

Author _____   Client _____
                                                            Company Name

                                             By _____
                                                            Authorized Signatory, Title

Invoice

Form 3, the Invoice, is rendered to the client when the assignment is completed. It can be handed over with the assignment or after the assignment has been approved. If Form 2, the Confirmation of Assignment, has already been signed by the client, then the invoice can be quite simple. It need only supply the fee and any expenses to be reimbursed, subtract advances paid against either the fee or the expenses, and show a total due. The time for payment would be that specified in Form 2, probably thirty days after delivery (although the author could certainly require payment on delivery, if the client is set up to pay that quickly). The title or description of the assignment would be referred to along with the author's job number. Restating the rights granted would also be wise.

Form 3 really cannot replace Form 1, the Estimate, or Form 2, the Confirmation of Assignment. Waiting until after an assignment is completed to show the terms and conditions which the author wants to govern the assignment is asking for trouble. If the client has not already given a letter or form with terms that contradict the invoice, the client may well respond to the terms of the invoice by payment with a check that has writing on its back that contradicts the terms of the invoice. Such a situation is filled with ambiguity and places at risk the business relationship. If the parties review proposed terms prior to working together, a disagreement can be resolved or the parties can agree not to work together on that particular project. Once the work has been done, disagreement over terms is far more difficult to resolve and is likely to leave the kind of bad feeling that makes future ventures dubious.

The invoice repeats almost exactly all the terms which either the estimate or the confirmation of assignment would have contained. As stated above, this would not be necessary if the author definitely had a confirmation of assignment signed by both parties. If an estimate alone has been supplied or the client has not signed the estimate or a confirmation of assignment, ambiguity remains as to the terms, and repeating the terms (on the invoice) may be of value since payment based on the invoice may be viewed by a court or arbitrator as acquiesence to its terms (although this cannot be guaranteed).

The negotiation checklist covers the terms which an invoice would need to contain if a confirmation of assignment has been signed by the client. If a confirmation of assignment has not been signed by the client, the negotiation checklist for Form 2 should also be reviewed.

Filling in the Form

Use the author's letterhead at the top of the form. Give the date, the client's name and address, and the author's job number. State the fee, expenses to be reimbursed, charges for revisions, advances (in parentheses to show that advances should be subtracted to arrive at the total due), and show the balance due. In Paragraph 1 describe the assignment briefly. In Paragraph 2, specify the delivery date. In Paragraph 3 give the limitations on the rights granted and specify whether the client's rights are exclusive or nonexclusive. In Paragraph 5 state the fee and any reuse percentage. In Paragraph 7 show the amount of any advance paid against expenses. In Paragraph 8 give a monthly interest rate for late payments. Fill in Paragraph 9 if advances on the fee were paid. Check the boxes in Paragraphs 11 and 12 to indicate whether copyright notice or authorship credit will be given in the name of the author. In Paragraph 13 state the percentages of the total fee payable for cancellation. In Paragraph 15 specify who will arbitrate disputes, and where, and give the maximum amount that can be sued for in small claims court. In Paragraph 16 give the state whose laws will govern the contract. Both parties should then sign the contract.

Negotiation Checklist

❏ Describe the assignment briefly. (Paragraph 1)

❏ Give the date of delivery. (Paragraph 2)

❏ State that the grant of rights takes place when the author is paid in full. (Paragraph 3)

❏ Limit the grant of rights and specify whether the client's use of the writing will include electronic rights. (Paragraph 3)

❏ All rights not granted to the client should be reserved to the author, including rights to preliminary research or materials. (Paragraph 4)

❏ The fee must be specified. (Paragraph 5)

❏ Detail the nature and amount of expenses which the client must reimburse to the author. (Paragraph 7)

❏ State the amount of any advance given against expenses. (Paragraph 7)

❏ Require payment within thirty days of delivery. (Paragraph 8)

❏ State the amount of any advances paid against the fee. (Paragraph 9)

❏ If the client has changed the nature of the assignment, additional fees must be charged for revisions. (Paragraph 10)

❏ With respect to revisions or the assignment itself, additional charges might be billed for work which had to be rushed or required unusual hours or other stresses.

❏ State whether the author's copyright notice will appear with the writing. (Paragraph 11)

❏ State whether the author will receive name credit with the writing. (Paragraph 12)

❏ If authorship credit should be given but is omitted, require payment of an additional fee.

❏ Fees for cancellation should be restated. (Paragraph 13)

❏ State that the author shall own all rights in the event of cancellation. (Paragraph 13)

❏ Specify a time for payment of cancellation fees, such as within thirty days of either the client's stopping work or the delivery of the work, whichever occurs first. (Paragraph 13)

❏ Specify that if the writing is not published within a certain time period, the rights shall revert to the author.

❏ State that the author owns the manuscript and any materials of value, such as photographic transparencies.

❏ Require the client to indemnify the author if the client does not request that the author obtain needed copyright permissions or privacy releases (such as for models in a photograph) or uses the assignment in a way that exceeds the use allowed by a permission or release. (Paragraph 14)

❏ Provide for arbitration, except for amounts which can be sued for in small claims court. (Paragraph 15)

❏ Compare the standard provisions in the introductory pages with Paragraph 16.

❏ Especially if the client has not signed Form 2, the Confirmation of Assignment, review the negotiation checklist for Form 2.

< Author's Letterhead >

Invoice

Client _____ Date _____

Address _____Job Number _____

Fee........................... $_____

Expenses................................. $_____

Revisions................................. $_____

Advances............................... ($_____)

Balance due........................... $_____

This Invoice is subject to the terms and conditions which follow.

1. Description. The Author has created and delivered to Client a Work of _____ words titled _____ for the following project _____.

2. Delivery Date. The Work was delivered on _____, 20_____.

3. Grant of Rights. Upon receipt of full payment, Author shall grant to the Client the following rights in the Work:

For use as _____ in the _____ language.

For the product or publication named _____

In the following territory _____

For the following time period _____

Other limitations _____

With respect to the usage shown above, the Client shall have ❏ exclusive ❏ nonexclusive rights.

If the Work is for use as a contribution to a magazine, the grant of rights shall be first North American serial rights only unless specified to the contrary above.

This grant of rights does not include electronic rights, unless specified to the contrary here_____ in which event the usage restrictions shown above shall be applicable. For purposes of this agreement, electronic rights are defined as rights in the digitized form of works that can be encoded, stored, and retrieved from such media as computer disks, CD-ROM, computer databases, and network servers.

4. Reservation of Rights. All rights not expressly granted are reserved to the Author, including but not limited to all rights in preliminary materials.

5. Fee. Client shall pay the following purchase price: $_____ for the usage rights granted. A reuse fee of ____ percent of the initial fee shall be paid in the following circumstances_____.

6. Additional Usage. If Client wishes to make any additional uses of the Work, Client shall seek permission from the Author and pay an additional fee to be agreed upon.

7. Expenses. If Author incurred reimbursable expenses, a listing of such expenses is attached to this Invoice with copies of supporting documentation. Author has received $_____ as an advance against expenses.

8. Payment. Payment is due to the Author within thirty days of the date of this Invoice, which is dated as of the date of delivery of the Work. Overdue payments shall be subject to interest charges of _____ percent monthly.

9. Advances. Author received $_____ as an advance against the total fee.

10. Revisions. The Author shall be given the first opportunity to make any revisions requested by the Client. If the revisions are not due to any fault on the part of the Author, an additional fee shall be charged. If the Author objects to any revisions to be made by the Client, the Author shall have the right to have his or her name removed from the published Work.

11. Copyright Notice. Copyright notice in the name of the Author ❏ shall ❏ shall not accompany the Work when it is published.

12. Authorship Credit. Authorship credit in the name of the Author ❏ shall ❏ shall not accompany the Work when it is published. If the Work is used as a contribution to a magazine or for a book, authorship credit shall be given unless specified to the contrary in the preceding sentence.

13. Cancellation. In the event of cancellation by the Client, the amount charged to the Client as the fee in this Invoice has been computed as follows based on the fee originally agreed upon: **(A)** Cancellation prior to the Work being turned in: ____ percent of fee; **(B)** Cancellation due to the Work being unsatisfactory: ____ percent of fee; and **(C)** Cancellation for any other reason after the Work is turned in: ____ percent of fee. In the event of cancellation, the Client shall pay any expenses incurred by the Author and the Author shall own all rights in the Work. The Invoice upon cancellation is payable within thirty days of the Client's notification to stop work or the delivery of the Work, whichever occurs sooner.

14. Permissions and Releases. The Client shall indemnify and hold harmless the Author against any and all claims, costs, and expenses, including attorney's fees, due to materials included in the Work at the request of the Client for which no copyright permission or privacy release was requested or uses which exceed the uses allowed pursuant to a permission or release.

15. Arbitration. All disputes shall be submitted to binding arbitration before _____ in the following location _____ and settled in accordance with the rules of the American Arbitration Association. Judgment upon the arbitration award may be entered in any court having jurisdiction thereof. Disputes in which the amount at issue is less than $_____ shall not be subject to this arbitration provision.

16. Miscellany. This Invoice shall be governed by the laws of the State of _____.

Author _____

Author–Agent Contract

An agent can be of immeasurable value to an author. Instead of seeking assignments, the author can devote full time to creative work and trust that the agent will provide marketing impetus. The cost to the author is the agent's commission, which is usually 10 to 15 percent, but the hope is that the agent will enable the author to earn more. The agent may have better contacts and be able to secure the largest amount of income by placing work with the right publisher.

The agent should not be given markets in which the agent cannot effectively sell. For example, an agent in New York may not be able to sell in Los Angeles or London. Nor should the agent be given exclusivity in markets in which the author may want to sell or want to have other agents sell. The length of the contract should not be overly long, or should be subject to a right of termination on notice. If the agent fails to sell, the author must take over sales or find another agent. The agent's promise to use best efforts is almost impossible to enforce. After termination, the agent will collect royalties and charge the agency fee for works placed during the term of the contract, but will not have any rights to commissions for works placed after the contract ended.

The author should resist signing an "intermediate rights" clause, which gives the agency the right to continue to license a work even if the book is out of print, the original agreement with a publisher has terminated, or the person who worked with the author has left the agency. If the agency seeks to put such a clause in the author's contract with a publisher, the author should also insist this not be done.

Another issue is whether commissions are payable on works placed by the author during the term of the contract. If the agent is unlikely to reach the markets in which the author is selling, probably no fee should be paid. Or the contract may state that no fee is payable if the amount earned by the author from a project is less than a certain amount.

The agent would handle billings and provide accountings. The author would want to be able to review the books and records of the agent. Since both the author and agent provide personal services, the contract should not be assignable.

Some agents may charge a reading fee when considering whether to accept an author as a client. On the one hand, authors have to understand that reputable agents do expend a great deal of time to read any submitted work. On the other hand, agents are in the business of looking for good authors to represent, so reading is simply part of this process. The greatest abuse is likely when agents charge fees on an ongoing basis to help authors revise work to be marketable. The risk is that the agent earns a living as an editor, not as an agent. The decisions whether to pay a reading fee or pay for an agent's editorial work will be made by each author, but certainly such fees suggest the value of investigating the professional standing of the agent. This can be done by asking for the list of authors represented by the agent and calling some of them, or perhaps by inquiring about the agent from organizations for authors or for agents.

Good sources to locate agents are the membership list for the Association of Author's Representatives, 10 Astor Place, Third Floor, New York, New York 10003, as well as the listings of agents in *Writer's Market* (Writer's Digest Books) and *Literary Market Place* (R.R. Bowker). Other helpful books are *Literary Agents: A Complete Guide* by Debby Mayer (Penguin), *Guide to Literary Agents* by Rachel Vater (Writer's Digest Books), and Jeff Herman's *Guide to Book Publishers, Editors, and Literary Agents* (Writer, Inc.).

Filling in the Form

In the Preamble fill in the date and the names and addresses of the author and agent. In Paragraph 1 indicate the geographical area and markets in which the agent will represent the author, whether the representation will be exclusive or nonexclusive, and how electronic rights will be handled. In Paragraph 5 fill in the commission rates, either entering none as the commission paid on work obtained by the author or showing exclusions to whatever commission rate is to be paid. Check the box as to commissions with respect to nonreimbursed expenses. In Paragraph 7 indicate the time for payment after receipt of fees and the interest rate for late payments. In Paragraph 12 give the names of arbitrators and the place for arbitration, as well as the maximum amount which can be sued for in small claims court. In Paragraph 16 fill in which state's laws will govern the contract. Both parties should sign the contract.

Negotiation Checklist

❏ Limit the scope of the agent's represention by geography and types of markets, including coverage of electronic rights. (Paragraph 1)

❏ State whether the representation is exclusive or nonexclusive. (Paragraph 1) If the representation is exclusive, the agent will have a right to commissions on assignments obtained by other agents. Assignments obtained by the author would fall under Paragraph 5.

❏ If the agent uses other agents for certain markets (for example, for foreign sales or film sales), review the impact of this on commissions.

❏ Any rights not granted to the agent should be reserved to the author. (Paragraph 1)

❏ Require that the agent use best efforts to sell the work of the author. (Paragraph 2)

❏ State that the agent shall keep the author promptly and regularly informed with respect to negotiations and other matters, and shall submit all offers to the author.

❏ State that any contract negotiated by the agent is not binding unless signed by the author.

❏ If the author is willing to give the agent power of attorney so the agent can sign on behalf of the author, the power of attorney should be very specific as to what rights the agent can exercise.

❏ Require that the agent keep confidential all matters handled for the author.

❏ Allow the author to accept or reject any assignment obtained by the agent. (Paragraph 2)

❏ Specify that a reasonable number of writing samples will be supplied to the agent by the author. (Paragraph 3)

❏ Provide for a short term, such as one year. (Paragraph 4) This interplays with the termination provision. Since termination is permitted on thirty days notice in Paragraph 10, the length of the term is of less importance in this contract.

❏ If the contract has a relatively long term and cannot be terminated on notice at any time, allow termination if the agent fails to generate a certain level of sales on a quarterly, semiannual, or annual basis.

❏ If the contract has a relatively long term and cannot be terminated on notice at any time, allow for termination if the specific agent dies or leaves the agency.

❏ Specify the commission percentage for assignments obtained by the agent during the term of the contract. This is usually 10 to 15 percent of the income, and may reach 20 percent for sales involving other agents.

❏ If expenses are substantial and are not reimbursed to the author, consider reducing the income by the expenses before computation of the agent's commission. If expenses are reimbursed, this should be excluded from income for purposes of computing the commission. (Paragraph 5)

❏ State that commissions are not payable on billings which have not been collected. (Paragraph 5)

❏ Confirm that the agent will not collect a commission for the author's speaking fees, grants, or prizes.

❏ In the case of an agent for a book, consider letting the agency do only that particular title or project.

❏ Require the agent to collect royalties and remit author's share to the author. (Paragraph 6)

❏ Require payments to be made quickly after billings are collected. (Paragraph 7)

❏ Charge interest on payments that are overdue. (Paragraph 7)

❏ Require the agent to treat money due the author as trust funds and to hold it in an account separate from the funds of the agency. (Paragraph 7)

❏ Require the agent to bear miscellaneous marketing expenses, such as messengers, shipping, phone calls, and the like.

❏ If the agent insists that the author bear certain expenses, require the author's approval for expenses in excess of a minimum amount.

❏ State that the author shall receive a copy of any statements of account received by the agent at the time the author is paid. (Paragraph 8)

❏ Provide for full accountings by the agent on a regular basis, such as every six months, if requested. (Paragraph 8)

❏ Provide the right to inspect books and records on reasonable notice. (Paragraph 9)

❏ Allow for termination on thirty days' notice to the other party. (Paragraph 10)

❏ State that the agreement will terminate in the event of the agent's bankruptcy or insolvency. (Paragraph 10)

❏ For book contracts, it is customary for the agent to continue to collect royalties and deduct the agent's commission even after termination of the agency contract. However, it would be better for the author to have the right to direct payment of his or her share after such termination. This might provide some protection against the agent's insolvency or holding of money in the event of a dispute, despite the fact that usually the author wants the agent to collect income. (Paragraph 10)

❏ Do not agree to an "agency coupled with an interest," since this language may make it impossible for the author to collect income directly from the publisher, even after termination. If the agent insists on such language, it should be limited to the amount of the agent's commissions so the author is able to collect his or her share directly.

❏ If the agent will insert a provision regarding payment to the agent into book publishing contracts, this provision should permit payment directly to the author of amounts due the author after termination of the contract between author and agent.

❏ Do not allow assignment of the contract, since both the agent and the author are rendering personal services. (Paragraph 11)

❏ Allow the author to assign payments due under the contract. (Paragraph 11)

❏ If the agent represents authors who are competitive with one another, decide what precautions might be taken against favoritism. Whether it is advantageous or disadvantageous to have an agent represent competing authors will depend on the unique circumstances of each case.

❏ If the agent requires a warranty and indemnity clause under which the author states that he or she owns the work and has the right to sell it, limit the liability of the author to actual breaches resulting in a judgment and try to place a ceiling on the potential liability.

❏ Provide for arbitration of disputes in excess of the amount which can be sued for in small claims court. (Paragraph 12)

❏ Compare the standard provisions in the introductory pages with Paragraphs 13–16.

Author–Agent Contract

AGREEMENT, entered into as of this _____ day of _____, 20_____, between _____ (hereinafter referred to as the "Author"), located at _____, and _____ (hereinafter referred to as the "Agent"), located at _____.

WHEREAS, the Author is an established author of proven talents; and

WHEREAS, the Author wishes to have an agent represent him or her in marketing certain rights enumerated herein; and

WHEREAS, the Agent is capable of marketing the writing created by the Author; and

WHEREAS, the Agent wishes to represent the Author;

NOW, THEREFORE, in consideration of the foregoing premises and the mutual covenants hereinafter set forth and other valuable consideration, the parties hereto agree as follows:

1. Agency. The Author appoints the Agent to act as his or her representative:

    (A) in the following geographical area _____

    (B) for the following markets: ❏ Book publishing ❏ Magazines ❏ Television ❏ Motion Picture ❏ Other, specified as _____

    (C) to be the Author's ❏ exclusive ❏ nonexclusive agent in the area and markets indicated.

    (D) Electronic rights are ❏ outside the scope of this agency contract ❏ covered by this agency contract insofar as the sale of such rights is incidental to the sale of nonelectronic rights ❏ covered by this agency contract. For purposes of this agreement, electronic rights are defined as rights in the digitized form of works that can be encoded, stored, and retrieved from such media as computer disks, CD-ROM, computer databases, and network servers.

Any rights not granted to the Agent are reserved to the Author.

2. Best Efforts. The Agent agrees to use his or her best efforts in submitting the Author's work for the purpose of securing assignments for the Author. The Agent shall negotiate the terms of any assignment that is offered, but the Author may reject any assignment if he or she finds the terms thereof unacceptable.

3. Samples. The Author shall provide the Agent with such samples of work as are from time to time necessary for the purpose of securing assignments. These samples shall remain the property of the Author and be returned on termination of this Agreement.

4. Term. This Agreement shall take effect as of the date first set forth above, and remain in full force and effect for a term of one year, unless terminated as provided in Paragraph 10.

5. Commissions. The Agent shall be entitled to a _____ percent commission for work obtained by the Agent during the term of this Agreement and a _____ percent commission for work obtained by the Author during the term of this Agreement, except that no commission shall be payable for the following types of work obtained by the Author_____.

It is understood by both parties that no commissions shall be paid on assignments rejected by the Author or for which the Author fails to receive payment, regardless of the reason payment is not made. Further, no commissions shall be payable for any part of the billing that is due to expenses incurred by the Author and reimbursed by the client. In the event that a flat fee is paid by the client, ❏ the Agent's commission shall be payable only on the fee as reduced for expenses ❏ the Agent's commission shall be payable on the full fee.

6. Billing. The Agent shall be responsible for all billings.

7. Payments. The Agent shall make all payments due within _____ days of receipt of any fees covered by this Agreement. Such payments due shall be be deemed trust funds and shall not be intermingled with funds belonging to the Agent. Late payments shall be accompanied by interest calculated at the rate of _____ percent per month thereafter.

8. Accountings. The Agent shall send copies of statements of account received by the Agent to the Author when rendered. If requested, the Agent shall also provide the Author with semiannual accountings showing all income for the period, the clients' names and addresses, the fees paid, the dates of payment, the amounts on which the Agent's commissions are to be calculated, and the sums due less those amounts already paid.

9. Inspection of the Books and Records. The Agent shall keep the books and records with respect to payments due each party at his or her place of business and permit the other party to inspect these books and records during normal business hours on the giving of reasonable notice.

10. Termination. This Agreement may be terminated by either party by giving thirty (30) days' written notice to the other party. In the event of the bankruptcy or insolvency of the Agent, this Agreement shall also terminate. The rights and obligations under Paragraphs 3, 6, 7, 8, and 9 shall survive termination, provided that in the event of termination the Author shall have the right to have payments (less commissions) paid directly to the Author rather than to the Agent as set forth in Paragraph 7 and the Agent shall no longer have the right to license any work placed for publication during the term of this Agreement.

11. Assignment. This Agreement shall not be assigned by either of the parties hereto. It shall be binding on and inure to the benefit of the successors, admininstrators, executors, or heirs of the Agent and Author.

12. Arbitration. Any disputes arising under this Agreement shall be settled by arbitration before _____ under the rules of the American Arbitration Association in the City of _____, except that the parties shall have the right to go to court for claims of $_____ or less. Any award rendered by the arbitrator may be entered in any court having jurisdiction thereof.

13. Notices. All notices shall be given to the parties at their respective addresses set forth above.

14. Independent Contractor Status. Both parties agree that the Agent is acting as an independent contractor. This Agreement is not an employment agreement, nor does it constitute a joint venture or partnership between the Author and Agent.

15. Amendments and Merger. All amendments to this Agreement must be written. This Agreement incorporates the entire understanding of the parties.

16. Governing Law. This Agreement shall be governed by the laws of the State of _____.

IN WITNESS WHEREOF, the parties have signed this Agreement as of the date set forth above.

Author _____   Agent _____

Book Publishing Contract

A book contract is worth celebrating, but it is like a celebration to mark the beginning of a long journey. The creation of the book may take years, the life of the book may span decades. And the book may be the source for innumerable spin-offs, such as a television series or films, and the licensing of electronic rights.

The book contract offers opportunities and presents pitfalls. Authors are well advised to seek expert assistance in negotiating these contracts. Since the book contract invariably originates with the publisher, the negotiation checklist will be especially valuable. Form 5 is worth study because it contains terms which are favorable to authors.

Form 5 might also be used when a nonprofessional publisher asks an author to do a book. For example, a charity, chamber of commerce, or even a corporation might want to contract for a book of specialized interest. If neither party has a standard contract to offer, Form 5 could be adapted for use.

The grant of rights gives the publisher certain rights, which the author carefully seeks to limit with respect to medium, time period, territory, and language. Beyond this, however, the publisher also seeks subsidiary rights, which are simply rights of exploitation in markets not encompassed by the grant of rights. If the grant of rights covers only the publication of books, then the sale of film, audio, or electronic versions would be a licensing of subsidiary rights.

The goal of the author in negotiating a book contract is to give the publisher only those rights that the publisher is capable of successfully exploiting. For those rights given to the publisher, fair compensation must be provided by the contract. Compensation usually takes the form of an advance and a royalty, so that the author profits from greater sales of the work. Advances are paid to the author in installments, often half when the contract is signed and half when the manuscript is turned in to the publisher. Accountings should take place on a regular basis and provide the author with as much information as possible.

Because compensation to the author is based on royalties, the computation of the royalty is crucial. First, is the royalty based on retail price or net price? Most publishers compute royalties based on retail price, which is best for authors. Net price is what the publisher receives from selling the book to wholesalers and bookstores, so net price is usually 40 to 50 percent less than retail price. The percentage rates for royalties are crucial. While these rates are subject to negotiation, somewhat standard rates are given in the negotiation checklist. And there is one important piece of information that many authors are not aware of. That is, royalty rates are reduced for a number of reasons, such as sales at a higher-than-normal discount. These reductions can have a devastating effect on royalties. The contract must be carefully reviewed to ascertain the impact of such royalty reduction provisions.

The author will want to have the work copyrighted in the author's name. The copyright lasts for the life of the author plus another seventy years and any publishing contract can be terminated after thirty-five to forty years under the termination provisions of the copyright law. To avoid any confusion as to who owns the copyright, the copyright notice in the book should be in the author's name.

The author will also want artistic control over the content of the book. No changes should be allowed without the author's approval. Certainly no advertising or unrelated content should be added without the consent of the author.

The publisher will request a warranty and indemnity provision from the author. In this provision the author states that the book contains no copyright infringements, no defamatory material, invades no one's privacy, and is not otherwise unlawful. If any of these warranties prove incorrect, the author agrees to reimburse the publisher for any damages and costs, including attorney's fees. Some publishers are now extending their publishers' liability insurance to cover authors for these risks. In the absence of such insurance, the author should seek to set a dollar limit or percent-of-royalty-income ceiling on his or her liability to the publisher.

The publisher will also want the option to publish the author's next work and will want to restrict the author from publishing competing works. The author should certainly try to have both these provisions stricken from the contract, since they may impair the author's ability to earn a livelihood.

If an author is creating a book with a coauthor, many publishers will simply have both the author and coauthor sign a book contract which specifies the division of royalties. This is satisfactory for the publisher, but leaves unresolved many important issues between the author and coauthor. They should have a collaboration agreement, such as that shown in Form 6.

Supplementary checklists for negotiating with book packagers and subsidy publishers follow the negotiation checklist for a book contract between an author and a commercial publisher. While many of the contractual issues are closely related, the key points for these other arrangements are highlighted in these checklists.

Filling in the Form

In the Preamble, fill in the date and the names and addresses of the parties. In the first Whereas clause, briefly describe the subject of the book. In Paragraph 1 enter the title of the book and specify the rights granted to the publisher with respect to form (such as hardcover, quality paperback, mass market paperback), territory, language, and term. In Paragraph 3 fill in the deadline for delivery of the manuscript as well as the approximate length of the book. Provide the amount of time to do revisions if requested and, in the event of rejection of the manuscript, specify what will happen to advances which have been paid. In Paragraph 4 fill in whatever materials, such as illustrations or an index, the author is also obligated to provide and specify a contribution by the publisher toward these costs. In Paragraph 5 specify a contribution by the publisher toward the costs of obtaining any permissions. In Paragraph 6 give the number of months in which the publisher must publish the book. In Paragraph 7 specify the royalty rates and situations in which royalties are discounted. In Paragraph 8 fill in the subsidiary rights which the publisher has the right to license and the division of income for each right. In Paragraph 9 specify the amount of the advance to the author. Indicate in Paragraph 10 how often the publisher will give accountings. In Paragraph 13 show the form of authorship credit which the author will receive. In Paragraph 14 place limits on how much the author can be forced to pay for a breach of warranty and how much the publisher can hold in escrow to cover the author's indemnity obligation. State in Paragraph 15 which artistic decisions will be determined by the author. In Paragraph 17 specify how many free copies the author will receive and give the discount at which the author may purchase additional copies. In Paragraph 24 state who will arbitrate and the place for arbitration. In Paragraph 28 fill in which state's law will govern the contract. Both parties should then sign the contract.

Negotiation Checklist

❑ Limit the grant of exclusive rights to publish with respect to medium, area, duration, and language, such as granting "book rights in the English language in the United States for a term of ten years." Note that publishers will want to expand the grant of rights and exploit the book over the long life of the copyright. (Paragraph 1)

❑ Consider reserving Canadian rights, in particular, for sale to a Canadian publisher.

❑ Specify with respect to medium whether the grant of rights covers hardcover, quality paperback, mass market paperback, etc.

❑ Reserve to the author all rights not specifically granted to the publisher, including electronic rights. (Paragraph 2)

❑ Specify a date for delivery of the manuscript. (Paragraph 3)

❏ Do not make time of the essence with respect to delivery of the manuscript.

❏ Extend the deadline in the event of illness of the author or other circumstances beyond his or her control which cause a delay.

❏ Provide for a margin of lateness in delivery, such as ninety days, before the publisher can terminate the agreement. (Paragraph 3) Any extensions of the time for delivery should be obtained in writing.

❏ Give the approximate length in words of the manuscript to be delivered. (Paragraph 3)

❏ Allow the author to deliver a "complete manuscript," rather than "a manuscript in form and content satisfactory to the publisher." (Paragraph 3 has a compromise provision.)

❏ If the author must deliver a manuscript which is satisfactory to the publisher, make an objective standard of reasonableness such as "reasonably satisfactory."

❏ Attach an outline or detailed description of the book to the contract so the manuscript can be judged against the outline. (Paragraph 3)

❏ Require the publisher to give detailed suggestions for revisions and a reasonable time to do the revisions. (Paragraph 3)

❏ If the manuscript is rejected by the publisher, determine whether advances will be kept, paid back, or paid back only if another contract for the book is signed with a different publisher. (Paragraph 3)

❏ If the author is submitting portions of the work in progress, have the publisher confirm in writing that these portions are satisfactory.

❏ Specify whether the author shall be responsible for delivering illustrations, photographs, maps, tables, charts, or an index, and give details as to the number and nature of any such additional items. (Paragraph 4)

❏ If the author must provide additional items which require the outlay of money, such as photographs or having an index created, state who will pay for this. (Paragraph 4)

❏ If the author is to pay for such additional items, such as an index or permission fees, provide for the publisher to make a nonrefundable payment toward these costs. (Paragraph 4)

❏ If the author is to create the index, allow for a certain amount of time in which to do this after the author has the paginated galleys.

❏ If the author fails to deliver any required materials, allow for a certain period of time, such as thirty days after notice from the publisher, for the author to provide what is missing.

❏ Require the publisher to publish the book within a certain time period, such as twelve or eighteen months. (Paragraph 6)

❏ If the publisher does not publish within the specified time period, give the author the right to terminate the contract and keep all money received. (Paragraph 6)

❏ Provide for royalties, which are usually preferable to a flat fee. (Paragraph 7)

❏ If a flat fee is offered, require a reuse fee after a certain number of books are printed so the flat fee becomes more like a royalty.

❏ Base the computation of royalties on suggested retail price, rather than net price, which is what the publisher receives from wholesalers and book stores. (Paragraph 7)

❏ If the contract provides for a freight pass-through (in which a book is priced at a slightly higher price to reimburse the bookstore for freight costs which the publisher normally pays but is not, in fact, paying), indicate that the amount of the freight pass-through is to be subtracted from the retail price prior to the computation of royalties.

❏ Have the royalty be a percentage of retail price, rather than a fixed dollar amount, since the price of the book may increase over time. (Paragraph 7)

All royalties are negotiable and the rates offered vary from one publisher to another, but what follows are general guidelines of what the author may expect:

❏ For an adult trade book in hardcover, a basic royalty of 10 percent of suggested retail price on the first 5,000 copies sold, 12 1/2 percent on the next 5,000 copies, and 15 percent on all copies sold in excess of 10,000.

❏ For a children's book in hardcover, a basic royalty starting at 10 percent and escalating to 15 percent after an agreed-upon number of copies are sold (but the practice varies widely with respect to children's books).

❏ For a quality paperback published by the publisher of the hardcover edition or as a paperback original, a royalty of 6 percent of retail price on the first 10,000 copies (or the first print run if it is less than 10,000 copies) with an increase to 7 1/2 percent for copies sold in excess of 10,000. Some publishers may offer 8 to 10 percent as a royalty, while others may escalate their rates only after the sale of 25,000 copies.

❏ For a mass market paperback published by the publisher of the hardcover edition, a royalty of 6 percent of retail price on the first 150,000 copies sold with an increase to 8 percent thereafter. A mass market original may have a similar or somewhat higher royalty rate structure.

❏ For professional, scientific, or technical books, a royalty is likely to be based on net price (which is what the publisher receives) rather than retail price. The royalty should be at least 15 percent of the net price. For hardcover textbooks, the royalty should escalate to 18 percent after 7,500 or 10,000 books have been sold and go even higher thereafter.

❏ For textbooks which originate in paperback, the royalty should be in the range of 10 to 15 percent of net price.

❏ Whenever escalations in royalty rates are provided in a contract, review carefully which sales are counted to reach the number of copies necessary for the royalty to escalate.

❏ Review with special care any provisions which reduce royalties and find out how many sales are likely to come within these provisions.

❏ Establish that the reduced royalties will in no event be less than half or three-quarters of what the regular royalties would have been.

Sales causing reduced royalties may include:

❏ Sales at a higher than normal discount to wholesalers or retailers. A normal discount might be 40 percent, and some publishers reduce royalties when the discount reaches 48 percent or more. This reduction may be gradual, such as 1 percent of royalty for each percent in excess of 48 percent discount, but the impact can be great. Moving the starting point for reductions from a 48 percent discount to perhaps a 51 percent discount may minimize the loss to a large degree, depending on the sales structure of the particular publisher. If such discounts are due to purchasing large quantities of books, the author should also consider requiring that different titles not be cumulated together for these purposes.

❏ Sales by mail order or direct response advertising may cause the royalty to be reduced to as little as half the regular royalty rate.

❏ Sales in Canada may cause the royalty to be reduced to two-thirds or even half of the regular royalty rate.

❏ Sales on small reprintings, such as 1,000 copies, may cause the royalty to be reduced to three-quarters of the regular rate. The author might allow this only if sales in the period prior to the reprinting were below a certain level and the reprinting did not take place until two years after first publication.

❑ Children's book authors should pay especially close attention to royalty reductions for sales in library bound editions outside normal trade channels.

❑ Sales for export, to reading circles, to book clubs, and to organizations outside regular book-selling channels may, if the discount from retail price is 60 percent or greater, cause the royalty to be reduced to 15 percent (for bound copies) or 18 percent (for unbound sheets) of what the publisher actually receives from the sale.

❑ Sales as a remainder (when excess inventory is liquidated), if at a discount of 70 percent or more, may cause the royalty to be reduced to 10 percent of what the publisher actually receives (or no royalty at all if the price is less than the publisher's manufacturing cost).

❑ Limit the percentage of copies which can be treated as sold at a discount.

❑ For royalties based on what the publisher actually receives, do not allow any reduction for discounts or bad debts.

❑ Finally, with respect to reduced royalties, promotional copies, author's copies, and copies which are destroyed are royalty free.

❑ Consider requiring that the publisher of the hardcover not bring out a paperback version until one year after the hardcover publication.

❑ Determine as to each subsidiary right which party controls that right and what the division of proceeds will be. (Paragraph 8) Subsidiary rights cover many possible sources of income which the publisher will exploit through marketing to other companies. Licensing of subsidiary rights may include abridgments, book clubs, reprints by another publisher, first and second serializa-

tions (which are magazine or newspaper rights before and after book publication), foreign or translation rights, syndication, advertising, commercial uses, films, plays, radio shows, television, audio tapes, and electronic versions (CD-ROM, online, etc.)

❑ State that the publisher has no right to share in subsidiary rights if the publisher does not fulfill all of its obligations under the contract. (Paragraph 8)

❑ Determine for each right whether the author, agent, or publisher can best sell that right.

❑ Reserve to the author all rights the publisher is not set up to sell.

❑ Retain a right of approval over subsidiary rights to be sold by the publisher.

❑ Reserve to the author all nonpublishing rights, such as stage, audio tape, novelty, television, film, and electronic rights.

❑ For first serial sales (the sale of part of the book to a magazine before first publication of the book), the author should receive 100 percent of the income. If the publisher acts as agent, the publisher might receive 10 to 20 percent. This approach would also apply to nonpublishing rights if, in fact, the publisher does obtain a right to share in the proceeds. However, for electronic rights (digitized versions of works for use in multimedia, CD-ROM, online, etc.), publishers are seeking 50 percent.

❑ For paperback licenses, book club licenses, abridgments and selections, and second serializations (the sale of part of the book to a magazine after first publication of the book), the author should seek 50 percent of the first $10,000 of income, 60 percent of the next $10,000, and 70 percent over $20,000.

❑ If the original publication is in paperback, the author should expect 50 to 75 percent of the income from licensing hardcover rights.

❏ For a paperback original, consider requiring that the paperback publisher wait a year before licensing hardcover rights.

❏ Allow the author 120 days to seek out a better offer for a paperback reprint.

❏ If the publisher insists on receiving part of the proceeds from licensing electronic rights, require that the negotiation for what the author will receive from the electronic license take place just before the electronic publication. This will allow a better assessment of the value of the electronic rights.

❏ If the publisher insists on having the right to license electronic rights, the author might seek a right of approval over all such licenses. This approval would be to insure that quality is maintained and that the work is not shortened, lengthened, or combined with other works in a detrimental way.

❏ If the print publisher is to do an electronic version of a book, insist on receiving an advance and royalty for the electronic version.

❏ Insist that the print publisher doing an electronic version not change the work in any way without the author's permission (such as addition of a sound track, abridgement, or combination with other works).

❏ Limit electronic rights to existing formats, specify which formats, and seek to make the usage nonexclusive.

❏ Seek assurance from the publisher that it and its licensees will take reasonable measures to prevent copying of the author's work.

❏ Make certain that any provision reserving or reverting rights to the author covers electronic rights.

❏ Carefully scrutinize the definition of licensing income. The author should always seek to have no reductions from such income. If the publisher uses "net income," the author must check which expenses will be deducted.

❏ Require that the author receive copies of any licenses negotiated by the publisher.

❏ Provide for the pass-through of licensing income received (perhaps in excess of a specified minimum amount, such as $100), so that such income is paid to the author within 10 days of receipt by the publisher and is not held for payment with other royalties.

❏ Provide for the payment of nonrefundable advances to the author, preferably paid in full at the time of signing the contract or half on signing the contract and half on delivery of the manuscript. (Paragraph 9)

❏ Provide that each book project is separate, so that money owed by the author on one book cannot be taken from money due to the author on another book.

❏ Consider whether income from licensing subsidiary rights, especially first serial rights, should be applied to unearned advances.

❏ Require periodic accountings at least every six months, which is common for the publishing industry, or as frequently as every three months if it can be negotiated. (Paragraph 10)

❏ Specify the information to be given in the accountings, so the author can appraise their accuracy. Ideally the accounting would show for the period and cumulatively to date the number of copies printed and bound, copies sold and returned at each royalty rate, copies distributed free for publicity, copies lost or destroyed, copies remaindered, and royalties due to the author. (Paragraph 10)

❏ Income from subsidiary rights should also be accounted for on these statements, even if such income is passed through to the author on receipt by the publisher. Copies of licenses should be provided at this time, if they have not already been provided.

❏ If the publisher wishes to create a reserve against returns of books, the amount of this reserve should be limited to a percentage of royalties due in any period (such as 20 percent) and the reserve should not be allowed to continue beyond a specified number of accounting periods. Since sales on first publication are most likely to be returned, the reserve might last for 3 accounting periods after first publication. (Paragraph 10)

❏ Require that any sums owing on the statements of account be paid when the statements are given. (Paragraph 11)

❏ In a very unusual case, after careful consultation with a tax advisor, the author may want a provision which limits royalties each year and causes any additional royalties to be spread forward into the future.

❏ State that the author may inspect the books and records of the publisher and, if a discrepancy of more than 5 percent is found to the publisher's advantage, the publisher shall pay the cost of the inspection. (Paragraph 12)

❏ Do not allow the publisher to place a time limit, such as one or two years after the mailing of the statement of account, on the author's right to inspect the books and have errors corrected.

❏ Require that copyright notice appear in the name of the author. (Paragraph 13)

❏ Require the publisher to register the copyright. (Paragraph 13)

❏ Specify that the author shall receive authorship credit. If there is a coauthor, indicate the sequence of names and, if necessary, size and placement. (Paragraph 13)

❏ Seek to have the publisher cover the author under the publisher's liability insurance policy for copyright infringements, libel, and related violations of rights. This will safeguard the author against many of the dangers in the warranty and indemnity provisions of publishers' contracts.

❏ If the publisher covers the author with its insurance, seek to have the publisher also pay or at least share in the cost of any deductible (which may be as high as $50,000 or $100,000) in the event of a claim.

❏ State that the author only warrants that to his or her knowledge the work does not libel anyone or violate anyone's rights of privacy. (Paragraph 14)

❏ Limit the indemnification to final judgments after all appeals have been taken. Avoid indemnifying for alleged breaches of the warranties. (Paragraph 14)

❏ Reserve the right not to pay for the publisher's costs and attorney's fees if the author selects and pays for the attorney to defend the action. (Paragraph 14)

❏ Do not indemnify for materials inserted at the publisher's request. (Paragraph 14)

❏ Require that the publisher indemnify the author for materials inserted in the book or placed on the cover at the publisher's request or choice.

❏ Limit the amount of the author's indemnification to the lesser of a dollar amount or a percentage of amounts payable under the contract. (Paragraph 14)

❏ Limit the right of the publisher to withhold royalties on account of the lawsuit to the lesser of a percentage of amounts payable under the contract or the amount of alleged damages. (Paragraph 14) Alternatively, the author might seek the right to post a surety bond.

❏ Do not agree to let sums payable under one contract be used to pay for a breach of a warranty under another contract.

❏ Retain a veto power over any settlements to be made by the publisher, since the money to pay the settlement may be the author's.

❏ If there is a joint author, determine whether both author and coauthor will be liable for a breach of warranty by one or the other. Review Form 6.

❏ Keep artistic control over the content of the book, including the right to do revisions if the publisher requests them. (Paragraph 15)

❏ Provide that licensees must agree not to add anything to the book, including advertising, without first obtaining the author's consent.

❏ Seek a right of consultation with respect to the price, print run, method of printing, publication date, design, paper, new printings, and similar matters. Most publishers will insist on having the ultimate control over these matters. (Paragraph 15)

❏ Agree to the book's final title, which can only be changed by the agreement of both parties.

❏ Give the author a veto power over material which the publisher wishes to place in the book or on the cover.

❏ Obtain the right to consult regarding the promotional budget, promotional campaign, or distribution of press releases and review copies. (Paragraph 15)

❏ Limit the amount of promotion the publisher can require the author to do.

❏ State that the author shall review proofs or galleys, and give a period of time in which to do this. (Paragraph 15)

❏ Most contracts require authors to pay for author's alterations once the manuscript is typeset, but this should be only in excess of a percentage of the typesetting cost (such as 15 percent), might be subject to a maximum dollar amount, and should exclude printer's errors or unavoidable updating.

❏ Require that the publisher send out a certain number of review copies to a list of people supplied by the author.

❏ Require the publisher to return the manuscript and all accompanying materials to the author within a certain time period after publication and to give the author page proofs if the author requests them prior to publication. (Paragraph 16)

❏ If valuable materials, such as original art or photographic transparencies, are submitted to the publisher, require that the publisher insure them and be strictly liable for loss or damage.

❏ Provide for the author to receive ten or more free copies of the book and any subsequent editions in a different form, such as a quality paperback after original hardcover publication. (Paragraph 17)

❏ Allow the author to purchase additional copies at a 40 or 50 percent discount from retail price. (Paragraph 17)

❏ Do not limit the author to personal use of copies purchased if the author wishes to sell these copies.

❏ If the author wants to sell a large quantity of the book, ask for a discount schedule. For example, 1 to 99 copies might have a 50 percent discount, 100 to 250 copies a 55 percent discount, 251 to 499 copies a 60 percent discount, 500 to 999 copies a 65 percent discount, and 1,000 or more copies a 70 percent or higher discount. If the author can order prior to the publisher's print run, a high discount is even more justifiable.

❏ Require that the publisher pay royalties on copies sold to the author.

❏ The author should have the first option to revise the book at the publisher's request. However, the publisher will want the right to have the revision done by someone else if the author cannot or will not do it. (Paragraph 18)

❏ If the book may be outdated quickly, state that the publisher must allow a revision within a certain time period, such as two or three years, and that the contract will terminate if the publisher refuses such a revision.

❏ If the author is to do a revision, state that an additional advance shall be negotiated and paid at that time.

❏ If a revision is done by someone else, the cost of this will come from royalties due the author. The cost should only come from royalties payable on the revised book, not the prior edition or other books by the author.

❏ Specify a minimum royalty the author will receive, even if a revision is done by someone else, or cap how much the royalties can be reduced to pay for the revision.

❏ Give the author the right to remove his or her name from the credits if the revision is not satisfactory.

❏ Make the agreement binding on successors and assigns of the parties. (Paragraph 19)

❏ Do not allow assignment by one party unless the other party consents to this in writing. (Paragraph 19)

❏ Allow the author to assign the right to royalties without obtaining the publisher's consent. (Paragraph 19)

❏ In the event of infringement, state that the parties can sue jointly and, after deducting expenses, share any recovery. If one party chooses not to sue, the other party can sue and, after deducting expenses, share any recovery. (Paragraph 20)

❏ With respect to rights retained by the author, the publisher should have no right to sue for an infringement.

❏ With respect to subsidiary rights in which the author receives more than 50 percent of income, the publisher's right to sue should be limited to the percentage the publisher would receive.

❏ Give the author the right to terminate the contract if the book remains out-of-print after a request by the author that it be put back in print. (Paragraph 21)

❏ Define out-of-print to include when in any 12 months sales are less than 750 copies or royalties are less than a specified amount.

❏ Define out-of-print to mean that the book is not available in bookstores, regardless of whether the publisher has copies.

❏ Define whether a book must be out-of-print in all editions or only those published by the publisher to be deemed out-of-print.

❏ Give the author the right to terminate if the publisher fails to give statements of account, fails to pay, or fails to publish. In all of these cases the author would retain the payments received from the publisher. (Paragraph 21)

❏ State that the contract will automatically terminate if the publisher goes bankrupt or becomes insolvent. (Paragraph 21)

❏ If the author fails to deliver a manuscript, the publisher will expect to receive back all payments. (Paragraphs 3 and 21)

❏ If the manuscript delivered in good faith is unsatisfactory to the publisher, the standard publishing contract will require the return of advances but the author can negotiate to retain them. (Paragraph 21)

❏ If possible, avoid any requirement to repay an advance if a book, after rejection by one publisher, is placed with another publisher.

❏ Provide for the reversion of all rights to the author upon termination. (Paragraph 21)

❏ Whatever the ground for termination, the author should have the right to purchase all production materials at scrap value and remaining copies at the lesser of cost or remainder value. (Paragraph 22)

❏ Allow the use of the author's name or picture to promote the work, but require that the promotion be in good taste. (Paragraph 23) The author might seek either to supply the biographical material or have a right of approval.

❏ If the author signs the contract first, a provision might be made to withdraw the offer if the publisher does not sign within thirty or sixty days after receipt of the contract.

❏ The author should resist giving the publisher a security interest in the work, which might entitle the publisher to seize the manuscript and related materials for money owed to the publisher (such as unrecouped advances) under the contract.

❏ If the author has an agent, the contract may provide for payment to the agent. A better approach would be to make the contract subject to the author–agent contract. In any case, the author should have the right to receive direct payment of all monies due other than the agent's commission.

❏ If an agency clause gives the agent a right to act on behalf of the author, review which actions the agent may take.

❏ The author should strike from the contract any provision which limits the creation of competitive works, since this may impair the range of work the author may later create. If the publisher insists on such a provision, the author should narrowly limit its scope with respect to the same subject matter, the same audiences, the same forms of book publication, duration, and geographic extent, and state that such a provision would be enforceable only when the sales of the original book would be impaired.

❏ The publisher may also seek an option for the author's next book. Ideally this will be stricken from the contract. If it is not stricken, it should be an option for one work only on terms to be agreed to (not terms identical to the existing contract). The publisher must accept or reject the work within a limited time period, such as thirty or sixty days, based on an outline (not a complete manuscript).

❏ State that a noncompetition clause or an option clause will be valid only if the publisher is not in breach of the contract and the contract has not been terminated.

❏ Include an arbitration clause. (Paragraph 24)

❏ Review the standard provisions in the introductory pages and compare with Paragraphs 25 to 28.

❏ If there is a joint author, review Form 6.

Negotiation Checklist for Use with Book Packagers

Book packagers have increased their presence in the publishing world in the last decade. The packager contracts with a publisher and agrees to deliver a book. The book may be delivered as a manuscript, finished mechanicals, or bound books. The publisher pays the packager, who in turn pays the author. The problem from the author's point of view is that the packager may take a substantial portion of the income which would normally be paid to the author. For example, the packager may take 50 percent of the author's royalties or pay the lowest possible flat fee and keep all of the royalties. The author must decide if such an arrangement is worthwhile.

A packager paying a flat fee may seek a work-for-hire or all rights contract with the author, in which case the author will be left with no residual interest in the work. In addition to the checklist for negotiating with a book publisher, the author should also use the following checklist to negotiate with a packager.

❏ Compare the royalty offered by the packager to what a publisher would pay for the same book.

❏ Compare the advance offered by the packager to what a publisher would pay.

❏ If the packager wants to pay a flat fee, consider whether a publisher would usually pay a royalty with an advance.

❏ Review the grant of rights to the packager and consider whether the packager needs such extensive rights to convey to the publisher.

❏ If the packager seeks to pay a flat fee in return for all rights or work for hire, consider whether it is fair for the packager to own the entire work as if the packager had been the author.

❏ Decide if the division of subsidiary rights income with the packager is fair.

❏ Under no circumstances should an author work without a guarantee of payment, which may happen if the packager is developing ideas for publishers but has not yet received a firm commitment from any publisher. In such a case the contract with the packager must provide for payments to the author regardless of whether the project is ever placed.

❏ The author's work should be accepted based on the contract with the packager, rather than depending on whether a publisher also finds it acceptable.

❏ Ascertain the authorship credit for the book, since the packager may want to be credited as author.

Review the negotiation checklist for the book contract, since those issues also exist with a packager. For example, the author dealing with a packager must be concerned about a schedule of payments, accountings, the right to inspect books, who owns the copyright, whether copyright notice is given, arbitration, and even who has the rights to the book if it goes out of print. Of course, the author should have a written contract with the packager setting forth the terms agreed upon between them.

Negotiation Checklist for Use with Subsidy Publishers

The subsidy publisher is paid by the author to bring out the author's book. The problem is that most books are relatively simple to print but far more difficult to market. While some authors are disappointed with the appearance of the books printed by a subsidy publisher, far more are disappointed by the failure of the book to find an audience.

Subsidy publishers, sometimes called vanity presses, offer authors the opportunity to place their books before the public. Nonetheless, subsidy publishing has a stigma. It almost certainly means the author has failed to find a commercial publisher willing to publish the book. Each author has to make an individual decision as to whether subsidy publishing is appropriate. Assuming the author wants to go forward, the following checklist supplements the negotiation checklist for the book contract with a commercial publisher.

❏ Obtain a firm fee from the publisher and determine what services are included for this fee.

❏ Make a schedule of payments, preferably based on stages of the book's completion.

❏ State the agreed upon publication date and include a production schedule that will allow that date to be met. Consider making time of the essence with respect to meeting that date.

❏ Specify what editorial evaluation and assistance will be available, since many authors complain that subsidy publishers are indiscriminate in what is accepted for publication and offer no assistance in improving the quality of the work.

❏ Require that the publisher provide copyediting for the manuscript.

❏ State that the author shall have the right to approve the design of the cover and interior of the book.

❏ Give the author the right to review galleys or page proofs so typographical errors can be corrected.

❏ Specify the type of binding (hardcover or softcover), whether the book has a jacket or not, how many colors will be used in printing the jacket or cover, the paper for the cover and interior of the book, and all relevant specifications. A shorthand way to handle this would be to state the book will be equal in quality to another title already published. This gives objectivity to the author's concerns about quality.

❏ Carefully determine where the publisher can sell the book. Do not give any markets to the publisher unless the publisher can sell effectively into those markets.

❏ Reserve all subsidiary rights to the author.

❏ Try not to give a noncompetition or option provision to the publisher.

❏ Specify the amount of money to be spent on promotion and the form this promotion will take. How many press releases and review copies will be sent out and to which lists? How much will be spent on advertising and in which publications? Will the publisher pay for a direct mail brochure? If so, how large will the direct mail campaign be and who will it be directed to? Will the publisher have a publicist seek talk shows on radio and television for the author? If so, specify in the contract exactly what the publicist will do.

❏ Give the author the right to approve the promotion and marketing of the book, including approving the content and appearance of press releases and direct mail brochures as well as the choice of lists to which mailings will be made.

❏ What royalty rate will the author receive? A rate of 40 percent of retail price on the first print run would not be unusual, since the publisher has already made its profit in the fee paid by the author.

❏ How many free books will the author receive?

❏ What must the author pay for additional copies of the book? Having paid to have the book printed, buying copies of the book may make the author feel he or she has paid twice for the same product.

❏ Will royalties be paid on copies of the book purchased by the author?

❏ Will the author be free to sell these books? Since most sales come through the author's efforts and the author will make far more by selling directly rather than creating sales for the publisher, this is an important point.

❏ How many of the books printed will actually be bound and jacketed? Many subsidy publishers bind a small number of books and keep the rest as unbound sheets. If sufficient copies are not sold during the term of the contract, the unbound sheets are never bound.

❏ If sales are low, will the author at some point receive ownership of the inventory and be able to sell it directly?

❏ Will the author also receive ownership of the mechanicals, computer disks, film, and related production materials?

❏ If the first print run sells out, will the publisher reprint the book at its own cost?

❏ If the book is reprinted, what will the author's royalty be? Many contracts drop the royalty rate to 20 percent of retail price. However, since the publisher made its profit before the book was printed, giving the publisher 80 percent of income requires scrutiny.

❏ Consider whether the author might prefer to own the books and simply have the publisher provide fulfillment services.

❏ To try and avoid the stigma of subsidy publishing, consider whether the author might not use his or her own imprint and have the publisher act as distributor.

❏ The checklist for negotiating with a commercial publisher must also be reviewed, and certainly there should be a written contract with any publisher.

An alternative to subsidy publishing is self-publishing, which is discussed later in this book. The author must give more time to the process, but also has the benefit of complete control. The author hires a designer and a printer and contracts with sales reps or a distributor. In this way, the author gives up no rights and avoids the stigma of subsidy publishing.

Negotiation Checklist for Use with E-Book Publishers

E-books are electronic versions of books on paper. E-books lack the touchable pleasure of paper and the ease of flipping through pages, but offer advantages in terms of portability, search features, and links to related materials. Depending on the type of e-book format, the e-book can be read on a computer or a special reader. Many e-books include security features to prevent unauthorized usage.

For the most part, the considerations of any book contract apply to e-books, so the negotiation checklists shown for a printed book would be very helpful when reviewing an e-book contract. In addition, e-books may be published by a "vanity" or "subsidy" publisher, so the negotiation checklist for use with subsidy publishers may also be relevant. In terms of conceptualization, especially with respect to the transfer of rights, it would also be of value to look at Form 21, the License of Electronic Rights. The following checklist focuses on the special issues that are likely to come up in an e-book contractual negotiation.

❑ Limit the grant of rights. Do not grant non-electronic rights and, even as to electronic rights, only grant what the publisher will be able to market.

❑ Reserve all rights not granted to the author, including but not limited to audio books, translations, film/television, and print-on-demand books (which are printed books produced by digital production).

❑ Do not grant rights that would allow the publisher to use content from the author's book in other publications of the publisher, unless payment is made or the promotional purpose is clear and acceptable to the author.

❑ Seek the highest possible royalty, as much as 50 percent of net income, especially if the print book already exists and the publisher is simply doing an e-book (and not creating the book from a manuscript). The rationale for such a high royalty is that the publisher has relatively little expense in creating the e-book.

❑ Define net income. This should be all income received by the publisher without any deductions other than perhaps the conversion costs (which should be specified at the outset). If deductions are to be taken, they should be carefully reviewed. Remember that the typical discount is 50 percent, so a 50 percent royalty will yield an effective rate of 25 percent of retail price.

❑ Seek an advance, but keep in mind that many e-book publishers do not pay advances.

❑ Find out as much as possible about the publisher's history and background, so that fly-by-night operations can be avoided.

❑ If the author has to pay production costs up front (because the publisher is a subsidy publisher), consider whether the costs are reasonable and whether the author would be in good company with the other authors published by that publisher. Would the author be better off paying for his or her own electronic conversion and retailing the book directly through Web-based retailers?

❑ With a subsidy publisher, the grant of rights should not only be limited but the grant should be nonexclusive. The rationale is that the author is prime mover here and should be free to go elsewhere.

❑ With a subsidy publisher, ascertain where the publisher's books are, in fact, sold, especially on the Web. Does the publisher itself have a good Web site where it sells its books and, if so, what volume does it achieve from the site?

❑ With a subsidy publisher, do not grant subsidiary rights unless the publisher can show an effective and acceptable way to market any such rights.

❑ With a subsidy publisher, be certain that such matters as editing, design, price, and promotion are all subject to the author's approval (or at least a right of consultation) and the publisher will honor its commitments (based on how it has handled books of other authors).

❑ Since promotion is extremely important, specify the nature of the online and off-line promotion that the publisher will undertake and to what degree the promotion will be ongoing. If the publisher fails to promote the book, it might be considered "out-of-promotion" and the author could have the right to terminate the contract.

❑ With a subsidy publisher, request contact information for other authors who can serve as references.

❑ Review works published by the publisher to determine the quality of editing, design, and similar matters.

❑ With a subsidy publisher, retain the right to terminate the contract on 30 or 60 days notice (subject to a reasonable grace period such as 90 days during which the publisher could continue to sell the book). This leaves the author free to accept a better offer from a commercial publisher (such an offer would, presumably, be exclusive). Obviously, the subsidy publisher should have no right to any income due to sales by other publishers on behalf of the author.

❑ With a commercial publisher, retain the right to terminate after a certain number of years (such as 1 or 3), especially if the publisher has merely taken a print book and converted it. The more work the publisher has done, such as creating many links to related materials, the more reasonable is the demand for a longer term.

❑ Permit the author to terminate if a certain level of income is not achieved (or a certain number of units are not sold) within a specified number of accounting periods.

❑ Permit the author to terminate if the book is not published, the publisher fails to pay royalties or goes bankrupt, or the book goes out of print.

❑ Consider the credentials of the editors and whether they will make a valuable contribution to the final version of the book.

❑ Specify which formats the e-book will be prepared in and sold as.

❑ Indicate the piracy protection features that will safeguard the e-book.

❑ Request monthly or quarterly statements of account with payment (instead of semiannual statements of account, which would be the norm with a printed book).

❑ If books are to be produced on disk or in CD-ROM format, how many free copies will the author receive?

❑ If books are to be produced on disk or in CD-ROM format, will the author have a special discount to buy copies?

❑ Keep in mind that many print publishers expect to obtain e-book rights, so the author should be able to deliver such rights if publishing the work as a printed book is a possibility.

❑ Assess whether the publisher is available on a prompt basis to handle issues that come up as well as to move through the normal publishing sequence of production, promotion, and sale.

Book Publishing Contract

AGREEMENT, entered into as of this _____ day of _____, 20___, between _____ (hereinafter referred to as the "Publisher"), located at _____, and _____ (hereinafter referred to as the "Author"), located at _____.

WHEREAS, the Author wishes to create a book on the subject of _____ (hereinafter referred to as the "Work")

WHEREAS, the Publisher is familiar with the work of the Author and wishes to publish a book by the Author; and

WHEREAS, the parties wish to have said publication performed subject to the mutual obligations, covenants, and conditions herein.

NOW, THEREFORE, in consideration of the foregoing premises and the mutual covenants hereinafter set forth and other valuable considerations, the parties hereto agree as follows:

1. **Grant of Rights.** The Author grants, conveys, and transfers to the Publisher in that unpublished Work titled _____, certain limited, exclusive rights as follows:

    (A) To publish, distribute, and sell the Work in the form of a _____ book;

    (B) In the territory of _____;

    (C) In the_____ language; and **(D)** For a term of _____years.

2. **Reservation of Rights.** All rights not specifically granted to the Publisher are reserved to the Author, including but not limited to electronic rights which are defined as rights in the digitized form of works that can be encoded, stored, and retrieved from such media as computer disks, CD-ROM, computer databases, and network servers.

3. **Delivery of Manuscript.** On or before the _____ day of _____, 20_____, the Author shall deliver to the Publisher a complete manuscript of approximately _____ words, which shall be reasonably satisfactory in form and content to the Publisher and in conformity with any outline or description attached hereto and made part hereof. The manuscript shall be in the following form: ❑ double-spaced hard copy ❑ computer files (specify format _____). The manuscript shall include the additional materials listed in Paragraph 4 (except that if an index is to be provided by the Author, it shall be delivered to the Publisher within thirty days of Author's receipt of paginated galleys). If the Author fails to deliver the complete manuscript within ninety days after receiving notice from the Publisher of failure to deliver on time, the Publisher shall have the right to terminate this Agreement and receive back from the Author all monies advanced to the Author pursuant to Paragraphs 4, 5, and 9. If the Author delivers a manuscript which, after being given detailed instructions for revisions by the Publisher and _____ days to complete such revisions, is not reasonably acceptable to the Publisher, then monies advanced to the Author pursuant to Paragraphs 4, 5, and 9 shall be ❑ retained by the Author ❑ repaid to the Publisher ❑ repaid to the Publisher only in the event the Author subsequently signs a contract with another Publisher for the Work.

4. **Additional Materials.** The following materials shall be provided by the Author _____ _____. The cost of providing these additional materials shall be borne by the Author, provided, however, that the Publisher at the time of signing this Agreement shall give a nonrefundable payment of $_____ to assist the Author in defraying these costs, which payment shall not be deemed an advance to the Author and shall not be recouped as such.

5. **Permissions.** The Author agrees to obtain all permissions that are necessary for the use of materials copyrighted by others. The cost of providing these permissions shall be borne by the Author, provided, however, that the Publisher at the time of signing this Agreement shall give a nonrefundable payment of $_____ to assist the Author in defraying these costs, which payment shall not be deemed an advance to the Author and shall not be recouped as such. Permissions shall be obtained in writing and copies shall be provided to the Publisher when the manuscript is delivered.

6. Duty to Publish. The Publisher shall publish the Work within _____ months of the delivery of the complete manuscript. Failure to so publish shall give the Author the right to terminate this Agreement ninety days after giving written notice to the Publisher of the failure to make timely publication. In the event of such termination, the Author shall have no obligation to return monies received pursuant to Paragraphs 4, 5, and 9.

7. Royalties. The Publisher shall pay the Author the following royalties: ____ percent of the suggested retail price on the first 5,000 copies sold; ____ percent of the suggested retail price on the next 5,000 copies sold; and ____ percent of the suggested retail price on all copies sold thereafter. These royalty rates shall be discounted only in the following circumstances: _____

All copies sold shall be cumulated for purposes of escalations in the royalty rates, including revised editions, except for editions in a different form (such as a paperback reprint of a hardcover original) which shall be cumulated separately. Copies sold shall be reduced by copies returned in the same royalty category in which the copies were originally reported as sold.

In the event the Publisher has the right pursuant to Paragraph 1(A) to publish the Work in more than one form, the royalty rates specified above shall apply to publication in the form of a _____ book and the royalty rates for other forms shall be specified here: _____

8. Subsidiary Rights. The following subsidiary rights may be licensed by the party indicated and the proceeds divided as specified herein:

Subsidiary Right	Right to License		Division of Proceeds	
	Author	Publisher	Author	Publisher
_____	_____	_____	_____	_____
_____	_____	_____	_____	_____
_____	_____	_____	_____	_____
_____	_____	_____	_____	_____
_____	_____	_____	_____	_____

If the division of proceeds for any subsidiary right changes after the sale of a certain number of copies, indicate which right, the number of copies required to be sold, and the new division of proceeds _____ _____

The Publisher shall have no rights pursuant to this Paragraph 8 if Publisher is in default of any of its obligations under this Agreement. The right to license any subsidiary right not set forth in this Paragraph is retained by the Author. Licensing income shall be divided as specified herein without any reductions for expenses.

Licensing income shall be collected by the party authorized to license the right and the appropriate percentage remitted by that party to the other party within ten days of receipt. Copies of all licenses shall be provided to both parties immediately upon receipt.

9. Advances. The Publisher shall, at the time of signing this Agreement, pay to the Author a nonrefundable advance of $_____, which advance shall be recouped by the Publisher from payments due to the Author pursuant to Paragraph 11 of this Agreement.

10. Accountings. Commencing as of the date of publication, the Publisher shall report every ____ months to the Author, showing for that period and cumulatively to date the number of copies printed and bound, the number of copies sold and returned for each royalty rate, the number of copies distributed free for publicity purposes, the number of copies remaindered, destroyed, or lost, the royalties paid to and owed to the Author, and licensing income. If the Publisher sets up a reserve against returns of books, the reserve may only be set up for the four accounting periods following the first publication of the Work and shall in no event exceed 15 percent of royalties due to the Author in any period.

11. **Payments.** The Publisher shall pay the Author all monies due Author pursuant to Paragraph 10 within thirty days of the close of each accounting period.

12. **Right of Inspection.** The Author shall, upon the giving of written notice, have the right to inspect the Publisher's books of account to verify the accountings. If errors in any such accounting are found to be to the Author's disadvantage and represent more than 5 percent of the payment to the Author pursuant to the said accounting, the cost of inspection shall be paid by the Publisher.

13. **Copyright and Authorship Credit.** The Publisher shall, as an express condition of receiving the grant of rights specified in Paragraph 1, take the necessary steps to register the copyright on behalf of the Author and in the Author's name and shall place copyright notice in the Author's name on all copies of the Work. The Author shall receive authorship credit as follows: _____.

14. **Warranty and Indemnity.** The Author warrants and represents that he or she is the sole creator of the Work and owns all rights granted under this Agreement, that the Work is an original creation and has not previously been published (except for those materials for which permissions have been obtained pursuant to Paragraph 5), that the Work does not infringe any other person's copyrights or rights of literary property, nor, to his or her knowledge, does it violate the rights of privacy of, or libel, other persons. The Author agrees to indemnify the Publisher against any final judgment for damages (after all appeals have been exhausted) in any lawsuit based on an actual breach of the foregoing warranties. In addition, the Author shall pay the Publisher's reasonable costs and attorney's fees incurred in defending such a lawsuit, unless the Author chooses to retain his or her own attorney to defend such lawsuit. The Author makes no warranties and shall have no obligation to indemnify the Publisher with respect to materials inserted in the Work at the Publisher's request. Notwithstanding any of the foregoing, in no event shall the Author's liability under this Paragraph exceed $_____ or _____ percent of sums payable to the Author under this Agreement, whichever is the lesser. In the event a lawsuit is brought which may result in the Author having breached his or her warranties under this Paragraph, the Publisher shall have the right to withhold and place in an escrow account _____ percent of sums payable to the Author pursuant to Paragraph 11, but in no event may said withholding exceed the damages alleged in the complaint.

15. **Artistic Control.** The Author and Publisher shall consult with one another with respect to the title of the Work, the price of the Work, the method and means of advertising and selling the Work, the number and destination of free copies, the number of copies to be printed, the method of printing and other publishing processes, the exact date of publication, the form, style, size, type, paper to be used, and like details, how long the plates or film shall be preserved and when they shall be destroyed, and when new printings of the Work shall be made. In the event of disagreement after consultation, the Publisher shall have final power of decision over all the foregoing matters except the following, which shall be controlled by the Author_____ _____. No changes shall be made in the complete manuscript of the Work by persons other than the Author, except for reasonable copy editing, unless the Author consents to such changes. Publisher shall provide the Author with galleys and proofs which the Author shall review and return to the Publisher within thirty (30) days of receipt. If the cost of the Author's alterations (other than for typesetting errors or unavoidable updating) exceeds _____ percent of the cost of the typography, the Publisher shall have the right to deduct such excess from royalties due Author hereunder.

16. **Original Materials.** Within thirty days after publication, the Publisher shall return the original manuscript and all additional materials to the Author. The Publisher shall provide the Author with a copy of the page proofs, if the Author requests them prior to the date of publication.

17. **Free Copies.** The Author shall receive ____ free copies of the Work as published, after which the Author shall have the right to purchase additional copies at a ____ percent discount from the retail price.

18. Revisions. The Author agrees to revise the Work on request by the Publisher. If the Author cannot revise the Work or refuses to do so absent good cause, the Publisher shall have the right to have the Work revised by a person competent to do so and shall charge the costs of said revision against payments due the Author under Paragraph 11 for such revised edition. In no event shall such revision costs exceed $ _____ .

19. Successors and Assigns. This Agreement may not be assigned by either party without the written consent of the other party hereto. The Author, however, shall retain the right to assign payments due hereunder without obtaining the Publisher's consent. This Agreement shall be binding on the parties and their respective heirs, administrators, successors, and assigns.

20. Infringement. In the event of an infringement of the rights granted under this Agreement to the Publisher, the Publisher and the Author shall have the right to sue jointly for the infringement and, after deducting the expenses of bringing suit, to share equally in any recovery. If either party chooses not to join in the suit, the other party may proceed and, after deducting all the expenses of bringing the suit, any recovery shall be shared equally between the parties.

21. Termination. The Author shall have the right to terminate this Agreement by written notice if: **(A)** the Work goes out-of-print and the Publisher, within ninety days of receiving notice from the Author that the Work is out-of-print, does not place the Work in print again. A work shall be deemed out-of-print if the work is not available for sale in reasonable quantities in normal trade channels; **(B)** if the Publisher fails to provide statements of account pursuant to Paragraph 10; **(C)** if the Publisher fails to make payments pursuant to Paragraphs 4, 5, 9, or 11; or **(D)** if the Publisher fails to publish in a timely manner pursuant to Paragraph 6. The Publisher shall have the right to terminate this Agreement as provided in Paragraph 3. This Agreement shall automatically terminate in the event of the Publisher's insolvency, bankruptcy, or assignment of assets for the benefit of creditors. In the event of termination of the Agreement, the Publisher shall grant, convey, and transfer all rights in the Work back to the Author.

22. Production Materials and Unbound Copies. Upon any termination, the Author may, within sixty days of notification of such termination, purchase the plates, offset negatives, or computer drive tapes (if any) at their scrap value and any remaining copies at the lesser of cost or remainder value.

23. Promotion. The Author consents to the use of his or her name, portrait, or picture for promotion and advertising of the Work, provided such use is dignified and consistent with the Author's reputation.

24. Arbitration. All disputes arising under this Agreement shall be submitted to binding arbitration before _____ in the following location _____ and shall be settled in accordance with the rules of the American Arbitration Association. Judgment upon the arbitration award may be entered in any court having jurisdiction thereof.

25. Notice. Where written notice is required hereunder, it may be given by use of first class mail addressed to the Author or Publisher at the addresses given at the beginning of this Agreement and shall be deemed received five days after mailing. Said addresses for notice may be changed by giving written notice of any new address to the other party.

26. Entire Agreement and Modifications. This Agreement represents the entire Agreement between the parties. All modifications of this Agreement must be in writing and signed by both parties.

27. Waivers and Defaults. Any waiver of a breach or default hereunder shall not be deemed a waiver of a subsequent breach or default of either the same provision or any other provision of this Agreement.

28. Governing Law. This Agreement shall be governed by the laws of _____ State.

IN WITNESS WHEREOF, the parties have signed this Agreement as of the date first set forth above.

Author_____   Publisher_____
                                                              Company Name

                                             By_____
                                                          Authorized Signatory, Title

Collaboration Contract

Collaboration presents the challenge and reward of blending two or more creative efforts into a single work. Publishers offer coauthors a publishing agreement to sign, but a publishing agreement does not resolve the issues likely to arise between the collaborators. That is why a collaboration agreement, such as Form 6, should also be entered into by the coauthors.

The first issue to be resolved is how the copyright in the collaboration will be owned. The copyright law provides that a joint work is "a work prepared by two or more authors with the intention that their contributions be merged into inseparable or interdependent parts of a unitary whole." The collaboration agreement can specify the intention of the parties.

If the copyright is owned jointly, either party can license the work as long as proceeds are equally shared. The collaboration agreement can override this, providing that the parties must agree before licensing the work or indicating that the income will not be equally shared. If one party dies, his or her heirs would inherit the rights in the copyright. Again, the collaboration agreement can alter this by stating that the surviving collaborator will own the entirety of the work and its copyright.

One advantage of a joint work is that the copyright term is the life of the survivor plus seventy years. The term for the collaboration agreement would usually be the same as the term of the copyright.

The responsibilities of the parties must be set out in the greatest detail possible. An outline or synopsis can be attached to the agreement, dividing these responsibilities and giving a schedule for the work.

The division of proceeds from sales of the work must be resolved, especially if the division is not equal or if different types of income will be shared differently. The contract can provide that both parties must agree to any disposition of rights, but it can also specify that one party will control certain rights. The agreement should state that the parties are independent of each other and have not formed a partnership, since a partner can legally bind the partnership even if he or she acted outside the authority of the partnership agreement.

The parties must decide how to authorize and share expenses, and what will happen if expenses are incurred but the project is either never completed or never sold. The failure to complete or sell the work raises complicated issues as to how the rights will be treated. It is likely that each party would want to retain the rights in his or her portion of the book and be free to publish that portion by itself or as part of a longer work. Whether this is fair will vary from project to project.

The agreement must determine what will happen if one collaborator fails to complete his or her portion of the work. Likewise, if one collaborator becomes disabled or dies, it is still necessary to complete, market, and revise the work. How will this be done? Probably both artistic and financial control of the project should be given to the active party at this point, rather than involving heirs or other people who were not parties to the original agreement.

The agreement must also deal with how each collaborator will avoid competing with the collaborative work, while not impairing either party's ability to earn a livelihood. For example, can one party create a similar work which might damage the market for the collaborative work? If not, should this be allowed after some period of time? Must the collaborators work together on sequels? Or can each one create his or her own sequels? Any agreement as to future works, whether written negatively as a noncompetition clause or positively as a right to collaborate on sequels, must be approached with the utmost caution. Otherwise the author may find that he or she has agreed to lifelong self-censorship.

If an agent is to be used, the contract should specify who the agent is or, at least, whether both parties must agree to the choice of an agent.

Authorship credit should be specified in the agreement. It is important that the credits accurately reflect what the parties did. The credit could be "by A and B" or "story by A and illustrations by B." "As told to" indicates one person telling their story to another; while "with" suggests that one person did some writing and the other person, usually a professional author, shaped and completed the book. It is against public policy for someone to take credit for writing a book which, in fact, was written by someone else.

The parties will have to give a warranty and indemnity to the publisher. If this clause is breached, both parties will be liable. The collaborators should determine who, in the event of a breach, should pay the publisher: both parties or only the party who created that portion of the work (assuming he or she has sufficient assets to pay for damages and legal fees).

Arbitration may be helpful in collaboration agreements, because certain issues do not lend themselves to determination in advance. For example, should the work be completed if one party is disabled? If it is completed, how should the disabled party's right to share income be affected? Should the nature of the authorship credit change, especially if a third party has been brought in to do substantial work? These and similar questions require a look at what has actually taken place before a fair result can be obtained.

The collaboration agreement is part of a process which will require the collaborators to contract with yet another party who will market the work. In the case of a book, a publisher will market what the collaborators create. Not only must the collaboration agreement resolve the issues likely to arise between the collaborators, it must also be compatible with reaching agreement with the publisher, who will disseminate the work to its ultimate audience. Form 5, the Book Publishing Contract, is therefore helpful to

keep in mind when negotiating Form 6 with a coauthor.

Filling in the Form

In the Preamble fill in the date and the names and addresses of the parties. In the second Whereas clause the tentative title of the work should be entered. In Paragraph 1 the work should be described and the appropriate boxes checked if a schedule, outline, or synopsis is attached to the agreement. In Paragraph 2 the obligations of each party should be described. In Paragraph 3 fill in the due date. In Paragraph 4 fill in a date for termination if no publishing agreement has been obtained. In Paragraph 5 fill in the first blank if the collaborators choose not to have a jointly owned copyright, and fill in the second blank if the parties choose either not to own jointly certain proprietary rights or not to work together on sequels. In Paragraph 6 provide a dollar limit for expenses for each party. Also in Paragraph 6 show how net proceeds will be divided for publishing and nonpublishing rights, filling in the final blank if certain rights are to be controlled or benefitted from in a way which is an exception to the general approach of the paragraph. Specify the name of any agent in Paragraph 7 and, if there is no agent, check the appropriate box as to whether the parties wish to obtain one. In Paragraph 8 give the credit line and state if the size or color of the names shall ever differ between the collaborators. In Paragraph 9 fill in the blank if one party is not to have artistic control over his or her portion of the work. In Paragraph 13 give the name of an arbitrator and a place for arbitration. In Paragraph 16 specify any limitations on the parties with respect to competitive works. In Paragraph 17 state how recoveries for infringements will be shared. In Paragraph 18 indicate which state's laws will govern the agreement. Have both parties sign.

ser ID:1222103270889

title:The locator
author:Dunn, Troy.
item id:0222103934139
    due:3/23/2006,23:59

title:Business and legal forms
author:Crawford, Tad, 1946-
item id:0222106448434
    due:3/23/2006,23:59

title:My fellow Americans : the
author:Waldman, Michael, 1960-
item id:0222105467930
    due:3/23/2006,23:59

Negotiation Checklist

❏ The project should be described in as much detail as possible. Any outline or synopsis can be attached to the contract. (Paragraph 1)

❏ Indicate precisely and in as much detail as possible the responsibilities of each party. (Paragraph 2)

❏ Specify a due date to complete the work. (Paragraph 3)

❏ If one party fails to complete his or her portion of the work by the due date, consider what should happen and whether there should be an extension, the other party should have the right to complete the work (or hire a third party to complete it), or the rights in each portion of the work should revert to the party creating that portion. (Paragraph 3)

❏ If the work is not completed and each party retains the rights in his or her portion, state that each party is free to do as he or she pleases with that portion.

❏ Specify a work schedule with a sequence of deadlines, so that missing any deadline would have the same consequences as missing the final due date. This may alert one party to difficulties that are developing with his or her collaborator.

❏ If the nature of the collaboration is such that each party will have some portion of work inextricably merged with the portion created by the other party, state whether such merged portions can or cannot be used by either party in the event the work is not completed.

❏ If either party could create a competitive work that would damage the market for the collaborative work, state that for a certain period of time neither party shall create such a work. (See other provisions.)

❏ State that the parties either have a publishing contract or agree to seek such a contract. (Paragraph 4)

❏ Indicate that any publishing contract must be acceptable to both parties, who must each sign it and obey its provisions. (Paragraph 4)

❏ If no publishing contract is obtained by a certain date, allow either party to terminate the contract on written notice to the other party and specify that each party shall keep the rights in the portion of the work that he or she has created. (Paragraph 4)

❏ Require each party to inform the other party regarding any negotiations. (Paragraph 4)

❏ State which party will control the disposition of the various rights, or whether the parties must both agree to any licensing of the work. (Paragraph 4)

❏ If one party negotiates all contracts and licenses, give the other party a veto right and require both parties to sign all documents.

❏ If there are three or more collaborators, state whether licensing, contracts, and artistic decisions will be controlled by one party, a majority vote, or unanimous agreement.

❏ Permit the use of a written power of attorney by one party on behalf of the other in specifically enumerated circumstances.

❏ Require that each collaborator receive an original or, at least, a copy of any contract or license which is entered into. (Paragraph 4)

❏ Specify whether the copyright will be held jointly in the whole work, or whether each party will retain copyright in that portion which he or she has created. (Paragraph 5)

❏ If the copyright is to be jointly owned, state that this will only happen if each party completes his or her portion. (Paragraph 5)

❏ If the copyright is jointly owned, decide whether each party's right in the joint copyright will pass on to heirs in the event of death or become the property of the other party. No provision has to be made if the choice is to have the right be inherited.

❏ If the copyrights are to be separately held by each party, provide for appropriate assignments of rights from each party so rights in the whole work are available for publication.

❏ If the work creates a trademark, characters, situations, or other rights which might be used later in sequels, determine whether both parties own the trademark or other rights and whether both have the right to do sequels. (Paragraphs 5 and 12)

❏ If both parties have a right to do sequels, consider whether this right shall be limited to a certain number of years after publication (perhaps two to four years) or should expire as of a specific date.

❏ State whether materials created or purchased in the course of developing the books (including research, tapes, interviews, books, equipment, etc.) shall be owned by both parties or by the party which obtained the material. (Paragraph 5)

❏ Specify how the expenses of the parties in creating the project will be shared, especially if the expenses are not shared in the same way income is or if different types of income are shared differently. (Paragraph 6)

❏ If the work is never completed, will one party have to contribute to cover expenses incurred by the other party? (Paragraph 3)

❏ Determine how income, including advances, will be divided. (Paragraph 6)

❏ Specify how advances will be paid back to a publisher if one party fails to complete his or her portion of the work and the entire work cannot be completed. (Paragraph 3)

❏ Determine whether different types of income should be divided differently. (Paragraph 6)

❏ If one party arranges the sale of certain rights, should that party receive an extra percentage as a reward?

❏ If one party has several capacities, such as being the author of the original work and the creator of a film version, should that party be free to receive payment in each capacity?

❏ Specify who will receive money owed and how and when the money will be distributed to the collaborators. Ideally, payment should be direct to each collaborator. (Paragraph 6)

❏ Specify whether money received will be kept in a joint bank account and, if so, whether both parties must sign on that account.

❏ To avoid any conflicts if both parties have agents, determine whether the parties will use an agent, specify the agent if known, and require both parties to sign and obey the contract with the agent. (Paragraph 7)

❏ Specify authorship credit, including the order, size, and color of the names and the use of the names on promotional or advertising materials. (Paragraph 8)

❏ Determine which party will have artistic control of the work, or whether each party will control his or her own portion. (Paragraph 9)

❏ Specify the conditions under which one party may make or authorize changes in the work of the other party. (Paragraphs 3, 9, and 12)

❏ Require each party to give a warranty and indemnity to the other party, so one party will have some protection against copyright infringements, invasions of privacy, and similar unlawful acts on the part of the other party. (Paragraph 10)

❏ Specify that each party will obtain any releases or licenses to use copyrighted materials in his or her portion of the work and determine how payment will be made for such materials. (Paragraph 10)

❏ Do not allow assignment of the contract, since the duties of an author are usually based on personal skills. (Paragraph 11)

❏ Consider carefully whether to allow assignment of money due under the contract, since a party who has no reward to look forward to may lose interest in the work. (Paragraph 11)

❏ If a party wishes to assign money to become due or any rights, give the other party the first option to purchase this right by matching the best terms offered by any outside party.

❏ In the event of the death or disability of a party prior to completing the work, decide if the other party should have the right to complete the work. (Paragraph 12)

❏ In the event of the death or disability of a party, determine how revisions of the work can be done and paid for. (Paragraph 12)

❏ If one collaborator dies, decide whether the survivor should control contractual and licensing decisions or whether the estate and heirs should be involved. (Paragraph 12)

❏ In the event of death or disability, create a formula for reallocating the shares of income.

❏ If all collaborators are deceased, provide for the heirs or personal representatives to make financial and artistic decisions. (Paragraph 12)

❏ An arbitration provision is probably wise, because it is usually quicker and less expensive than a court proceeding. (Paragraph 13)

❏ In addition to arbitration, include a mediation provision so that the parties will have an independent mediator seek to resolve disputes before going to arbitration. Unlike arbitration, mediation is not binding on either party.

❏ Specify the agreement's term. (Paragraph 14)

❏ State that the agreement does not create a partnership or joint venture between the parties. (Paragraph 15)

❏ If the promotional or marketing commitment of either party is important to the project, specify what activities that party must undertake.

❏ Have both parties agree to allow the use of their name, portrait, or picture to promote the work.

❏ If the parties agree not to compete with the work, the exact limitations must be specified. (Paragraph 16. See other provisions.)

❏ If the work is infringed by others, determine how to bring suit, share costs, and share any recovery. (Paragraph 17)

❏ Review the standard provisions in the introductory pages and compare to Paragraph 18.

Other Provisions that can be added to Form 6:

❏ Exclusivity. This provision is designed for the situation in which a person tells his or her story to an author and agrees not to share the story with anyone else if it would impair the value of the book being created by the author.

Exclusivity. The parties hereto agree that this Agreement is an exclusive agreement in that neither party will enter into any other agreements for books or for magazine articles which will diminish the value of any of the parties' respective rights in this Agreement. The Author acknowledges that the following activities by the Coauthor do not violate the preceding sentence: _____

_____

_____

_____

_____

_____

_____.

_____.

Further, the Author agrees that the Coauthor is free to sell the publishing and nonpublishing rights to his or her story if such sales will not diminish the value of the parties' respective rights and do not deal with those aspects of the Coauthor's story embodied in the Work, and that all proceeds derived by the Coauthor from the granting of such rights are the sole property of the Coauthor.

❏ Noncompetition. The danger of such a non-competition clause is that one party or the other may be barred from earning a portion of his or her livelihood.

Noncompetition. The parties agree that for a period of _____ years neither party shall authorize the publication of any other work in book form which directly competes with and would significantly diminish the market for the Work. This noncompetition provision shall not apply in the following circumstances:_____

_____

_____.

Collaboration Contract

AGREEMENT, entered into as of this _____ day of _____, 20___, between _____ (hereinafter referred to as the "Author"), located at _____, and _____ (hereinafter referred to as the "Coauthor"), located at _____.

WHEREAS, each party is familiar with and respects the work of the other; and

WHEREAS, the parties hereto wish to collaborate on a book project tentatively titled _____ _____ (hereinafter referred to as the "Work"); and

WHEREAS, the parties wish to have the creation of the Work governed by the mutual obligations, covenants, and conditions herein;

NOW, THEREFORE, in consideration of the foregoing premises and the mutual covenants hereinafter set forth and other valuable considerations, the parties hereto agree as follows:

1. Description. The Work shall be approximately _____ words on the subject of_____ _____ _____.

Materials other than text include _____ _____ _____.

A ❑ schedule ❑ outline ❑ synopsis is attached to and made part of this agreement.

2. Responsibilities. The Author shall be responsible for writing approximately _____ words to serve as the following parts of the text _____ _____.

The Author shall also provide the following materials _____ _____ _____.

The Coauthor shall be responsible for writing approximately _____ words to serve as the following parts of the text _____ _____.

The Coauthor shall also provide the following materials_____ _____ _____.

3. Due Date. Both Author and Coauthor shall complete their portions of the Work by _____, 20 _____, or by the date for delivery of the manuscript as specified in a publishing contract entered into pursuant to Paragraph 4. If such a publishing contract requires sketches or other materials prior to the date for delivery of the manuscript, the party responsible for same shall provide it to the publisher. In the event either party fails to complete his or her portion of the Work by the due date for reasons other than death or disability, the parties may agree to an extension of the due date or agree to allow a nondefaulting party to complete the Work as if the other party were deceased or disabled. If no agreement can be reached, the arbitrator may award a nondefaulting party the right to complete the Work as if the other party were deceased or disabled or may convey to each party the rights of copyright in that party's completed portion of the Work and specify how the parties shall contribute to any expenses incurred and repay any advances.

4. **Contracts and Licenses.** If a contract for the Work has not already been entered into with a publisher, both Author and Coauthor agree to seek such a contract. Such publishing contract shall be entered into in the names of and signed by both the Author and the Coauthor, each of whom shall comply with and perform all required contractual obligations. If a mutually agreeable publishing contract for initial publication of the Work is not entered into with a Publisher by _____, 20_____, then either party may terminate this agreement by giving written notice to the other party prior to such time as a mutually agreeable publishing contract for initial publication is entered into. Each party shall fully inform the other party of all negotiations for such a publishing contract or with respect to the negotiation of any other licenses or contracts pursuant to this Agreement. The disposition of any right, including the grant of any license, shall require written agreement between both parties hereto. Each party shall receive a copy of any contract, license, or other document relating to this Agreement.

5. **Copyright, Trademarks, and Other Proprietary Rights.** Author and Coauthor agree that the Work shall be copyrighted in both their names, and that upon completion of the Work it is their intention that their respective contributions shall be merged into a joint work with a jointly owned copyright, unless provided to the contrary here:_____. If either party does not complete their portion of the Work, the nature of copyright ownership shall be governed by Paragraph 3. It is further agreed that trademarks, rights in characters, titles, and similar ongoing rights shall be owned by both parties who shall both participate in any sequels under the terms of this Agreement, unless provided to the contrary here:_____. A sequel is defined as a work closely related to the Work in that it is derived from the subject matter of the Work, is similar in style and format to the Work, and is directed toward the same audience as that for the Work. Material of any and all kinds developed or obtained in the course of creating the work shall be ❑ jointly owned ❑ the property of the party who developed or obtained it.

6. **Income and Expenses.** Net proceeds generated by the Work shall be divided as set forth in this Paragraph. Net proceeds are defined as gross proceeds from the sale or license of book rights throughout the world (including but not limited to serializations, condensations, and translations), including advances, minus reasonable expenses. Such expenses shall include agents' fees and the parties' expenses incurred in the creation of the Work, provided that the parties' expenses shall be supported by appropriate verification and shall not exceed $_____ for the Author and $_____ for the Coauthor. Each party shall provide verification for expenses to the other party within ten days of a written request. Unless otherwise provided, the parties' expenses shall be reimbursed from first proceeds received, including but not limited to advances.

Net proceeds from the sale or license of nonelectronic publishing rights shall be divided _____ percent to the Author and _____ percent to the Coauthor.

Net proceeds from the sale or license of electronic publishing rights shall be divided _____ percent to the Author and _____ percent to the Coauthor. For purposes of this Agreement, electronic rights are defined as rights in the digitized form of works that can be encoded, stored, and retrieved from such media as computer disks, CD-ROM, computer databases, and network servers.

Net proceeds from the sale or license of nonpublishing rights in the Work (including but not limited to audio, merchandising, motion picture, stage play, or television rights to the Work), whether such sale or license occurs before or after initial publication of the Work, shall be divided _____ percent to the Author and _____ percent to the Coauthor, unless provided to the contrary here, in which case the following rights shall be treated with respect to division of net proceeds and control or disposition as follows:_____ _____.

If possible, net proceeds shall be paid directly to each party in accordance with the divisions set forth in this Paragraph. If either party is designated to collect such net proceeds, that party shall make immediate payment to the other party of such amounts as are due hereunder.

7. **Agent.** If the parties have entered into an agency agreement with respect to the Work, it is with the following agent:_____. If a contract for the Work has not already been entered into with an agent, both Author and Coauthor agree ❑ to seek such a contract ❑ not to seek such a contract. Any agency contract shall be mutually acceptable to and entered into in the names of and signed by both the Author and the Coauthor, each of whom shall comply with and perform all required contractual obligations.

8. **Authorship Credit.** The credit line for the Work shall be as follows wherever authorship credit is given in the Work or in promotion, advertising, or other ancillary uses:_____
_____. The color and type size for such authorship credit shall be the same for both authors unless provided to the contrary here:_____
_____.

9. **Artistic Control.** Each party shall have artistic control over his or her portion of the Work, unless provided to the contrary here, in which case artistic control of the entire Work shall be exercised by _____
_____. The parties shall share ideas and make their work in progress available to the other party for discussion and coordination purposes. Except as provided in Paragraphs 3 and 12, neither party shall at any time make any changes in the portion of the Work created by the other party.

10. **Warranty and Indemnity.** Author and Coauthor each warrant and represent to the other that the respective contributions of each to the Work are original (or that appropriate releases have been obtained and paid for) and do not libel or otherwise violate any right of any person or entity, including but not limited to rights of copyright or privacy. Author and Coauthor each indemnify and hold the other harmless from and against any and all claims, actions, liability, damages, costs, and expenses, including reasonable legal fees and expenses, incurred by the other as a result of the breach of such warranties, representations, and undertakings.

11. **Assignment.** This Agreement shall not be assignable by either party hereto, provided, however, that after completion of the Work, either party may assign the right to receive money pursuant to Paragraph 6 by giving written notice to the other party.

12. **Death or Disability.** In the event that either party dies or suffers a disability that will prevent completion of his or her respective portion of the Work, or of a revision thereof or a sequel thereto, the other party shall have the right to complete that portion or to hire a third party to complete that portion and shall adjust the authorship credit to reflect the revised authorship arrangements. The deceased or disabled party shall receive payments pursuant to Paragraph 6 pro rata to the proportion of his or her work completed or, in the case of a revision or sequel, shall receive payments pursuant to Paragraph 6 after deduction for the cost of revising or creating the sequel with respect to his or her portion of the Work. The active party shall have the sole power to license and contract with respect to the Work, and approval of the personal representative, heirs, or conservator of the deceased or disabled party shall not be required. If all parties are deceased, the respective heirs or personal representatives shall take the place of the parties for all purposes.

13. **Arbitration.** All disputes arising under this Agreement shall be submitted to binding arbitration before _____ in the following location _____ and shall be settled in accordance with the rules of the American Arbitration Association. Judgment upon the arbitration award may be entered in any court having jurisdiction thereof.

14. Term. The term for this Agreement shall be the duration of the copyright, plus any renewals or extensions thereof.

15. Independent Parties. The parties to this Agreement are independent of one another, and nothing contained in this Agreement shall make a partnership or joint venture between them.

16. Competitive Works. If the parties wish to restrict future activities to avoid competition with the Work, any such restrictions must be stated here: _____

_____

17. Infringement. In the event of an infringement of the Work, the Author and Coauthor shall have the right to sue jointly for the infringement and, after deducting the expenses of bringing suit, to share in any recovery as follows:_____. If either party chooses not to join in the suit, the other party may proceed and, after deducting all the expenses of bringing the suit, any recovery shall be shared between the parties as stated in the preceding sentence.

18. Miscellany. This Agreement shall be binding upon the parties hereto, their heirs, successors, assigns, and personal representatives. This Agreement constitutes the entire understanding between the parties. Its terms can be modified only by an instrument in writing signed by both parties. Each party shall do all acts and sign all documents required to effectuate this Agreement. A waiver of any breach of any of the provisions of this Agreement shall not be construed as a continuing waiver of other breaches of the same or other provisions hereof. This Agreement shall be governed by the laws of the State of _____.

IN WITNESS WHEREOF, the parties hereto have signed this Agreement as of the date first set forth above.

Author _____   Coauthor _____

Contract to License Audio Rights

There has been a dramatic growth in the market for audio works. This growth has brought changes in the way audio rights are treated. Instead of simply allowing audio rights to be passed on as a subsidiary right, with the book publisher assuming control over disposition of the right and sharing in licensing proceeds, some authors are seeking to reserve their audio rights. This is especially important for books that are likely to have an audio market, such as self-help and how-to books or novels.

If the author believes his or her book may achieve success as an audio work and is able to reserve the audio rights in the initial book contract, then the author may be offered a contract like Form 11 by an audio publisher (who may also be a publisher of books).

The concepts of audio and book publishing are closely related, but there are significant differences. The audio contract licenses audio rights only; it should not allow the publisher to acquire any other rights. While book publishers insist on acquiring exclusive rights, audio publishers will sometimes accept nonexclusive rights or overlapping markets (i.e., one publisher for direct mail sales and another publisher for retail sales). Authors must be careful not to allow the grant of audio rights to interfere with possible movie deals.

Royalties for audio sales are computed on the publisher's net receipts, rather than on retail price as in book publishing. The discount given to retailers is similar for audio works and books (40 percent or more off retail price). This means that a 10 percent royalty on a $10 book is $1, while a 10 percent royalty on a $10 audiotape, CD, or DVD-audio is $.60 ($10 multiplied by the 60 percent of retail price which the publisher will receive and multiplied again by the 10 percent royalty). Since many audiotapes, CDs, or DVDs-audio are sold by direct mail, the royalty rate for direct mail sales is especially important. If the publisher has worldwide English-language rights, the royalty rate for export sales has to be carefully scrutinized.

Advances are paid on audio contracts, but these advances are low compared to book advances due to the much smaller size of the market for audiotapes. Accountings are often rendered quarterly or even monthly for audio works, which is advantageous for the author compared with the semiannual accountings and payments made by book publishers.

Artistic control is an important issue, since an audio work will rarely represent the entirety of the original book. How will the book be abridged? And who will have the final decision regarding transitional narration to be added or sound effects and music? The author may want to read the work, but it is likely the publisher will prefer to use professionals with trained voices (and unlikely that the publisher will pay the author who does double as a reader for doing the reading). If performers are used, the publisher will probably seek to own the copyright in the sound recording, while the author would continue to own the copyright in the underlying literary work.

Many other issues are similar to those raised by book publishing contracts. These include the author's reservation of rights, the duty of the publisher to publish within a certain time, the right to inspect the publisher's books and records, authorship credit, a warranty and indemnity provision, how infringements by third parties will be handled, promotion, free copies for the author, termination, and the various boilerplate provisions. The negotiation checklist for Form 5, Book Publishing Contract, should be reviewed as a helpful supplement to the negotiation checklist for Form 7.

Filling in the Form

In the Preamble fill in the date and the names and addresses of the parties. In Paragraph 1 fill in the title of the book, indicate the limits on the grant of rights and whether the grant is exclusive or nonexclusive, and specify how long a segment of the tape may be used for advertising or promotion. In Paragraph 4 state a deadline for publication. In Paragraph 5 indicate the amount of the advance. In Paragraph 6 state the royalty rates. If any subsidiary rights are granted, show this in Paragraph 7. In Paragraph 8 indicate the frequency of the accountings. In Paragraph 10 show how the copyright notice for the literary work and the copyright notice for the sound recording will appear, as well as filling in who will own the copyright in the sound recording. In Paragraph 11 place limits on the author's liability for a breach of warranty and also limit what amount of royalties may be placed in escrow in the event of a lawsuit. In Paragraph 13 indicate if the author will have certain rights of artistic control. In Paragraph 14 detail the publisher's promotional obligations. In Paragraph 15 indicate how many free copies of the tape the author will receive and what discount will be given to the author for additional copies purchased. In Paragraph 19 fill in the arbitrator and the place for arbitration. In Paragraph 20 specify which state's laws will govern the contract. Both parties should then sign the contract.

Negotiation Checklist

❑ Specify the title of the book from which the audio work will derive. (Paragraph 1)

❑ Indicate that the grant is to do a nondramatic reading. This should avoid any conflict with a movie sale that would include the right to exploit the soundtrack of the movie. (Paragraph 1)

❑ State that the copies for sale will be on magnetic tape in the form of audiocassettes, CDs, or DVDs-audio, to avoid any confusion as to other possible ways in which the audio work could be reproduced. (Paragraph 1)

❑ Limit the grant of rights by territory, language, term, markets, and exclusivity. While publishers may want worldwide rights, the author will probably be able to limit this to English language rights and reserve the right to make translations. If the author has a better way to sell English language tapes abroad, then he or she should try to limit the territory to the United States and whatever other countries the publisher can reach effectively. The markets would include sales through normal trade channels, direct mail, direct response, export, and so on. If the publisher can sell effectively to all markets (subject to the other restrictions on the grant of rights), the author might permit this. Exclusivity should also depend on how effectively the publisher can reach the markets involved. (Paragraph 1)

❑ Specify how long an excerpt from the audio work may be used by the publisher for advertising or promotional purposes. (Paragraph 1)

❑ Any rights not granted to the publisher should be expressly reserved to the author. Reference may be made here to the reservation of sound track rights based on a movie or electronic rights. (Paragraph 2)

❑ The author should provide whatever materials are necessary for script preparation, and these materials should be returned to the author after the script has been prepared. (Paragraph 3)

❑ Specify a deadline for the publisher to publish the audio work, after which the author would have the right to terminate the contract. (Paragraph 4)

❑ Indicate the amount of the advance to the author. (Paragraph 5)

❑ Specify the royalty rates for copies sold through normal trade channels, such as wholesalers and bookstores. These rates might start at 10 percent and escalate to 15 percent or more after the sale of 5,000 to 10,000 copies. Some contracts start the royalty rates in the range of 7 percent, so expect to negotiate. (Paragraph 6)

❑ Specify the royalty rate for sales by direct mail, which may be 5 percent but is based on retail price rather than net receipts. It is worth finding out what proportion of sales are made by direct mail and perhaps seeking an escalation in the rate over a certain sales figure. Of course, it is also possible to seek a higher initial royalty for direct mail. (Paragraph 6)

❑ If the publisher has worldwide English language rights, a royalty rate must be specified for export sales. If this is based on net receipts, it is likely to yield less to the author than sales in the United States. This is because the publisher receives less from foreign distributors. Information about the amount of net receipts generated on a foreign sale would be helpful in evaluating the royalty rate. A rate of 15 percent of net receipts would be a good target for the author, if the publisher sells abroad at a discount in the range of 50 to 60 percent. (Paragraph 6)

❑ Seek to have all copies sold cumulated for purposes of royalty escalations. (Paragraph 6)

❑ Copies given free to the author or as part of the promotional campaign will be royalty free. (Paragraph 6)

❑ If a reserve against returns is to be created, limit the amount of the reserve and state that such reserve shall not last for more than three accounting periods after publication.

❑ In an audio contract, do not license subsidiary rights. If any subsidiary rights are to be licensed, be absolutely certain these rights have not already been licensed in the book contract. (Paragraph 7)

❑ Require accountings with payment on a monthly or quarterly basis. (Paragraph 8)

❑ Reserve the right to inspect the publisher's books and records and charge the expense of the inspection to the publisher if errors of 5 percent or more are discovered. (Paragraph 9)

❑ Determine who will own the copyright in the sound recording. This is likely to be the publisher unless the author takes an active role in the creation of the sound recording. (Paragraph 10)

❑ Determine who will own the master recording from which copies are made. This is likely to be the publisher.

❑ State that copyright notice for the literary work shall be in the name of the author and copyright notice for the sound recording shall be in the name of the owner of that copyright. (Paragraph 10)

❑ Have the publisher register the copyrights with the Copyright Office. (Paragraph 10)

❑ If the author must give a warranty and indemnity provision, exclude any materials inserted in the work at the publisher's request. (Paragraph 11)

❑ Limit the warranty and indemnity provision to final judgments after all appeals have been exhausted and provide limits on the amount the author will have to pay. (Paragraph 11)

❑ Allow the author to retain his or her own attorney to defend any action, in which case the author would not be responsible for the publisher's legal fees. (Paragraph 11)

❑ Limit the amount which may be held in escrow during a lawsuit based on a breach of warranty. (Paragraph 11)

❏ If the rights granted are infringed by a third party, determine how the author and publisher will sue and divide any costs and recovery. (Paragraph 12)

❏ Give the author a right to approve the script and, perhaps, the right to approve the readers and background music and sounds or even the finished recording. (Paragraph 13)

❏ If the author is to read his or her work, seek an additional fee for this.

❏ Allow the publisher to use the author's name and image to promote the work. (Paragraph 14)

❏ Specify what steps the publisher will take to promote the work, perhaps including a budget. (Paragraph 14)

❏ Indicate how many free copies of the audio tape will be given to the author, such as ten or twenty copies, and the discount at which the author may purchase additional copies. This discount might be 40 or 50 percent off retail price. (Paragraph 15)

❏ If the author can sell large quantities, the discount might be structured to increase with the size of the author's orders.

❏ Allow the author to terminate the contract if the tapes or CDs are not available to be purchased in stores, if the publisher fails to give any accountings or make any payments when due, or if the publisher fails to publish.

❏ State that the contract shall automatically terminate if the publisher becomes bankrupt or insolvent. (Paragraph 16)

❏ In the event of termination, state that all rights will be conveyed back to the author. (Paragraph 16)

❏ In the event of termination, give the author the right to purchase the master recording and related materials at scrap value and any remaining copies at the lesser of unit production cost or remainder value. (Paragraph 17)

❏ Allow a limited extension of the publisher's time to perform due to wars, floods, or other acts beyond the control of the publisher.

❏ Do not agree to give the publisher an option to do the author's next audio work or book.

❏ Do not agree to a noncompetition provision.

❏ Because of the similarity between audio and book publishing contracts, a review of the negotiation checklist for Form 5 is helpful.

❏ Compare the standard provisions in the introductory pages with Paragraphs 18–20.

Contract to License Audio Rights

AGREEMENT, entered into as of this _____ day of _____, 20___, between_____ _____ (hereinafter referred to as the "Author"), located at _____, and _____ (hereinafter referred to as the "Publisher"), located at _____.

WHEREAS, the Author wishes to license audio rights in a certain book created by the Author; and

WHEREAS, the Publisher is familiar with this book by the Author and wishes to produce, distribute, and sell such an audio presentation (hereinafter referred to as the "Work"); and

WHEREAS, the parties wish to have said Work created and distributed subject to the mutual obligations, covenants, and conditions herein.

NOW, THEREFORE, in consideration of the foregoing premises and the mutual covenants hereinafter set forth and other valuable considerations, the parties hereto agree as follows:

1. **Grant of Rights.** The Author grants, conveys, and transfers to the Publisher in the book titled_____ _____, certain limited rights as follows:

    (A) To make a recording of a nondramatic reading of the book and produce, distribute, and sell copies of the Work on magnetic tape in the form of audiocassettes, as CDs, or as DVDs-audio; **(B)** In the territory of _____; **(C)** In the _____language; **(D)** For a term of _____years; **(E)** In the following markets_____; and **(F)** This grant of rights shall be ❑ exclusive ❑ nonexclusive. The Publisher shall have the right to excerpt up to _____ minutes from the Work for broadcast for purposes of advertising, publicity, or promotion.

2. **Reservation of Rights.** All rights not specifically granted to the Publisher are reserved to the Author, including but not limited to the retention of audio and video rights in any recording based on a dramatic adaptation or dramatization in connection with the grant of motion picture, television, radio, or dramatic rights, and the retention of electronic rights which are defined as rights in the digitized form of works that can be encoded, stored, and retrieved from such media as computer disks, CD-ROM, computer databases, and network servers.

3. **Original Materials.** The Author shall provide the Publisher with a copyedited manuscript for script preparation and a bound galley for final editing of the Work, unless the book has been published in which case a copy of the book itself shall be provided. These materials shall be delivered within thirty days of signing this Agreement or of the materials becoming available, whichever date is later. Within thirty days after publication, the Publisher shall return all original materials to the Author.

4. **Duty to Publish.** The Publisher shall publish the Work no later than _____, 20_____. Failure to so publish shall give the Author the right to terminate this Agreement ninety days after giving the Publisher written notice of the failure to make timely publication.

5. **Advances.** The Publisher shall, at the time of signing this Agreement, pay to the Author a nonrefundable advance of $_____, which advance shall be recouped by the Publisher from payments due to the Author pursuant to Paragraph 8 of this Agreement.

6. **Royalties.** The Publisher shall pay the Author the following royalties: ____ percent of net receipts on the first _____ copies sold; ____ percent of net receipts on the next _____ copies sold; and ____ percent of net receipts on all copies sold thereafter. "Net receipts" shall mean actual cash proceeds received by the Publisher, less returns, taxes, and shipping and handling charges which may be included in the sales price. For copies sold directly to the consumer by direct mail or coupon advertising, the Publisher shall pay ____ percent of the amount

received. For copies sold for export the Publisher shall pay ____ percent of the net receipts. All copies sold shall be cumulated for purposes of royalty escalations. No royalty shall be payable on copies furnished without charge to the Author or distributed without charge for purposes of advertising, publicity, or promotion.

7. Subsidiary Rights. The following subsidiary rights may be licensed by the party indicated and the proceeds divided as specified herein:

Subsidiary Right	Right to License		Division of Proceeds	
	Author	Publisher	Author	Publisher
_____	_____	_____	_____	_____
_____	_____	_____	_____	_____
_____	_____	_____	_____	_____
_____	_____	_____	_____	_____

The right to license any subsidiary right not set forth in this Paragraph is retained by the Author.

Licensing income shall be divided as specified herein without any reductions for expenses of any kind.

Licensing income shall be collected by the party authorized to license the right and the appropriate percentage remitted by that party to the other party within ten days of receipt. Copies of all licenses shall be provided to both parties immediately upon receipt.

8. Accountings. Commencing with the date of publication, the Publisher shall give a statement of account every ____ months to the Author, showing for that period and cumulatively to date the number of copies manufactured, the number of copies sold and returned for each royalty rate, the number of copies distributed free for publicity purposes, the number of copies remaindered, destroyed, or lost, the royalties paid to and owed to the Author, and licensing income. Payment due the Author shall accompany each statement of account.

9. Right of Inspection. The Author shall, upon the giving of written notice, have the right to inspect the Publisher's books of account to verify the accountings. If errors in any such accounting are found to be to the Author's disadvantage and represent more than 5 percent of the payment to the Author pursuant to the said accounting, the cost of inspection shall be paid by the Publisher.

10. Copyright and Authorship Credit. The Publisher shall, as an express condition of receiving the grant of rights specified in Paragraph 1, place copyright notice in the Author's name on all copies of the Work. Notwithstanding the foregoing, the exclusive right, title, and interest in the copyright in the performance embodied in the sound recording shall be the property of _____. The copyright notice for the Work shall read © (Author's Name) 20___ and ℗ _____20____. The Publisher shall take the necessary steps to register the copyrights on behalf of the owners thereof.

11. Warranty and Indemnity. The Author warrants and represents that he or she is the sole creator of the Work and owns all rights granted under this Agreement, that the Work is an original creation (except for material obtained with the written permission of others or material from the public domain), that the Work does not infringe any other person's copyrights or rights of literary property, nor, to his or her knowledge, does it violate the rights of privacy of, or libel, other persons. The Author agrees to indemnify the Publisher against any final judgment for damages (after all appeals have been exhausted) in any lawsuit based on an actual breach of the foregoing warranties. In addition, the Author shall pay the Publisher's reasonable costs and attorney's fees incurred in defending such a lawsuit, unless the Author chooses to retain his or her own attorney to defend such lawsuit. The Author makes no warranties and shall have no obligation to indemnify the Publisher with respect to materials inserted in the Work at the Publisher's request. Notwithstanding any of the foregoing, in no event shall the Author's liability under this Paragraph exceed $_____ or _____ percent of sums payable to the Author under this Agreement, whichever is the lesser. In the event a lawsuit is brought that may result in the Author having breached his or her warranties under this Paragraph, the Publisher shall have the right to withhold and place in an escrow account _____ percent of sums payable to the Author pursuant to Paragraphs 7 and 8, but in no event may said withholding exceed the damages alleged in the complaint.

12. Infringement. In the event of an infringement of the rights granted under this Agreement to the Publisher, the Publisher and the Author shall have the right to sue jointly for the infringement and, after deducting the expenses of bringing suit, to share equally in any recovery. If either party chooses not to join in the suit, the other party may proceed and, after deducting all the expenses of bringing the suit, any recovery shall be shared equally between the parties.

13. Artistic Control. The Publisher shall select one or more readers for the nondramatic reading of the Work. The Work may be a complete, condensed, or abridged version of the book. Any such version shall include verbatim selections from the book and, if supplied by the Publisher, connecting narrative passages as well as background music and sounds. The Author shall have the right to approve the recording script, which approval shall not be unreasonably withheld. The Author shall not have the right to approve the selection of readers, to approve the background music or sounds, or to approve the recording, unless specified here:_____

_____,

in which case such approval shall not be unreasonably withheld.

14. Promotion. The Author consents to the use of his or her name, portrait, or picture in connection with the promotion and advertising of the Work, provided such use is dignified and consistent with the Author's reputation. The Publisher agrees to implement the following program with respect to promotion of the Work:_____

_____

_____

15. Free Copies. The Author shall receive ____ free copies of the Work as published, after which the Author shall have the right to purchase additional copies at a ____ percent discount from the retail price.

16. Termination. The Author shall have the right to terminate this Agreement by written notice if: **(1)** the Work is not available in reasonable quantities through normal trade channels and the Publisher, within ninety days of receiving notice from the Author that the Work is not available, does not make the Work available again; **(2)** if the Publisher fails to provide statements of account pursuant to Paragraph 8; **(3)** if the Publisher fails to make payments pursuant to Paragraphs 5, 7, or 8; or **(4)** if the Publisher fails to publish in a timely manner pursuant to Paragraph 4. The Publisher shall have the right to terminate this Agreement if the Author fails to comply with the requirements of Paragraph 3. This Agreement shall automatically terminate in the event of the Publisher's insolvency, bankruptcy, or assignment of assets for the benefit of creditors. In the event of termination of the Agreement, the Publisher shall grant, convey, and transfer all rights in the Work back to the Author.

17. Production Materials and Copies. Upon any termination, the Author may, within sixty days of notification of such termination, purchase the master recording or any related materials at their scrap value and any remaining copies at the lesser of cost or remainder value.

18. Successors and Assigns. This Agreement may not be assigned by either party without the written consent of the other party hereto. The Author, however, shall retain the right to assign payments due hereunder without obtaining the Publisher's consent.

19. Arbitration. All disputes arising under this Agreement shall be submitted to binding arbitration before_____ in the following location _____ and shall be settled in accordance with the rules of the American Arbitration Association. Judgment upon the arbitration award may be entered in any court having jurisdiction thereof.

20. Miscellany. This Agreement represents the entire understanding between the parties. All modifications of this Agreement must be in writing and signed by both parties. Any waiver of a breach or default hereunder shall not be deemed a waiver of a subsequent breach or default of either the same provision or any other provision of this Agreement. This Agreement shall be binding on the parties and their respective heirs, administrators, successors, and assigns. This Agreement shall be governed by the laws of _____ State.

IN WITNESS WHEREOF, the parties have signed this Agreement as of the date first set forth above.

Author _____   Publisher _____

                                                 Company Name

                                     By _____

                                             Authorized Signatory, Title

Author's Lecture Contract

Many authors find lecturing to be an important source of income as well as a rewarding opportunity to express their feelings about their creativity and being an author. High schools, colleges, literary societies, and other institutions often invite authors to lecture.

A contract ensures that everything goes smoothly. For example, who will pay for transportation to and from the lecture? Will the author have to give one lecture in a day or, as the institution might prefer, many more? Will the author have to review writing by students? Resolving these kinds of questions, as well as the amount of and time to pay the fee, will make any lecture a more rewarding experience.

Filling in the Form

In the Preamble give the date and the names and addresses of the parties. In Paragraph 1 give the dates when the author will lecture, the nature and extent of the services the author will perform, and, if relevant, the form in which the author is to bring examples of his or her work. In Paragraph 2 specify the fee to be paid to the author and when it will be paid during the author's visit. In Paragraph 3 give the amounts of expenses to be paid (or state that none or all of these expenses are to be paid), specify which expenses other than travel and food and lodging are covered, and show what will be provided by the sponsor, such as food or lodging. In Paragraph 5 state the interest rate for late payments. In Paragraph 8 give which state's law will govern the contract. Then have both parties sign the contract.

Negotiation Checklist

❏ How long will the author have to stay at the sponsoring institution? (Paragraph 1)

❏ What are the nature and extent of the services that the author will have to perform? (Paragraph 1)

❏ What special materials, if any, must the author bring? (Paragraph 1)

❏ Specify the work facilities which the sponsor will provide the author.

❏ Specify the fee to be paid to the author. (Paragraph 2)

❏ Give a time for payment of the fee. (Paragraph 2)

❏ Consider having part of the fee paid in advance.

❏ Specify the expenses which will be paid by the sponsor, including the time for payment of these expenses. (Paragraph 3)

❏ Indicate what the sponsor may provide in place of paying expenses, such as giving lodging, meals, or a car. (Paragraph 3)

❏ If illness prevents the author from coming to lecture, state that an effort will be made to find another date. (Paragraph 4)

❏ If the sponsor must cancel for a reason beyond its control, indicate that the expenses incurred by the author must be paid and that an attempt will be made to reschedule. (Paragraph 4)

❏ If the sponsor cancels within 48 hours of the time the author is to arrive, consider requiring the full fee as well as any expenses be paid.

❏ Provide for the payment of interest on late payments by the sponsor. (Paragraph 5)

❏ Retain for the author all rights, including copyrights, in any recordings of any kind which may be made of the author's visit. (Paragraph 6)

❏ If the sponsor wishes to use a recording of the author's visit, such as a video, require that the sponsor obtain the author's written permission and that, if appropriate, a fee be negotiated for this use. (Paragraph 6)

❏ Compare the standard provisions in the introductory pages with Paragraphs 7–8.

Author's Lecture Contract

AGREEMENT, entered into as of the _____ day of _____, 20 _____, between_____ (hereinafter referred to as the "Author"), located at _____and

_____(hereinafter referred to as the "Sponsor"), located

at _____.

WHEREAS, the Sponsor is familiar with and admires the work of the Author; and

WHEREAS, the Sponsor wishes the Author to visit the Sponsor to enhance the opportunities for its students to have contact with working professional authors; and

WHEREAS, the Author wishes to lecture with respect to his or her work and perform such other services as this contract may call for;

NOW, THEREFORE, in consideration of the foregoing premises and the mutual covenants hereinafter set forth and other valuable considerations, the parties hereto agree as follows:

1. **Author to Lecture.** The Author hereby agrees to come to the Sponsor on the following date(s):_____

_____ and perform the following services:

_____.

The Author shall use best efforts to make his or her services as productive as possible to the Sponsor. The Author further agrees to bring examples of his or her own work in the form of _____

_____.

2. **Payment.** The Sponsor agrees to pay as full compensation for the Author's services rendered under Paragraph 1 the sum of $_____. This sum shall be payable to the Author on completion of the _____ day of the Author's residence with the Sponsor.

3. **Expenses**. In addition to the payments provided under Paragraph 2, the Sponsor agrees to reimburse the Author for the following expenses:

   (A) Travel expenses in the amount of $_____.

   (B) Food and lodging expenses in the amount of $_____.

   (C) Other expenses listed here:_____in the amount of $_____.

The reimbursement for travel expenses shall be made fourteen (14) days prior to the earliest date specified in Paragraph 1. The reimbursement for food, lodging, and other expenses shall be made at the date of payment specified in Paragraph 2, unless a contrary date is specified here:_____.

In addition, the Sponsor shall provide the Author with the following:

(A) Tickets for travel, rental car, or other modes of transportation as follows: _____

_____

(B) Food and lodging as follows: _____

_____

(C) Other hospitality as follows: _____

_____

4. Inability to Perform. If the Author is unable to appear on the dates scheduled in Paragraph 1 due to illness, the Sponsor shall have no obligation to make any payments under Paragraphs 2 and 3, but shall attempt to reschedule the Author's appearance at a mutually acceptable future date. If the Sponsor is prevented from having the Author appear by Acts of God, hurricane, flood, governmental order, or other cause beyond its control, the Sponsor shall be responsible only for the payment of such expenses under Paragraph 3 as the Author shall have actually incurred. The Sponsor agrees in such a case to attempt to reschedule the Author's appearance at a mutually acceptable future date.

5. Late Payment. The Sponsor agrees that, in the event it is late in making payment of amounts due to the Author under Paragraphs 2, 3, or 8, it will pay as additional liquidated damages _____ percent in interest on the amounts it is owing to the Author, said interest to run from the date stipulated for payment in Paragraphs 2, 3, or 8 until such time as payment is made.

6. Copyrights and Recordings. Both parties agree that the Author shall retain all rights, including copyrights, in relation to recordings of any kind made of the appearance or any works shown in the course thereof. The term "recording" as used herein shall include any recording made by electrical transcription, tape recording, wire recording, film, videotape, or other similar or dissimilar method of recording, whether now known or hereinafter developed. No use of any such recording shall be made by the Sponsor without the written consent of the Author and, if stipulated therein, additional compensation for such use.

7. Modification. This contract contains the full understanding between the parties hereto and may only be modified in a written instrument signed by both parties.

8. Governing Law. This contract shall be governed by the laws of the State of _____.

IN WITNESS WHEREOF, the parties hereto have signed this Agreement as of the date first set forth above.

Author_____   Sponsor_____
                                                                    Company Name

                                             By_____
                                                                    Authorized Signatory, Title

Privacy Release Form

Authors and self-publishers often accompany writing with photographs of people. Both text and photographs (or other images of people) raise the risk of violating an individual's rights to privacy and publicity. While these laws are intricate, this summary will help alert the author to potential dangers.

The right to privacy can take a number of forms. For example, state laws and court decisions forbid the use of a person's name, portrait, or picture for purposes of advertising or trade. This raises the question of the definitions for the terms "advertising" and "trade." Public display of an image which showed or implied something embarrassing and untrue about someone would also constitute a violation of the right to privacy. And physically intruding into a private space such as a home or office, perhaps to take a photograph for use with an article, can be an invasion of privacy.

The right of publicity is the right which a celebrity creates in his or her name, image, and voice. To use the celebrity's image for commercial gain violates this right of publicity. And, while the right of privacy generally protects only living people, a number of states have enacted laws to protect the publicity rights of celebrities even after death. These state laws supplement court decisions which held that celebrities who exploited the commercial value of their names and images while alive had publicity rights after death.

On the other hand, use of people's images for newsworthy and editorial purposes is protected by the First Amendment. No releases need be obtained for such uses, which serve the public interest.

What should the author do about all this? If the author is certain that the image will only be used for newsworthy and editorial purposes, no privacy release need be obtained. This should cover most of the images used by authors. If, on the other hand, there is a possibility of commercial use, a release should be obtained. For example, a photograph can be used for posters, postcards, and T-shirts, all of which are clearly trade uses. Or the photograph can be used in an advertisement. Only by having a privacy release can the author ensure the right to exploit the commercial value of the image in the future.

Form 9 allows the author to use a person's image for advertising and trade. While some states may not require written releases or the payment of money for a release, it is always wise to use a written release and make at least a small payment as consideration. By the way, Form 9 is intended for use with friends and acquaintances who pose, as well as with professional models or people connected with a piece of writing.

It is also important to be aware that if the release is intended to cover one use, and the image is then used in a distorted and embarrassing way for a different purpose, the release may not protect the author, regardless of what it says. An example of this would be a privacy release signed by a model for a bookstore's advertisement, in which she was to appear in bed reading a book. This advertisement was later changed and used by a bedsheet manufacturer known for its salacious advertisements. The title on the book became pornographic and a leering old man was placed next to the bed looking at the model. This invaded the model's privacy despite her having signed a release.

In general, a minor must have a parent or guardian give consent. While the author should check the law in his or her state, the age of majority in most states is eighteen.

The author should have any release signed at the same time the image is obtained. If the author, for example, is taking photographs, the privacy release should be signed during the session. While a witness isn't a necessity, having one can help if a question is later raised about the validity of the release.

If the author is asked to use a release form supplied by someone else, the author must make certain that the form protects the author. The negotiation checklist will be helpful in reviewing the provided form and suggesting changes to strengthen the form.

Is a privacy release necessary when an author wants to have exclusivity with respect to a newsworthy story? It is not, because this exclusivity is obtained by entering into an agreement between the author and the person who is the subject of the story or knows the information to be contained in the story. This might take the form of a collaboration agreement, but it might also take the form of an agreement to provide information only to the author in return for some compensation. Since the information is newsworthy, no privacy release need be obtained. However, the exclusivity provision that appears in the other provisions with Form 6 would be appropriate to use (changing the word "coauthor" to suit the circumstances) and the provisions of the privacy release might be added as an extra safeguard.

Filling in the Form

Fill in the dollar amount being paid as consideration for the release. Then fill in the name of the person giving the release and the name of the author. Have the person and a witness sign the form. Obtain the addresses for both the person and the witness and date the form. If the person is a minor, have the parent or guardian sign. Have the witness sign and give the addresses of the witness and the parent or guardian as well as the date.

Negotiation Checklist

❑ Be certain that some amount of money, even a token amount, is actually paid as consideration for the release.

❑ Have the release given not only to the author, but also to the author's estate and anyone

else the author might want to assign rights to (such as a manufacturer of posters or T-shirts).

❑ If someone else has obtained the release, be certain that it covers successors and assigns such as the author.

❑ State that the grant is irrevocable.

❑ Cover the use of the name as well as the image of the person.

❑ Include the right to use the image in all forms, media, and manners of use.

❑ Include the right to make distorted or changed versions of the image as well as composite images.

❑ Allow advertising and trade uses.

❑ Allow any other lawful use.

❑ Have the person waive any right to review any finished artwork, including written copy to accompany the artwork.

❑ Have the person recite that he or she is of full age.

❑ If the person is a minor, have a parent or guardian sign the release.

Privacy Release Form

In consideration of _____ dollars ($_____), receipt of which is acknowledged, I, _____ , do hereby give _____ , his or her assigns, licensees, and legal representatives the irrevocable right to use my name (or any fictional name), picture, portrait, or photograph in all forms and media and in all manners, including composite or distorted representations, for advertising, trade, or any other lawful purposes, and I waive any right to inspect or approve the finished version(s), including written copy that may be created in connection therewith. I am of full age.* I have read this release and am fully familiar with its contents.

Witness_____

Signed_____

Address_____

Address_____

Date _____, 20 ___

Consent (if applicable)

I am the parent or guardian of the minor named above and have the legal authority to execute the above release. I approve the foregoing and waive any rights in the premises.

Witness_____

Signed_____

Address_____

Address_____

Date _____, 20 ___

* Delete this sentence if the subject is a minor. The parent or guardian must then sign the consent.

Permission Form

Some projects require obtaining permission from the owners of copyrighted materials such as illustrations, paintings, articles, lyrics, poems, or books. The author ignores obtaining such permissions at great peril. Not only is it unethical to use someone else's work without permission, it can also lead to liability for copyright infringement and breach of contract.

Of course, some copyrighted works have entered the public domain, which means that they can be freely copied by anyone. For works published by United States authors on or before December 31, 1977, the maximum term of copyright protection is ninety-five years. However, copyrights have expired on all United States works registered or published prior to 1923. Copyrights obtained from 1923–1963 have a ninety-five year term if these copyrights were renewed, while copyrights obtained from 1964–1977 benefit from automatic renewal and definitely have a ninety-five year term. Authors should also keep in mind that foreign countries may confer different terms of copyright protection.

For works published on or after January 1, 1978, the term of protection is usually the life of the author plus seventy years, so these works would only be in the public domain if copyright notice had been omitted or improper. This complicated topic is discussed fully in *The Writer's Legal Guide*. The absence of a copyright notice on works published between January 1, 1978 and February 28, 1989 (when the United States joined the Berne Copyright Union) does not necessarily mean the work entered the public domain. On or after March 1, 1989, copyright notice is no longer required to preserve copyright protection, although such notice does confer some benefits under the copyright law. A basic rule would be to obtain permission for any work published on or after January 1, 1978, unless the author is certain the work is in the public domain.

Fair use offers another way in which the author may avoid having to obtain a permission, even though the work is protected by a valid copyright. The copyright law states that copying "for purposes such as criticism, comment, news reporting, teaching (including multiple copies for classroom use), scholarship, or research, is not an infringement of copyright." To evaluate whether a use is a fair use depends on four factors set forth in the law: "(1) the purpose and character of the use, including whether such use is of a commercial nature or is for nonprofit educational purposes; (2) the nature of the copyrighted work; (3) the amount and substantiality of the portion used . . . and (4) the effect of the use upon the potential market for or value of the copyrighted work." These guidelines have to be applied on a case-by-case basis. If there is any doubt, it is best to seek permission to use the work.

One obstacle to obtaining permissions is locating the person who owns the rights. A good starting point, of course, is to contact the publisher of the material, since the publisher may have the right to grant permissions. If the author's address is available, the author can be contacted directly. In some cases, permissions may have to be obtained from more than one party. Authors' societies and agents may be helpful in tracking down the owners of rights.

For an hourly fee, the Copyright Office will search its records to aid in establishing the copyright status of a work. Copyright Office Circular R22, "How to Investigate the Copyright Status of a Work," explains more fully what the Copyright Office can and cannot do. Circulars and forms can be ordered from the Copyright Office by calling (202) 707-9100.

Obtaining permissions can be time-consuming, so starting early in a project is wise. A log should be kept of each request for a permission. In the log, each request is given a number. The log describes the material to be used, lists the name and address of the owner of the rights, shows when the request was made and when any reply was received, indicates if a fee must be paid, and includes any special conditions required by the owner.

Fees may very well have to be paid for certain permissions. The standard book publishing agreement does not provide for the publisher to pay these fees, although the author can negotiate for such a contribution. Also, publisher's agreements usually make the author liable if lawsuits develop for permissions which should have been obtained by the author. In any case, the author should keep in mind that permission fees are negotiable and vary widely in amount. For a project that will require many permissions, advance research as to the amount of the fees is a necessity.

Filling in the Form

The form should be accompanied by a cover letter requesting that two copies of the form be signed and one copy returned. The name and address of the author, the title of the author's book (or other project), and the name of the author's publisher or client, should be filled in. Then the nature of the material should be specified, such as text, photograph, illustration, poem, and so on. The source should be described along with an exact description of the material. If available, fill in the date of publication, the publisher, and the author. Any copyright notice or credit line to accompany the material should be shown. State after other provisions any special limitations on the rights granted and also indicate the amount of any fee to be paid. If all the rights are not controlled by the person giving the permission, then that person will have to indicate who else to contact. If more than one person must approve the permission, make certain there are enough signature lines. If the rights are owned by a corporation, add the company name and the title of the authorized signatory. A stamped, self-addressed envelope and a photocopy of the material to be used might make a speedy response more likely.

Negotiation Checklist

❏ State that the permission extends not only to the author, but also to the author's successors and assigns. Certainly the permission must extend to the author's publisher (or client).

❏ Specify how the material will be used, whether for a book, a product, or some other use.

❏ Describe the material to be used carefully, including a photocopy if that would help.

❏ Obtain the right to use the material in future editions, revisions, and electronic versions, as well as in the present use.

❏ State that nonexclusive world rights in all languages are being granted.

❏ In an unusual situation, seek exclusivity for certain uses of the material. This form does not seek exclusivity.

❏ Negotiate a fee, if requested. Whether a fee is appropriate, and its amount, will depend on whether the project is likely to earn a substantial return.

❏ If a fee is paid, add a provision requiring the party giving the permission to warrant that the material does not violate any copyright or other rights and to indemnify the author against any losses caused if the warranty is incorrect.

❏ Keep a log on all correspondence relating to permission forms and be certain one copy of each signed permission has been returned for the author's files.

Permission Form

The Undersigned hereby grant(s) permission to _____ (hereinafter referred to as the "Author"), located at _____ , and to the Author's successors and assigns, to use the material specified in this Permission Form in the book titled _____ to be published by _____ .

This permission is for the following material:

Nature of material _____

Source _____

Exact description of material, including page numbers_____

If published, date of publication _____

Publisher _____

Author(s) _____

This material may be used in the Author's book and in any future revisions, editions, and electronic versions thereof, including nonexclusive world rights in all languages.

It is understood that the grant of this permission shall in no way restrict republication of the material by the Undersigned or others authorized by the Undersigned.

If specified here, the material shall be accompanied on publication by a copyright notice as follows_____ _____

and a credit line as follows _____ .

Other provisions, if any: _____

If specified here, the requested rights are not controlled in their entirety by the Undersigned and the following owners must be contacted: _____ _____

One copy of this Permission Form shall be returned to the Author and one copy shall be retained by the Undersigned.

_____   _____
Authorized Signatory   Date

_____   _____
Authorized Signatory   Date

Nondisclosure Agreement for Submitting Ideas

What can be more frustrating than having a great idea and not being able to share it with anyone? If the idea has commercial value, sharing it is often the first step on the way to realizing the remunerative potential of the concept. The author wants to show the idea to a publisher, manufacturer, or producer. But how can the idea be protected?

Ideas are not protected by copyright, because copyright only protects the concrete expression of an idea. The idea to write a guide to the White House is not copyrightable, but the written guide certainly is protected by copyright. The idea to have a television series in which each program would have a narrator teach local history at a well-known landmark in his or her locale is not copyrightable, but each program would be protected by copyright. Of course, copyright is not the only form of legal protection. An idea might be patentable or lead to the creation of a trademark, but such cases are less likely and certainly require expert legal assistance. How does an author disclose an idea for an image, a format, a product, or other creations without risking that the listener, or potential business associate, will simply steal the idea?

This can be done by the creation of an express contract, an implied contract (revealed by the course of dealing between the parties), or a fiduciary relationship (in which one party owes a duty of trust to the other party). Form 11, the Nondisclosure Agreement, creates an express contract between the party disclosing the idea and the party receiving it. Form 11 is adapted from a letter agreement in *Licensing Art & Design* by Caryn Leland (Allworth Press).

What should be done if a company refuses to sign a nondisclosure agreement or, even worse, has its own agreement for the author to sign? Such an agreement might say that the company will not be liable for using a similar idea and will probably place a maximum value on the idea (such as a few hundred dollars). At this point, the author has to evaluate the risk. Does the company have a good reputation or is it notorious for appropriating ideas? Are there other companies that could be approached with the idea, ones that would be willing to sign a nondisclosure agreement? If not, taking the risk may make more sense than never exploiting the idea at all. A number of steps, set out in the negotiation checklist, should then be taken to try and gain some protection. The author will have to make these evaluations on a case-by-case basis.

Filling in the Form

In the Preamble fill in the date and the names and addresses of the parties. In Paragraph 1 describe the information to be disclosed without giving away what it is. Have both parties sign the agreement.

Negotiation Checklist

❑ Disclose what the information concerns without giving away what is new or innovative. For example, "an idea for a new format for a series to teach history" might interest a producer but would not give away the particulars of the idea (i.e., using different narrators teaching at landmarks in different locales). (Paragraph 1)

❑ State that the recipient is reviewing the information to decide whether to embark on commercial exploitation. (Paragraph 2)

❑ Require the recipient to agree not to use or transfer the information. (Paragraph 3)

❏ State that the recipient receives no rights in the information. (Paragraph 3)

❏ Require the recipient to keep the information confidential. (Paragraph 4)

❏ State that the recipient acknowledges that disclosure of the information would cause irreparable harm to the author. (Paragraph 4)

❏ Require good faith negotiations if the recipient wishes to use the information after disclosure. (Paragraph 5)

❏ Allow no use of the information unless agreement is reached after such good faith negotiations. (Paragraph 5)

If the author wishes to disclose the information despite the other party's refusal to sign the author's nondisclosure form, the author should take a number of steps:

❏ First, before submission, the idea should be sent to a neutral third party (such as a notary public or professional authors' society) to be held in confidence.

❏ Anything submitted should be marked with copyright and trademark notices, when appropriate. For example, the idea may not be copyrightable, but the written explanation of the idea certainly is. The copyright notice could be for that explanation, but might make the recipient more hesitant to steal the idea.

❏ If an appointment is made, confirm it by letter in advance and sign any log for visitors.

❏ After any meeting, send a letter that covers what happened at the meeting (including any disclosure of confidential information and any assurances that information will be kept confidential) and, if at all possible, have any proposal or followup from the recipient be in writing.

Nondisclosure Agreement for Submitting Ideas

AGREEMENT, entered into as of this _____ day of _____, 20____, between_____ (hereinafter referred to as the "Author"), located at _____, and _____ (hereinafter referred to as the "Recipient"), located at _____.

WHEREAS, the Author has developed certain valuable information, concepts, ideas, or designs, which the Author deems confidential (hereinafter referred to as the "Information"); and

WHEREAS, the Recipient is in the business of using such Information for its projects and wishes to review the Information; and

WHEREAS, the Author wishes to disclose this Information to the Recipient; and

WHEREAS, the Recipient is willing not to disclose this Information, as provided in this Agreement.

NOW, THEREFORE, in consideration of the foregoing premises and the mutual covenants hereinafter set forth and other valuable considerations, the parties hereto agree as follows:

1. **Disclosure.** Author shall disclose to the Recipient the Information, which concerns:_____ _____.

2. **Purpose.** Recipient agrees that this disclosure is only for the purpose of the Recipient's evaluation to determine its interest in the commercial exploitation of the Information.

3. **Limitation on Use.** Recipient agrees not to manufacture, sell, deal in, or otherwise use or appropriate the disclosed Information in any way whatsoever, including but not limited to adaptation, imitation, redesign, or modification. Nothing contained in this Agreement shall be deemed to give Recipient any rights whatsoever in and to the Information.

4. **Confidentiality.** Recipient understands and agrees that the unauthorized disclosure of the Information by the Recipient to others would irreparably damage the Author. As consideration and in return for the disclosure of this Information, the Recipient shall keep secret and hold in confidence all such Information and treat the Information as if it were the Recipient's own proprietary property by not disclosing it to any person or entity.

5. **Good Faith Negotiations.** If, on the basis of the evaluation of the Information, Recipient wishes to pursue the exploitation thereof, Recipient agrees to enter into good faith negotiations to arrive at a mutually satisfactory agreement for these purposes. Until and unless such an agreement is entered into, this nondisclosure Agreement shall remain in force.

6. **Miscellany.** This Agreement shall be binding upon and shall inure to the benefit of the parties and their respective legal representatives, successors, and assigns.

IN WITNESS WHEREOF, the parties have signed this Agreement as of the date first set forth above.

Author_____   Recipient_____
                                                          Company Name

                                              By_____
                                                      Authorized Signatory, Title

Contract with Book Designer

The author with a finished manuscript must choose between two roads. One road leads to the world of commercial publishing where the author submits the manuscript to publishers (and perhaps agents) and hopes for success. The other road, less traveled (but becoming familiar to more and more authors), leads to the domain of self-publication. Here the author does not give up control of his or her manuscript. Instead, the author oversees the processes of design, printing, and sales, using contracts like Forms 12 to 15 to establish successful business arrangements.

Should an author self-publish? Subjective factors weigh heavily in this decision. Is the author someone who can work with a designer, a printer, a sales rep, or a distributor? Is it worthwhile to give up time from writing to do all that (and probably a lot more, such as creating direct mail brochures and filling orders from the dining room table)? Are the author's expectations reasonable, or so high that disappointment is bound to result? From a more objective viewpoint, the most important issue is whether there is a market for the book that can be reached by the author. What are the likely sales for the book? If these sales are by direct mail, how much will the direct mail piece, postage, and handling cost? Once sales have been estimated, all the costs can be put together to see whether the venture is likely to be profitable.

After the decision has been made to self-publish, the next step is to have a designer fashion a design for the book (unless the self-publisher does this, perhaps through desktop publishing). The designer is a creator too, so the relationship can have the joys and agonies of any creative collaboration. By looking at samples of the designer's work and perhaps speaking with several prior clients, it should be possible to find a designer whose skills and temperament will meet the requirements of the self-publisher.

What will the designer do? Will the cover be designed as well as the interior of the book? What will the self-publisher be given as the finished product? Will it be ready for the printer or require additional work? Will the designer take responsibility for overseeing the printing? If photography or illustration is needed for the cover (or interior), will the designer commission or locate this, pay the fees, and obtain the necessary releases?

Of course, there must be agreement as to the fee. Many designers have switched to computers for their design work. This can be very cost efficient for certain projects. It is worth asking if the designer uses a computer and, if so, whether this has cost advantages. If the designer does use a computer, the author might save money by giving the designer computer disks (instead of a manuscript that would have to be scanned).

Expenses are the other significant aspect of the cost. The designer will incur a variety of expenses, from the dispatching of messengers to the procuring of reproduction-quality type (or film). A big expense might be the hiring of an illustrator or photographer to create a cover image or even interior spots. The self-publisher must know the likely range of these expenses, and perhaps control it by placing a ceiling on the budget. Whether or not the designer marks up these expenses can be another point of controversy, although the designer may argue that the advancing of the expense money and the amount of paperwork justify a markup.

Changes and revisions are another source of expense. If the self-publisher initiates changes or revisions outside the scope of the initial assignment, the designer will expect additional payment. A fair method for determining such payment (such as an hourly rate) should be included in the contract.

The self-publisher must have the rights to use the design for the book and any related advertising or promotion. It would be unusual for the design of a book's interior to have other sales potential (such as for T-shirts), but in such a case the self-publisher would seek additional usage rights from the designer. If the design is so unique that the self-publisher does not want a similar design used on a competitive book, the contract might provide that the designer would not reuse the design without the self-publisher's approval. If the designer uses art or photography, the designer should pay the necessary fees and obtain releases that allow use of the images in a book or on a book's cover.

The designer must also work on schedule. Failure to do this should be a ground for the self-publisher to terminate the contract. To ensure the self-publisher's satisfaction, approval should be required for representative page layouts and type samples as well as for the complete book. Most designers work with computers and can provide a printout of the complete book without paying for reproduction-quality type.

Unless the self-publisher has skills as a graphic artist, the designer should deliver materials ready to be given to the printer. These may take the form of mechanicals (many printers take mechanicals in as electronic files), film, or separations. The parties should determine if the designer will render additional services, such as overseeing the printing. Some designers will deliver finished books, which means they take responsibility for assuring that the printer delivers a satisfactory job. In this situation, designers also markup the printing, which can be an expensive way to try and guarantee quality. In any case, the exact services to be rendered by the designer should be discussed in detail before the commencement of work and reflected in a contract like Form 12.

Filling in the Form

Fill in the date and the names and addresses for the designer and the self-publisher. In Paragraph 1 give the project title and description, indicate if the designer is to do the interior of the book or the cover of the book, give any other specifications, state the form in which the designed book will be delivered ready for printing, and specify any other services the designer will perform. In Paragraph 2 specify the amount of time the designer has to complete the various phases of the work. In Paragraph 4 fill in the amount of the design fee. In Paragraph 5 fill in the maximum amount the designer is allowed to bill for expenses. In Paragraph 7 indicate how extra work will be charged for by the designer. In Paragraph 8 indicate whether or not the designer shall receive design credit for the design. In Paragraph 10 the blank space should only be filled in if the designer is not retaining ownership of the preliminary materials. In Paragraph 13 fill in who will arbitrate, the place of arbitration, and the maximum amount which can be sued for in small claims court. In Paragraph 16 specify which state's laws will govern the contract. Both parties should then sign the contract.

Negotiation Checklist

❑ Give the title of the book and describe the assignment in whatever detail is required, attaching another sheet to the contract if necessary (in which case the line for "Subject Matter" would refer to the attached sheet). It is very important to determine exactly what the designer is agreeing to do. (Paragraph 1)

❑ State whether the designer will do the cover design, interior design, or both. (Paragraph 1)

❑ Give specifications in detail, such as book size, number of colors, number of pages, and whatever else is known at the time of signing the agreement. (Paragraph 1)

❑ State that the designer will deliver materials ready for the printer. Indicate the form these materials will take, such as mechanicals (usually as electronic files), film, or separations.

❑ Specify if the designer is to render other services, such as coordinating with the printer or going on press while the book is being printed. (Paragraph 1)

❑ If the designer is to handle the printing and the designer's fee includes the cost of the printing, the self-publisher must be certain that the printing process will be reviewed in such a way that the final product will be satisfactory and, if it is not satisfactory, that recourse against both the designer and the printer is provided for. Since the designer stands in the position of the printer in such an arrangement, Form 13 should be reviewed.

❑ If the designer is paid to handle the printing, consider whether the amount of the designer's markup is fair.

❑ Approve the design at as many stages as possible, including samples for layouts and typefaces. (Paragraph 2)

❑ Give a due date for the work at each approval stage, which can be expressed as a number of days after the self-publisher's approval of the prior stage. (Paragraph 2)

❑ If possible, approve the finished book before reproduction quality type or film is created. Many designers can use computers to provide such a printout. (Paragraph 2)

❑ If the self-publisher is to provide reference materials, the due date can be expressed as a number of days after the designer's receipt of these materials. (Paragraph 2)

❑ If even a short delay would cause serious problems, make time of the essence.

❑ State that illness or other delays beyond the control of the designer will extend the due date, but only up to a limited number of days.

❑ Be certain the grant of rights encompasses all the rights needed by the self-publisher. Usually worldwide book rights, including electronic versions as well as advertising and promotion, is sufficient. (Paragraph 3)

❑ If it is likely a certain type of additional usage will be made, the amount of the reuse fee can be specified. The reuse fee can also be expressed as a percentage of the original fee, or the original fee can be increased and the grant of rights expanded. If the self-publisher will want to use a unique design for a poem on T-shirts, it would be wise to obtain novelty rights in the initial contract. Another approach would be to seek all rights, but designers (like authors) object to selling rights which may not be used and for which nothing is presumably being paid. In any case, the fact that usage fees must be paid (and permission obtained) for uses beyond the grant of rights should be kept in mind at all times.

❑ Specify the fee. (Paragraph 4)

❑ Determine whether sales tax must be paid. Since most books are for resale, it is quite likely sales tax need not be paid on mechanicals or other materials used to create the books. However, the sales tax laws vary from state to state and must be checked for the particular state involved. (Paragraph 4)

❑ Any expenses the self-publisher will reimburse to the designer should be specified to avoid misunderstandings. Some designers include expenses in their fee (especially if the expenses are minimal), and the self-publisher can certainly ask that this be done, but most bill separately for expenses. (Paragraph 5)

❏ If expenses are to be reimbursed, consider putting a maximum amount on how much will be reimbursed. Any expenses beyond this amount would have to be absorbed by the designer. (Paragraph 5)

❏ Determine whether the designer marks up expenses, such as billing 15 to 20 percent of the expenses as an additional charge. If expenses are going to be marked up, this should be stated. One rationale for marking up expenses is the depletion of the designer's funds until reimbursement and the extra paperwork. Sometimes, however, the self-publisher is paying a fee that may be large enough to cover such overhead items as carrying charges and staff time.

❏ If expenses will be significant, consider whether an advance against expenses is justified. If an advance against expenses is given, it should certainly have to be repaid if the expenses are never incurred.

❏ State that payment shall be made within a certain number of days after delivery of the finished design, usually within thirty days after such delivery. (Paragraph 6)

❏ Deal with the issue of payment for work-in-progress that is postponed but not cancelled. A pro rata billing might be appropriate. (Paragraph 6)

❏ The fee for cancellation at different stages of the assignment should be specified. The self-publisher should have the right to stop work on the project without being liable for more than the work done to date by the designer, unless special circumstances have caused the designer to have other losses. (Paragraph 6)

❏ Specify advances to be paid against the fee. Book design would not ordinarily require such an advance but a schedule of payments would probably be necessary for an extensive job.

❏ Revisions can be a problem. The designer should be given the first opportunity to make revisions, after which the self-publisher should be able to have the revisions done by another designer. (Paragraph 7)

❏ If revisions are the fault of the designer, no additional fee should be charged. However, if the self-publisher changes the nature of the assignment, additional fees must be charged for revisions. (Paragraph 7)

❏ If the designer is to receive credit for the design, the self-publisher may allow the designer to remove his or her name if the revisions are done by someone else. (Paragraph 7)

❏ With respect to revisions or the assignment itself, the self-publisher should seek to avoid forcing the designer to rush or work unusual hours since the fees for work under such stress may be higher.

❏ Document any revisions or changes in the assignment in writing, since there may later be a question as to whether the changes were executed accurately and whether they came within the initial description of the project. Paragraph 16 requires that all modifications to the agreement be written.

❏ State whether the designer will receive name credit for the book design. This would be especially likely for a cover or a unique design for an interior. (Paragraph 8)

❏ Copyright notice for the design, or photographs or illustrations used in the design, will not lessen the right of the self-publisher to bring suit for the infringement of his or her exclusive rights in the design as well as for any writing that is infringed. (Paragraph 9)

❏ The self-publisher should retain ownership of the physical design in its ready-to-print form, since this may be used to incorporate future changes. (Paragraph 10)

❏ Unless there is a special reason to obtain ownership of preliminary materials used to create the design, the ownership of these materials can be retained by the designer. (Paragraph 10)

❏ The designer must obtain needed releases with respect both to using copyrighted work or, in some cases, using the images of people. (Paragraph 11)

❏ The self-publisher should obtain a warranty and indemnity provision, in which the designer states that the work is not a copyright infringement and not libelous and agrees to pay for the self-publisher's damages and attorney's fees if this is not true. Such a warranty should not extend to materials provided by the self-publisher for insertion in the book. (Paragraph 12)

❏ If the design is unique and the self-publisher does not want it used elsewhere, a provision against competitive uses might be added. (See other provisions.)

❏ Include a provision for arbitration, excluding amounts that can be sued for in small claims court. (Paragraph 13)

❏ Specify a short term. (Paragraph 13)

❏ Allow the self-publisher to terminate if the designer does not meet the project's specifications, falls behind schedule, or becomes insolvent. (Paragraph 14)

❏ Allow the designer the right to assign money payable under the contract, unless there is a particular reason not to do so. (Paragraph 14)

❏ Give the self-publisher the right to assign the contract or rights under the contract. This might happen if, for example, the self-publisher licensed rights to reprint the book as a book club selection. (Paragraph 14)

❏ Consider whether purchasing publisher's liability insurance might be advisable.

❏ Compare the standard provisions in the introductory pages with Paragraph 16.

Other provisions that can be added to Form 12:

❏ Noncompetition. If a book has a unique look, the self-publisher may not want the designer to create books in a similar style that might damage the book's market. One solution would be to insist on an all-rights contract, since the designer would have no right to reuse the work at all. A less extreme solution is to have a noncompetition provision, although even this can be objectionable since the designer cannot risk his or her livelihood by agreeing not to work in a particular style. For books using familiar formats, such a provision would presumably not be appropriate.

Noncompetition. The Designer agrees not to make or permit any use of the Design or similar designs which would compete with or impair the use of the Design by the Publisher. The Designer shall submit any proposed uses of the Design or similar designs to the Publisher for approval, which approval shall not be unreasonably withheld.

Contract with Book Designer

AGREEMENT, entered into as of the _____ day of _____ , 20 _____ , between _____ , located at _____ (hereinafter referred to as the "Designer"), and _____ , located at _____ (hereinafter referred to as the "Publisher"), with respect to a book design (hereinafter referred to as the "Design").

WHEREAS, Designer is a professional book designer of good standing;

WHEREAS, Publisher wishes the Designer to design a book as described more fully herein; and

WHEREAS, Designer wishes to create such Design and implement the Design pursuant to this Agreement;

NOW, THEREFORE, in consideration of the foregoing premises and the mutual covenants hereinafter set forth and other valuable considerations, the parties hereto agree as follows:

1. **Description.** The Designer agrees to create the Design in accordance with the following specifications:
   Project title and description:_____
   ❑ Interior design to be created by Designer   ❑ Cover design to be created by Designer
   Other specifications:_____
   Designer shall deliver the Design ready for printing, as follows:_____
   Other services to be rendered by Designer:_____

2. **Due Date.** The Designer agrees to deliver representative layouts with type samples within _____ days after the later of the signing of this Agreement or, if the Publisher is to provide reference, layouts, or specifications, after the Publisher has provided same to the Designer. The entire Design shall be designed and presented to the Publisher no later than _____ days after the Publisher's approval of the representative layouts and type samples. If possible, the entire Design shall be shown to the Publisher prior to generation of reproduction-quality type, mechanicals, film, or separations. After Publisher's approval of the entire Design, the Design in the form ready for printing shall be delivered no later than _____ days thereafter.

3. **Grant of Rights.** Designer hereby grants to the Publisher exclusive worldwide book rights in the Design for the full term of any copyright therein (or in perpetuity if the design is not copyrightable), including the right to use the Design in electronic versions of the book and in advertising and promotion related to the book.

4. **Fee.** Publisher agrees to pay the following purchase price: $_____ for the usage rights granted. Publisher agrees to pay sales tax if required by the applicable state laws.

5. **Expenses.** Publisher agrees to reimburse the Designer for expenses incurred for stats, type, photography, illustration, and similar production expenses, provided that such expenses shall be itemized and supported by invoices, shall not be marked up, and shall not exceed $_____ in total.

6. **Payment.** Publisher agrees to pay the Designer within thirty days of the date of Designer's billing, which shall be dated as of the date of delivery of the Design in the form ready for printing. In the event that work is postponed or cancelled at the request of the Publisher, the Designer shall have the right to bill and be paid pro rata for work completed through the date of that request, but the Publisher shall have no further liability hereunder.

7. **Revisions.** The Designer shall be given the first opportunity to make any revisions requested by the Publisher. If the revisions are not due to any fault on the part of the Designer, an additional fee shall be charged as follows:_____. If the Designer objects to any revisions to be made by the Publisher, the Designer shall have the right to have any design credit and copyright notice in his or her name removed from the published Design.

8. **Design Credit.** Design credit in the name of the Designer   ❑ shall   ❑ shall not accompany the Design when it is reproduced.

9. **Copyright Notice.** Copyright notice in the name of the Designer   ❑ shall   ❑ shall not accompany the Design when it is reproduced.

10. Ownership of Physical Design. The ownership of the physical Design in the form delivered ready for printing shall be the property of the Publisher. Sketches and any other materials created in the process of making the finished Design shall remain the property of the Designer, unless indicated to the contrary here: _____.

11. Releases. The Designer agrees to obtain releases for any art, photography, or other copyrighted materials to be incorporated by the Designer into the Design.

12. Warranty and Indemnity. The Designer warrants and represents that he or she is the sole creator of the Design and owns all rights granted under this Agreement, that the Design is an original creation (except for materials obtained with the written permission of others or materials from the public domain), that the Design does not infringe any other person's copyrights or rights of literary property, nor does it violate the rights of privacy of, or libel, other persons. The Designer agrees to indemnify and hold harmless the Publisher against any claims, judgments, court costs, attorney's fees, and other expenses arising from any alleged or actual breach of this warranty.

13. Arbitration. All disputes arising under this Agreement shall be submitted to binding arbitration before _____ _____ in the following location _____ and settled in accordance with the rules of the American Arbitration Association. Judgment upon the arbitration award may be entered in any court having jurisdiction thereof. Disputes in which the amount at issue is less than $_____ shall not be subject to this arbitration provision.

14. Assignment. The Publisher shall have the right to assign any or all of its rights and obligations pursuant to this Agreement. The Designer shall have the right to assign monies due to him or her under the terms of this Agreement, but shall not make any other assignments hereunder.

15. Term and Termination. This Agreement shall have a term of _____ months after delivery pursuant to Paragraph 2. The Publisher may terminate this Agreement at any time prior to the Designer's commencement of work and may terminate thereafter if the Designer fails to adhere to the specifications or schedule for the Design. This Agreement shall also terminate in the event of the Designer's bankruptcy or insolvency. The rights and obligations of the parties pursuant to Paragraphs 3, 8, 9, 10, 11, 12, and 13 shall survive termination of this Agreement.

16. Miscellany. This Agreement shall be binding upon the parties hereto and their respective heirs, successors, assigns, and personal representatives. This Agreement constitutes the entire understanding between the parties. Its terms can be modified only by an instrument in writing signed by both parties, except that the Publisher may authorize expenses or revisions orally. A waiver of a breach of any of the provisions of this Agreement shall not be construed as a continuing waiver of other breaches of the same or other provisions hereof. This Agreement shall be governed by the laws of the State of _____.

IN WITNESS WHEREOF, the parties hereto have signed this Agreement as of the date first set forth above.

Designer_____   Publisher_____
                                                                        Company Name

                                             By:_____
                                                                   Authorized Signatory, Title

Contract with Printer

The author who decides to self-publish will have to work with a printer. In a large publishing company, the printing process would be managed by a production supervisor. For the self-publisher who knows nothing of printing, it would be worthwhile to find an advisor to fill the role of production supervisor. This might be the designer of the book, although some designers know little about printing. Another possibility would be to locate a production manager or supervisor who could offer advice. Or, if the self-publisher were fortunate, the printer might be trustworthy enough to ensure proper production techniques and quality. Certainly the self-publisher would need to review samples of the printer's work to see if the quality is satisfactory.

This section elaborates the ramifications of dealing with the printer. However, the production aspects have been dealt with at length in books such as *Pocket Pal* (International Paper Company) and *Getting It Printed* by Mark Beach and Eric Kenley (North Light Books). The more the self-publisher learns about the printing process, the greater the likelihood that each book will meet appropriate quality standards.

The first step in dealing with a printer is to request a price quotation. To do this, detailed specifications must be given for the book. It is always wise to seek more than one bid, since prices vary widely. One reason for great price variation is that printers have different equipment. The equipment may make the printer effective for one size of book but not another, which is reflected in the price. Asking each printer about their best book size and print-run length may give helpful insights into matching a book with the most efficient printer.

Since the self-publisher will probably be seeking printing bids when the book is still being written or designed, the specifications initially given to the printer are always subject to change. Thus, estimates often include variable costs for increasing or decreasing the number of pages and the size of the print run. Schedule A can be used as a Request for Printing Quotation or, when the job is ready to print, it can be used as Printing Specifications to accompany Form 13. When requesting quotations, always keep the specifications identical for each printer. This may be difficult if, for example, a printer has a special house paper (which is purchased in large quantities to create a cost savings) and bases its bid on such paper. Of course, the self-publisher is free to supply his or her own paper and ink, but is unlikely to go to this level of sophistication. Also, find out how long a quotation will hold before the printer will insist on rebidding the job (and may increase the price).

Once a printer has given an acceptable printing quotation, the self-publisher will want to know that the books will be of good quality and delivered on time. It is important to check the printer's proofs before allowing the book to be printed. After approval, the printer is free to print the book in conformity with the approved proofs. Some publishers will send a production specialist to watch the press run, especially for color printing.

The printing industry has developed what it calls "trade customs," which are a set of rules intended to govern the relationship of printer to client. Notwithstanding these self-serving rules, the self-publisher can certainly create his or her own contractual arrangement by having the printer sign a contract with explicit terms such as those contained in Form 13.

The price will usually be expressed as a certain amount for a certain quantity (such as $7,500 for 5,000 books). Trade custom allows for the printer to deliver 10 percent more or less than the agreed upon quantity. These "overs" or "unders" are paid for at the marginal unit cost (which might be $1 per book, even if the average unit cost is $1.50 per book, since the initial cost of the film work and setting up the press are not part of the marginal unit cost). If the self-publisher will not accept either overs or unders, this should be stated in the specifications. In such a case the printer will probably adjust its price upward.

The self-publisher will certainly keep ownership over whatever materials he or she gives to the printer, such as electronic files, mechanicals, or art. If these materials are valuable, they should be insured and returned as soon as possible after printing. A more sensitive issue is ownership of the materials created by the printer in the course of the project. If, for whatever reason, the self-publisher wishes to have a future printing of the book done by a different printer, the self-publisher must have the right to receive any film and separations back from the printer. The best way to accomplish this is to own the film, require the printer to store it without charge, and pay only for delivery charges if the self-publisher decides to move the film to another printer. Printers should agree to this, since the film will never have to be moved if they satisfy the self-publisher.

Printers will seek to limit their liability to the amount paid by the self-publisher for the printing job. This does not appear fair if a job costs $10,000, but the self-publisher loses $30,000 because the printer never delivers books or delivers them too late (for example, delivers a children's book about Santa Claus on January 15th and misses the Christmas season). The printer will also prefer to deliver the books "F.O.B. printing plant," which means that the printer will load the books at the printing plant without charge but has no responsibility after that. The self-publisher will either arrange to pay shipping and insurance costs to the final destination or ask the printer to ship "C.I.F. Bridgeport, Connecticut," if that is the destination for the books. C.I.F. means that the cost of the merchandise, insurance, and freight charges to the destination are paid by the shipping party (in this case, the printer). If the printer does arrange this, it will no doubt want to bill an extra charge. In any case, the self-publisher must be assured that if the books are lost or damaged in shipment, the insurance funds are available to cover the loss and, if feasible, reprint.

Filling in the Form

In the Preamble fill in the date and the names and addresses of the parties. In Paragraph 1 check the appropriate box and either fill in the specifications in Paragraph 1 or in Schedule A. In Paragraph 2 specify the delivery date, the place of delivery, and the terms (probably F.O.B. or C.I.F.). In Paragraph 3 restate the number of copies, give the price, indicate the amount of overs and unders which are acceptable, and specify the price per book for the overs and unders. In Paragraph 4 specify when payment must be made after delivery (usually thirty days for United States printers, although sixty days is sometimes agreed to). In both Paragraph 5 and Paragraph 6 indicate whether the printer must insure the materials and, if so, for how much. In Paragraph 6 also indicate which party will pay the expense of returning the materials. In Paragraph 8 specify the arbitrator, the place of arbitration, and the amount beneath which claims can be brought in small claims court. In Paragraph 9 specify a term for the contract. In Paragraph 10 indicate which state's laws will govern the contract. Have both parties sign and append Schedule A, if necessary. Detailed instructions on filling out Schedule A are not included here because the self-publisher should fill out that schedule with the assistance of a skilled production manager.

Negotiation Checklist

❏ Fill out the specifications to attain the book that the self-publisher wants, including quantity, stock, trim size, number of pages, binding (if any), whether proofs (such as blue lines, match prints, or color keys) will be provided, packing, and any other specifications. (Paragraph 1 or Schedule A)

❏ Specify a delivery date. (Paragraph 2)

❏ Specify a delivery location. (Paragraph 2)

❏ Indicate the terms of delivery, such as F.O.B. or C.I.F., and be certain the books are sufficiently insured. (Paragraph 2)

❏ State that the risk of loss is borne by the printer until the books are delivered according to the terms of the contract. (Paragraph 2)

❏ State that time is of the essence. The printer will resist this, since late delivery will be an actionable breach of contract. (Paragraph 2)

❏ Do not allow the printer to limit damages for nondelivery or late delivery to the purchase price of the books.

❏ State the price for the quantity ordered. (Paragraph 3)

❏ Specify whether 10 percent overs or unders is acceptable. (Paragraph 3)

❏ Determine whether any sales or other tax must be paid on the printing, and ascertain whether this tax has been included in the price or will be an additional charge. Most books are sold by the printer to publishers for resale, so sales tax should not be payable. However, this must be checked with the sales tax authorities in both the printer's and self-publisher's states if there is any uncertainty on this point.

❏ State when payment will be made after delivery, which is usually within thirty or sixty days. (Paragraph 4)

❏ Do not give the printer a security interest in the books, which the printer might want until full payment has been made for the books. Such a security interest, when perfected by filing with the appropriate government agencies, would give the printer a right to the books themselves or their sale proceeds.

❏ State that all materials supplied by the self-publisher remain the property of the self-publisher and must be returned when no longer needed. (Paragraph 5)

❏ Do not give the printer a security interest in materials supplied by the self-publisher.

❏ Indicate that the printer shall pay the expense of returning the materials supplied by the self-publisher. (Paragraph 5)

❏ State whether materials supplied by the self-publisher will be insured by the printer and, if so, for how much. (Paragraph 5)

❏ State that all materials created by the printer are the property of the self-publisher, must be stored without charge, and must be returned when no longer needed. (Paragraph 6)

❏ Indicate who will pay for the return to the publisher of materials created by the printer. (Paragraph 6)

❏ State whether materials created by the printer and owned by the self-publisher will be insured by the printer and, if so, for how much. (Paragraph 6)

❏ Decide whether the printer may use other companies to do part of the production process. Printers may have color inserts, binding, shrink-wrapping, or other production done by other companies. If the self-publisher's trust is with a particular printer, this practice may be ill-advised. In any case, the self-publisher should be familiar with the true capabilities of the printer. Jobbing work out may cause production delays. Also, a printer's bid that seems too high may be the result of the printer marking up work to be done by others, instead of doing that work itself.

❏ If the printer requests a provision to extend the delivery date in the event of war, strikes, or similar situations beyond its control, the self-publisher should specify that after some period of time the contract will terminate. This period of time might be relatively brief if the books have not yet been printed.

❏ Require proofs for both the cover and interior of the book, and hold the printer to matching these proofs. Or, if the self-publisher prefers to avoid this extra expense, be aware of the risk that the printing may have defects that could have been avoided. (Paragraph 7)

❏ Require that the printer meet a quality standard reflected in samples shown by the printer.

❏ Do not allow the printer to make a blanket disclaimer of warranties, since these warranties are to protect the buyer. A warranty is a fact the buyer can rely upon, such as the printer's statement that a certain kind of paper will be used for a book or simply the fact that the printer has title to the books and can sell them.

❏ The self-publisher should ascertain any extra expenses, such as charges for changes in the specifications after an order has been placed; charges to use paper and ink provided by the self-publisher; charges for delays caused by the self-publisher's tardiness in reviewing pre-press proofs; charges for press proofing (that is, having someone review sheets and make adjustments while the press is running); charges for samples to be air freighted or for extra covers; charges for storage of unbound sheets or bound books; charges for shipping; and any other charges.

❏ State that disputes shall be arbitrated, but not at the printer's sole option or at its place of business. (Paragraph 8)

❏ Specify a short term for the contract. (Paragraph 9)

❏ Allow the self-publisher to terminate without charge prior to the printer's starting work or if the printer fails to meet the production specifications or schedule. (Paragraph 9)

❏ State that the contract will terminate if the printer becomes bankrupt or insolvent. (Paragraph 9)

❏ Specify that the self-publisher's right to materials it supplied or materials the printer created will survive termination of the contract. (Paragraph 9)

❏ If there is to be any charge for cancellation of an order, make certain such a charge bears a reasonable relationship to expenses actually incurred by the printer for that order.

❏ If work beyond the original specifications is needed, a method or standard that the printer will use to bill such extra work should be agreed upon.

❏ Do not allow the printer to limit the time to inspect the books and complain about defects, since the self-publisher should certainly have a reasonable amount of time to do this. Of course, defects should be looked for and documented in writing to the printer as soon as discovered.

❏ If at all possible, refuse any provision stating that the self-publisher warrants the book is not a copyright infringement, libelous, obscene, or otherwise unlawful, and indemnifies the printer if this is not true. Another variation to be avoided would allow the printer to refuse to bind the book in the event of a breach of such a warranty.

❏ Compare the standard provisions in the introductory pages with Paragraphs 8 and 10.

Contract with Printer

AGREEMENT, entered into as of the _____ day of _____ 20____, between _____ (hereinafter referred to as the "Publisher"), located at _____, and _____ (hereinafter referred to as the "Printer"), located at _____, with respect to the printing of certain materials (hereinafter referred to as the "Work").

WHEREAS, the Publisher has prepared the Work for publication and wishes to have the Work printed in accordance with the terms of this Agreement; and

WHEREAS, the Printer is in the business of printing and is prepared to meet the specifications and other terms of this Agreement with respect to printing the Work;

NOW, THEREFORE, in consideration of the foregoing premises and the mutual covenants hereinafter set forth and other valuable consideration, the parties hereto agree as follows:

1. **Specifications.** The Printer agrees to print the Work in accordance with ❏ Schedule A or ❏ the following specifications:

   Title _____

   Description _____

   Quantity _____

   Repro Materials

      Text _____

      Cover _____

   Trim Size _____

   Number of Pages _____

   Illustrations _____ black-and-white _____ color

   Stock _____

      Text _____

      Cover _____

   Presswork _____

   Proofs _____

   Binding _____

   Packing _____

   Other Specifications _____

2. **Delivery and Risk of Loss.** Printer agrees to deliver the order on or before _____, 20_____ to the following location _____ and pursuant to the following terms _____. The Printer shall be strictly liable for loss, damage, or theft of the books until delivery has been made as provided in this Paragraph. Time is of the essence with respect to the delivery date.

3. **Price and Quantity.** The price for the _____ copies ordered shall be $_____. The Publisher shall not accept less than _____ copies or more than _____ copies. Copies under or over the quantity ordered shall be subtracted or added to the price at the rate of $_____ per copy.

4. **Payment.** The price shall be payable within _____ days of delivery.

5. **Ownership and Return of Supplied Materials.** All electronic files, camera-ready copy, artwork, film, separations, and any other materials supplied by the Publisher to the Printer shall remain the exclusive property of the Publisher and be returned by the Printer at its expense as soon as possible upon the earlier of either the printing of the Work or the Publisher's request. The Printer shall be liable for any loss or damage to such materials from the time of receipt

until the time of return receipt by the Publisher. The Printer ❑ shall ❑ shall not insure such materials for the benefit of the Publisher in the amount of $_____.

6. Ownership and Return of Commissioned Materials. All materials created by the Printer for the Publisher, including but not limited to flats, plates, or belts, shall become the exclusive property of the Publisher and shall be stored without expense by the Printer and be returned at the Publisher's request. The expense of such return of materials shall be paid by the ❑ Printer ❑ Publisher. The Printer shall be liable for any loss or damage to such materials from the time of creation until the time of return receipt by the Publisher. The Printer ❑ shall ❑ shall not insure such materials for the benefit of the Publisher in the amount of $_____.

7. Proofs. If proofs are requested in the specifications, the Work shall not be printed until such proofs have been approved in writing by the Publisher. The finished copies of the Work shall match the quality of the proofs.

8. Arbitration. All disputes arising under this Agreement shall be submitted to binding arbitration before _____ _____ at the following location _____ and the arbitration award may be entered for judgment in any court having jurisdiction thereof. Notwithstanding the foregoing, either party may refuse to arbitrate when the dispute is for less than $_____.

9. Term and Termination. This Agreement shall have a term ending _____ months after delivery pursuant to Paragraph 2. The Publisher may terminate this Agreement at any time prior to the Printer's commencement of work and may terminate thereafter if the Printer fails to adhere to the specifications or production schedule for the Work. This Agreement shall also terminate in the event of the Printer's bankruptcy or insolvency. The rights and obligations of the parties pursuant to Paragraphs 5, 6, and 8 shall survive termination of the Agreement.

10. Miscellany. This Agreement contains the entire understanding between the parties and may not be modified, amended, or changed except by an instrument in writing signed by both parties. A waiver of any breach of any of the provisions of this Agreement shall not be construed as a continuing waiver of other breaches of the same or other provisions hereof. This Agreement shall be binding upon the parties hereto and their respective heirs, successors, assigns, and personal representatives. This Agreement shall be interpreted under the laws of the State of_____ _____.

IN WITNESS WHEREOF, the parties have signed this Agreement as of the date first set forth above.

Printer_____   Publisher_____
            Company Name   Company Name

By_____   By_____
        Authorized Signatory, Title   Authorized Signatory, Title

Schedule A   ❏ **Request for Printing Quotation**   ❏ **Printing Specifications**

Printer _____   Designer_____

Address _____   Address_____

_____   _____

Contact Person _____   Contact Person _____

Phone _____   Phone_____

Job Name _____   Job Number _____

Description _____   Date for Quotation _____

_____   Date Job to Printer _____

_____   Date Job Needed _____

Quantity: 1) _____   2) _____   3) _____   ❏ Additional _____

Size: Flat Trim_____ x _____   Folded/Bound to _____ x _____

Number of Pages _____   ❏ Self Cover   ❏ Plus Cover   ❏ Cover Bleed

Design includes: ❏ Page Bleeds #_____   ❏ Screen Tints #_____   ❏ Reverses #_____

Halftones Print: ❏ Halftone (black) # _____   ❏ Duotone (black plus PMS _____) #_____

Size of Halftones _____

Color Requirements:

Cover: ❏ 4 Color Process   ❏ Spot Colors PMS #s_____ plus Black

Inside: ❏ Full Color   ❏ Spot Color PMS #s _____   ❏ Color Signatures only #_____

Color Separations: ❏ transparencies #_____   ❏ reflective art #_____   ❏ film provided by client

Original art will be supplied as separated electronic files, or ____ b&w and ____ color images must be scanned.

Resolution of finished separations _____

Coatings:	Overall Varnish	Spot Varnish	UV Coating	Film Lam	Gloss	Matte
Cover	❏	❏	❏	❏	❏	❏
Inside	❏	❏	❏	❏	❏	❏

Special instructions _____

_____

_____

Electronic Files:

File name(s) for print output _____

Software used and version _____

Included: ❑ fonts ❑ images files ❑ hard copy print out ❑ color proof

Mechanicals: (if supplied)

Color breaks shown: ❑ on acetate overlays ❑ on tissues ❑ # of pieces of separate line art _____

Paper Stock: Name   Weight   Grade   Finish   Color

Cover _____ _____ _____ _____ _____

Inside _____ _____ _____ _____ _____

Insert / Other _____ _____ _____ _____ _____

❑ Send samples of paper   ❑ Make book dummy

Other Printing Specifications:

❑ Special Inks _____

❑ Die Cutting ❑ Embossing ❑ Engraving ❑ Foil Stamping ❑ Thermography ❑ Serial Numbering

❑ Other _____

_____

Proofs: ❑ Digital ❑ Blues ❑ Color Keys ❑ Chromalins ❑ Pictro Proof ❑ Press Proofs

Details _____

Bindery: ❑ Hard Bound ❑ Perfect Bound ❑ Spiral Bound ❑ Ring Binder ❑ Saddle Stitch

❑ Score ❑ Perforate ❑ Fold ❑ Drill ❑ Punch ❑ Round Corners ❑ Tip In

Details _____

Packing: ❑ Rubber/String/Paper Band in #_____ ❑ Shrink Wrap in #_____ ❑ Bulk in Cartons

❑ Maximum weight per carton _____ lbs ❑ Skids ❑ Pallets ❑ Other _____

Shipping:

Deliver To _____

_____

_____

❑ Truck ❑ Rail ❑ Sea ❑ Air ❑ Drop Ship ❑ UPS/Other _____

❑ Customer pick up ❑ Separate shipping costs ❑ Send cheapest way ❑ Other _____

Shipment terms _____ ❑ Insure for _____ percent of printing cost

Miscellaneous instructions: _____

_____

_____

_____

Contract with Sales Representative

The author who publishes his or her own book must find an effective method to bring the book to its intended audience. Many self-publishers rely on direct mail, direct response advertising (in which the advertisement includes a way to order the book), and sending catalogs or even making personal sales visits to bookstores. However, the vast number of bookstores makes it difficult to reach them effectively without help.

One way to reach the bookstores would be to contract with a distributor, a method elaborated in Form 15. The distributor, which might also be a publisher, may employ a sales staff. It is more likely, however, that the distributor will have many independent sales representatives. The self-publisher may wish to emulate this approach.

Form 14, Contract with Sales Representative, covers the key issues to be resolved when a self-publisher retains a sales representative. The scope of representation is specified, both with respect to the type of accounts (usually only bookstores and wholesalers) and the territory. Since this is an exclusive sales contract, the sales representative has a right to payment for sales made by others (for example, if a bookstore in the territory simply sends an order directly to the publisher). The schedule of house accounts can be used to exclude certain accounts from the sales representative's right to receive a commission. House accounts might be accounts which have a special history, such as accounts handled by the in-house sales manager or accounts that order directly from the publisher.

Sales representatives work to earn commissions: 10 percent of net receipts (sales less returns) for sales to retail bookstores and 5 percent of net receipts for sales to wholesalers. Net receipts will require a definition enumerating any items subtracted from the self-publisher's gross receipts to reach net receipts. For a book with good sales potential, the self-publisher should be able to create a network of sales representatives. Each sales representative covers a particular territory, which is why many such sales representatives are necessary to ensure thorough coverage.

The self-publisher must understand what sales representatives do, and what they do not do. A sales representative goes to the accounts in his or her territory, shows catalogs and sales materials such as jackets to the account buyers, and takes orders for the books. The sales representative does not publish a catalog, advertise the books, warehouse and ship the books, bill accounts, or handle collections of delinquent accounts. All of these functions must be handled by the self-publisher. This is in sharp contrast to dealing with a distributor, but the distributor is likely to charge 25 to 30 percent of net receipts instead of 5 to 10 percent.

The term of the agreement is closely tied with the right of termination. If a sales representative does not sell successfully, the self-publisher has to have the right to replace that sales representative immediately. The self-publisher will have to give statements of account and make payments on a regular basis, probably each month. It should be made clear that the representative is an independent contractor, not an employee or agent of the self-publisher. Assignment of rights and obligations under the contract should not be allowed, except that the sales representative can be given the right to employ other sales representatives if that appears necessary.

The self-publisher interested in finding sales representatives might look at publishers' lists which complement the books of the self-publisher. Publishers will list their sales representatives in their catalogs (since the catalogs are tools to encourage accounts to place orders). The self-publisher will then be able to contact sales representatives who are familiar with similar lines of books. Another alternative is to look up the listings of sales representatives in *Literary Market Place*, which is updated annually.

Filling in the Form

In the Preamble fill in the date and the names and addresses of the parties. In Paragraph 1 fill in the geographical territory in which the sales representative will have exclusive rights. In Paragraph 2 fill in the term. In Paragraph 4 specify any items to be subtracted in reaching net receipts. In Paragraph 6 state when the monthly statement of account must be rendered. In Paragraph 11 specify an arbitrator and a place for arbitration. In Paragraph 12 indicate if notices should be sent to addresses other than those given in the Preamble. In Paragraph 13 specify which state's laws will govern the contract. Fill in Schedule A with a listing of House Accounts. Have both parties sign the contract.

Negotiation Checklist

❏ Specify the territory to be given to the sales representative. (Paragraph 1)

❏ Limit the types of accounts covered, usually to retail and wholesale booksellers, and exclude house accounts. (Paragraph 1)

❏ Exclude from the scope of the representation all types of sales which the representative is unlikely to make, such as sales to book clubs, corporations (for premiums), libraries, and individuals. (Paragraph 1)

❏ Decide whether the contract is an exclusive sales agreement, in which case the sale representative will receive commissions on sales within the scope of the contract even if he or she does not make the sale. (Paragraph 1)

❏ Determine which accounts shall be house accounts. (Paragraph 1 and Schedule A)

❏ Specify a term for the contract, preferably a short term unless the contract can be terminated at will. (Paragraph 2)

❏ Require the sales representative to use best efforts to sell books. (Paragraph 3)

❏ State that the self-publisher shall use best efforts to fulfill orders, but do not make the publisher liable for commissions on orders which cannot be fulfilled. If a book is never published or has gone out of print, of course the self-publisher would be unable to fulfill the order and would not want to pay any commission. (Paragraph 3)

❏ Specify the commissions to be received by the sales representative, usually 5 percent for sales to wholesalers and 10 percent for sales to bookstores. (Paragraph 4)

❏ Define "net receipts," which is the amount against which commissions will be paid. Net receipts will be amounts received by the publisher from wholesalers and bookstores, perhaps reduced by certain expenses. For example, the bookstore would usually pay shipping charges. If the self-publisher pays for freight (perhaps as part of an arrangement in which the retail price is increased to cover freight costs), the retail price would be reduced by the amount of the allowance for freight charges prior to the computation of the commission. (Paragraph 4)

❏ State that commissions shall be reduced for bad debts and returns at the time of declaring the bad debt or receiving the returns. (Paragraph 4)

❏ Specify a time for the payment of commissions. (Paragraph 5)

❏ Create a reserve against bad debts and returns, which would be a certain percentage of commissions to be held back by the publisher until the amount of bad debts and returns can be determined.

❑ State that the publisher shall give monthly statements of account and specify what information the accountings will provide. (Paragraph 6)

❑ Indicate that the parties are independent of each other. (Paragraph 7)

❑ Require the sales representative to indemnify the publisher for injuries to the sales representative or others while traveling. (Paragraph 7)

❑ Do not allow assignment of the agreement by either party. If there will be a change of sales representatives, the publisher will want to choose the new person. (Paragraph 8)

❑ Consider whether to allow the sales representative to employ others to make sales visits. (Paragraph 8)

❑ Allow each party to inspect the other party's books on reasonable notice. (Paragraph 9)

❑ Specify that by giving a short advance notice, such as thirty or sixty days, the contract can be terminated. (Paragraph 10)

❑ State that the contract can be terminated immediately for cause. (Paragraph 10)

❑ If the contract has a longer term and cannot be terminated quickly, provide that certain minimum sales levels must be achieved or the contract will terminate.

❑ State that the contract shall automatically terminate in the event of the bankruptcy or insolvency of either party. (Paragraph 10)

❑ Compare the standard provisions in the introductory pages with Paragraphs 11–13.

Contract with Sales Representative

AGREEMENT, entered into as of the _____ day of _____, 20_____, between _____
(hereinafter referred to as the "Publisher"), located at _____, and
_____ (hereinafter referred to as the "Sales Representative"),
located at _____.

WHEREAS, Publisher has published or will publish certain books for which it seeks sales representation; and

WHEREAS, Sales Representative is in the business of representing publishers for the sale of books to both retail and wholesale accounts;

NOW, THEREFORE, in consideration of the foregoing premises and the mutual covenants hereinafter set forth and other valuable consideration, the parties hereto agree as follows:

1. **Scope of Representation.** The Publisher appoints the Sales Representative to act as Publisher's exclusive sales representative in selling Publisher's books to retail and wholesale booksellers in the following sales territory: _____ _____. House accounts, which are listed in Schedule A, are excluded from this Agreement and no commissions shall be payable on such accounts. Other accounts excluded from this Agreement include but are not limited to book clubs, direct mail sales or other sales to individual buyers, national book chains, premium sales, sales to libraries, and sales for institutional use.

2. **Term.** This Agreement shall have a term of _____ months, which shall be automatically renewed until the date of termination.

3. **Duties of the Parties.** The Sales Representative agrees to use his or her best efforts to promote and sell the Publisher's books in the sales territory. The Publisher shall use best efforts to have inventory sufficient to meet market demand in the territory handled by the Sales Representative, and shall make deliveries of all books sold by the Sales Representative, but shall have no liability for commissions with respect to orders which are not fulfilled for causes including but not limited to titles which were not published, titles which are out of stock, or titles which are out of print.

4. **Commissions.** For the services of the Sales Representative, the Publisher agrees to pay Sales Representative a commission of 10 percent of the net receipts from all sales made by the Sales Representative to retail booksellers and 5 percent of the net receipts from all sales made by the Sales Representative to wholesale booksellers. Net receipts shall be all payments due the Publisher for the books sold, less any deductions specified here: _____. Commissions paid on sales which result in returns or bad debts shall be deducted from commissions due for the month in which the returns or bad debts are recorded.

5. **Payment.** Commissions shall be paid to the Sales Representative on a monthly basis at the time of rendering the Statement of Account for the month.

6. **Statements of Account.** Statements of account shall be given by the Publisher to the Sales Representative on a monthly basis _____ days after the last day of the month accounted for. Each statement shall show for the month the net receipts from sales made by the Sales Representative to eligible accounts, the appropriate commission rates, the commissions due, and any deductions from commissions.

7. **Relationship of the Parties.** The parties hereto are independent entities and nothing contained in this Agreement shall be construed to constitute the Sales Representative an agent, employee, partner, joint venturer, or any similar relationship with or of the Publisher. Further, the Sales Representative hereby indemnifies the Publisher against any claim by the Sales Representative or others accompanying him or her with respect to injuries or damages sustained or caused while traveling, including but not limited to those caused while traveling by automobile or any other form of transportation.

8. **Assignment.** This Agreement shall not be assignable by either party hereto, provided, however, that the Sales Representative shall have the right to employ or commission at its own cost and expense other sales representatives to sell the Publisher's works in the territory of the Sales Representative.

9. Inspection of Books. Each party shall maintain accurate books and documentation with respect to all transactions entered into pursuant to this Agreement. Within two weeks of receipt of a written request by either party, the other party shall permit the requesting party or its authorized representative to examine these books and documentation during normal business hours.

10. Termination. Either party may terminate this Agreement by giving the other party sixty (60) days written notice. In the event either party is in default of any of its obligations hereunder, the other party may terminate this Agreement at any time by giving written notice of termination. This Agreement shall automatically terminate in the event of the insolvency or bankruptcy of either party. The rights and obligations of the parties pursuant to Paragraphs 4, 5, and 7 shall survive termination hereunder.

11. Arbitration. All disputes arising under this Agreement shall be submitted to binding arbitration before_____ _____ in the following location _____ and the arbitration award may be entered for judgment in any court having jurisdiction thereof.

12. Notices and Changes of Address. All notices shall be sent by registered or certified mail, return receipt requested, postage prepaid, to the Publisher and Sales Representative at the addresses first given above unless indicated to the contrary here: _____ _____. Each party shall give written notification of any change of address prior to the date of said change.

13. Miscellany. This Agreement contains the entire understanding between the parties hereto and may not be modified, amended, or changed except by an instrument in writing signed by both parties. A waiver of any breach of any of the provisions of this Agreement shall not be construed as a continuing waiver of other breaches of the same or other provisions hereof. This Agreement shall be binding upon the parties and their respective heirs, successors, assigns, and personal representatives. This Agreement shall be governed by the laws of the State of _____.

IN WITNESS WHEREOF, the parties hereto have signed this Agreement as of the date first set forth above.

Sales Representative_____
Company Name

Publisher_____
Company Name

By_____
Authorized Signatory, Title

By_____
Authorized Signatory, Title

Schedule A: House Accounts

Account Name | Address

1._____
2._____
3._____
4._____
5._____
6._____
7._____
8._____
9._____

Contract with Book Distributor

The author who has determined to self-publish his or her book needs distribution. Any publisher with a small number of titles is likely to want a larger company to handle its distribution. This larger company may be a distributor or another publisher. One of the best ways to find a distributor is to find a company that has successfully sold books similar to the ones to be published by the author. If this company is a publisher, of course, tension may develop if the books are so similar as to be competitive.

If the book has already been printed, the potential distributor may have an easier time evaluating its market potential. On the other hand, if the book is in manuscript form, the distributor may be able to make helpful suggestions that will increase its marketability (not the least of which may be to include the distributor's name and address on the book so additional orders can be generated). In contacting a distributor or publisher, the sales manager is a good person to speak with. The sales manager can give a great deal of insight into the market that company can reach effectively and direct the self-publisher to the final decision maker with respect to taking on a book or line of books for distribution.

A fundamental issue is whether to sell the books outright or consign the books to the distributor. Each arrangment has its advantages. If the books are sold, the self-publisher does not have to worry about how the public will receive the books. The distributor has taken this risk. The print run can be matched to the order from the distributor, so the printing costs are kept to a minimum. Arrangements for payment vary, but a partial payment might be made when the contract is signed with the balance due thirty to sixty days after delivery. The distributor would be likely to pay 30 to 35 percent of the retail price, although these percentages can be lower or higher and may become better for the self-publisher as the dollar volume of sales increases.

Assuming a price set at 32 1/2 percent of retail price, a $20 book would yield $6.50 for the self-publisher.

If the books are consigned, the self-publisher retains title until the distributor sells the books on behalf of the self-publisher. Despite the retention of title, consignment has a number of risks. There is no guarantee the books will ever be sold, in which case the self-publisher will receive no payment. The distributor, as a merchant, has the right to pass good title to the books even if it sells them in violation of the agreement with the self-publisher. If creditors of the distributor believe the books belong to the distributor, they may be able to seize these books in the event the distributor goes bankrupt. Certainly the capability to sell, integrity, and financial condition of any potential distributor must be reviewed carefully by the self-publisher.

For consigned books, the distributor will usually pay 70 to 80 percent of its net receipts to the self-publisher. Net receipts are the wholesale prices received by the distributor (reduced by certain items which must be carefully defined, such as sales taxes collected). Net receipts vary from one distributor to another, but might average 50 percent of the retail price. Taking the same $20 book and assuming the distributor pays 75 percent of net receipts to the self-publisher, the self-publisher will now receive $20, multiplied by the 50 percent received by the distributor, and multiplied again by the 75 percent paid to the self-publisher. This results in the payment of $7.50 per book to the self-publisher, a lot better than the $6.50 received when the books were sold outright to the distributor.

Is the extra payment per book worth the risks of consignment? That is a question each self-publisher must answer based on his or her unique circumstances. If the self-publisher has a small list, little capital, low overhead, and low printing costs, selling outright might be the way to go.

Later, when the number of titles and volume of sales has grown and the self-publisher has come to know the distributor, it might make sense to change to a consignment arrangement. Of course, many distributors will feel that they do not want to take the risk of forecasting sales and will insist on a consignment arrangement.

Form 15 is drafted for a continuing relationship between the self-publisher and distributor. For each title, a memorandum is prepared that begins by stating: "The following is to confirm the distribution for the book listed below pursuant to the Contract dated _____, 20___, between _____ and _____." This would continue by giving the title, author, a brief description of the book, page size, number of pages, binding, any additional specifications (such as using two colors or visuals in the text), quantity, retail price, delivery date, and publication date. Both parties would sign and date the memorandum. If the contract is for only one book, then only one such memorandum need be prepared. Or Paragraph 1 can be amended to state that the contract is for one book and the information that would have been given in the memorandum can be given in Paragraph 1.

Whether the books are sold or consigned, the distributor may want to have a voice in such matters as price, content, design, and paper quality. The distributor taking consigned books must sell the books to earn a profit, while the distributor that has purchased books will lose money if it cannot resell the books. Especially if the distributor has purchased the books, it may insist on a right of approval (over the manuscript, cover design and copy, cover and interior stock, text design, and so on) to ensure that quality standards will be maintained.

The rights granted to the distributor to sell books must be carefully limited. As in any grant of rights, only those rights that can be effectively exploited by the other party should be granted to that party. If the distributor sells to bookstores in the United States, that should be the limited grant of rights given to the distributor. The self-publisher is free to seek another distributor for the rest of the world, whether that proves to be one distributor (working with sub-distributors in each country) or many distributors (perhaps one in each country). The distributor may need nonexclusive direct mail rights as well, although the self-publisher may resist giving this if the direct mail campaigns will compete with one another.

The distributor may also want the right to sell to book clubs or for premium use (such as when a corporation buys a large quantity of books to use in promoting the corporation or its products). If the books are consigned, sales to either book clubs or for premium use will probably not work well for the self-publisher. This is because the discounts for such sales may be 65 to 80 percent off the retail price. If the distributor keeps 25 to 30 percent of these proceeds, the self-publisher may actually suffer a loss. These sales should either have a lower percentage for the distributor (such as 10 percent) or be allowed only with the written consent of the self-publisher. On the other hand, even if the books have been sold, the self-publisher may not want the distributor to sell to book clubs and for premium use if these are sales (or licences) the self-publisher could make himself.

The term of the contract has to be long enough to let the distributor sell the books, but not so long that the self-publisher cannot get back the rights granted if the distributor is unable to sell effectively. The time for payment, periodic statements of account, and the right to inspect the records of the distributor will all be covered in the contract. If the books are consigned, the self-publisher will want the right to perfect a security interest in the books. This means that if certain filings are made with the appropriate government agency, the self-publisher will have priority over unsecured creditors of the distributor with respect to the consigned inventory in the event of the distributor's bankruptcy. The risk of loss or damage to the consigned books, and insurance coverage, must also be dealt with.

One of the most important issues is the responsibility for and nature of the promotion of the books. What will each party do and who will bear the expenses? Will the distributor do more than place the book in its catalog? For example, will the distributor have booths at the major trade shows and perhaps advertise the books in appropriate media? Who will supply press releases and review copies and pay the cost of distributing them? Even the costs of preparing art for the catalog or facsimile covers for the sales conference can be expensive. Who will pay for this? It is likely that both the self-publisher and the distributor should actively promote the books, in which case the contract offers the opportunity to divide the responsibilities in a way that will make the promotional campaign most effective.

Filling in the Form

In the Preamble fill in the names and addresses of the parties. Keep in mind that Paragraph 1 requires the signing of a separate memorandum for each title to be distributed. In Paragraph 2 specify the rights granted to the distributor with respect to types of markets and territories. Check the appropriate box to select either Paragraph 4 (if the books are being sold) or Paragraph 5 (if the books are being consigned). For Paragraph 4, fill in the amount of the discount from retail price to reach the price to be paid for the books. For Paragraph 5, fill in what percentage of the net receipts will be paid to the self-publisher. In Paragraph 7 specify for books sold to the distributor whether any payment will be made at the time of signing the memorandum for each title and how many days after delivery payment of the balance will be made. In Paragraph 8 specify when the statement of account must be given for each monthly accounting period. In Paragraph 11 fill in the number of months after termination during which the distributor may sell off purchased inventory. In Paragraph 12 specify for consigned books the amount of insurance to be maintained. In Paragraph 13 state the promotion to be done by the distributor and the information about the distributor to be placed in the books. In Paragraph 14 state when remainder sales may be commenced for books purchased by the distrib-

utor. In Paragraph 18 specify the arbitrator and the place of arbitration. In Paragraph 19 indicate the addresses for notice if these addresses are not those shown in the Preamble. In Paragraph 20 specify which state's laws will govern the contract. Both parties should then sign the contract.

Negotiation Checklist

❏ Specify whether the contract will cover one title or many titles, in which case the information to appear in the separate memorandum for each title should be listed. (Paragraph 1)

❏ State any requirements which may cause extra expense, such as a requirement for shrink-wrapping or boxing the books. If there are special requirements as to the quality of the cover or paper stock, the number of images to be stripped into the books, or the fact that a certain number of images must be printed in color, these types of specifications should be set forth in the memorandum for each book.

❏ Limit the grant of rights to what the self-publisher wants the distributor to sell and what the distributor can effectively sell, such as "exclusive trade distribution and nonexclusive direct mail rights in the United States." For each type of distribution, specify the territory and whether the right is exclusive or nonexclusive. (Paragraph 2)

❏ If the distributor cannot sell effectively in Canada or other foreign countries, these territories should be reserved to the self-publisher. (Paragraph 2)

❏ If the distributor is to sell in foreign countries, have the distributor bear the expense of any freight forwarding, customs duties, or taxes.

❏ Reserve to the self-publisher all rights not granted to the distributor. (Paragraph 2)

❑ Agree that the parties will consult to avoid creating titles which are in direct competition.

❑ Specify a term for the contract. Unless termination is permitted on sixty or ninety days' written notice, the term should be relatively brief, such as one year after publication. (Paragraph 3)

❑ State whether the books are being sold or consigned. (Paragraphs 4 and 5)

❑ If the books are being sold, seek the highest price per book. This may be approximately 35 percent of retail price and might escalate upward as the sales volume increases. (Paragraph 4)

❑ Make all books purchased nonreturnable. (Paragraph 4)

❑ If books are being consigned, be very specific as to what net receipts include and what is excluded from the definition. Net receipts should include the gross receipts (all money received by the distributor) from the sale of the books. To arrive at net receipts, gross receipts might be reduced by discounts which the distributor gives its customers for early payment, money received to reimburse the distributor for expenses to be incurred (such as shipping and handling charges for direct mail orders), and similar items, each of which should be carefully evaluated. (Paragraph 5)

❑ For a consignment, seek the highest pass-through of net receipts to the self-publisher. This might be 75 percent of net receipts and escalate upward with increasing sales volume. (Paragraph 5)

❑ For consigned books do not allow the distributor to make sales at more than a certain discount from retail price (such as a 55 or 60 percent discount) without obtaining the self-publisher's consent. (Paragraph 5) In such cases, which may include sales to book clubs or premium sales, consider whether the dis-

tributor should receive a lower proportion of the net receipts, such as 5 or 10 percent.

❑ If the distributor is also a publisher, do not allow the distributor to sell the self-publisher's books at a higher discount than the distributor sells its own books.

❑ Seek to have the distributor pay the freight and insurance charges to deliver the books from the printer. (Paragraph 6) Keep in mind that "C.I.F. Dallas, Texas" stands for cost, insurance, and freight, and means that the cost of the merchandise, packing, shipping to the destination (in this case, Dallas, Texas), and insuring during shipment are all included in the quoted price. On the other hand, "F.O.B. Taos, New Mexico" stands for free on board and means that the goods will be loaded for shipment without charge (in this case, loaded at Taos). If the printer sells books F.O.B. at the location of the printing plant, this means that the cost of shipping and insurance will have to be paid by either the self-publisher or the distributor.

❑ If books are sold outright, payment should be made as quickly as possible. Thirty days after delivery would be reasonable, but it might be possible to receive a partial payment at the time of signing the contract. (Paragraph 7)

❑ If books are consigned, payment will be made as books are sold. If the distributor considers books sold when orders are received, the distributor will probably want to pay based on the average amount of time it takes to collect payment after receipt of an order. This may be sixty to ninety days, but the self-publisher should certainly seek payment sooner, such as twenty days after the close of the month for which the accounting is being given. (Paragraphs 7 and 8)

❑ For consigned books, negotiate for an advance payment at the time of signing the memorandum for each title. Such advances are recouped against future payments for each title and help cash flow, especially if payment is to be made sixty to ninety days after the receipt of orders.

❏ State that consigned books shall be considered sold when the order is received by the distributor, not when the payment is received by the distributor. (Paragraph 7)

❏ Specify that consigned books which are returned shall be subtracted from sales when returned. (Paragraph 7)

❏ Do not allow the distributor to impose any charge for consigned books which are returned other than reducing net receipts by an appropriate amount for the loss of a previously recorded sale.

❏ State that for consigned books the distributor shall bear the risk of loss for uncollectible accounts. (Paragraph 7)

❏ Make time of the essence with respect to payment. (Paragraph 7)

❏ Bill interest on late payments, but do not violate state usury laws. (Paragraph 7)

❏ State that sales proceeds due to the self-publisher shall be kept in a trust account segregated from the funds of the distributor. This provides some protection in the event of the distributor's bankruptcy.

❏ Require periodic statements of account, preferably on a monthly basis, providing information as to the sales and returns for each title and, in the case of consigned books, showing net receipts and the amount due the self-publisher. (Paragraph 8)

❏ Give the self-publisher the right to inspect the books and records of the distributor. (Paragraph 9)

❏ If an inspection of the books and records reveals an underpayment to the self-publisher of more than 5 percent, require the distributor to pay the cost of the inspection. (Paragraph 9)

❏ State that title in the books does not pass to the distributor until payment in full has been received. (Paragraph 10)

❏ Give the self-publisher a right to perfect a security interest in the books, so that the inventory (especially if consigned) can be protected from creditors of the distributor. (Paragraph 10)

❏ Allow termination of the contract by either party on thirty or sixty days' written notice. It is especially detrimental to the self-publisher to be locked into a contract when the distributor is not successful in selling the books. To increase flexibility, this termination can be for single titles and does not have to terminate the distribution contract itself. (Paragraph 11)

❏ If the distributor resists allowing termination on thirty or sixty days' written notice, specify that termination will be allowed if specified minimum sales figures are not met. This could be either a certain number of copies sold or a certain dollar amount generated for the self-publisher.

❏ Allow the self-publisher to terminate on written notice if the distributor is in default under the contract. (Paragraph 11)

❏ State that the contract shall automatically terminate if the distributor is bankrupt or insolvent. (Paragraph 11)

❏ For books purchased by the distributor, give a six or nine month sell-off period after termination. (Paragraph 11) During the sell-off period, the distributor is allowed to sell inventory that remains on hand. The distributor may demand that the sell-off right include the right to remainder the inventory. Remainder sales are made in bulk at discounts that usually range from 75 to 95 percent off retail price. Remainder books are then sold at a high discount, often 50 or more percent off retail price, to the public. If the distributor is at fault in failing to sell a book, remaindering it may injure the future potential of the book with a different distributor.

❏ After termination, require that any consigned books be returned to the self-publisher at the expense of the distributor. (Paragraph 11)

❏ If the distributor wants to keep a reserve fund after termination to cover the expense of returns of the books, limit the time during which such a fund may be kept and the maximum amount of money that can be placed in the fund.

❏ For consigned books, state that the distributor shall bear the risk of loss or damage from any cause from the time of delivery to the distributor until the time the books are returned to the self-publisher. This would include the risk that books returned to the distributor by bookstores may be damaged. (Paragraph 12)

❏ If the distributor will not agree to bear the risk of loss or damage to the books, specify how inventory shrinkage will be documented. For example, such shrinkage could be documented by a written report and photographs. Without documentation, the distributor can claim loss or damage and the self-publisher will have difficulty in verifying the claim and making his or her own insurance claim (if the distributor is not providing insurance and the self-publisher is).

❏ Require the distributor to insure consigned books for the benefit of the self-publisher and specify the amount of the insurance. (Paragraph 12) This should be enough to cover the cost of reprinting the inventory in the event of loss or damage. If the distributor argues that the cost of insurance, or even the cost of the warehousing of the books, should be paid by the self-publisher, it can be pointed out that the books are in the distributor's warehouse so the distributor can benefit from selling them and that insurance and warehousing for such books should simply be a normal overhead expense of the distributor's operation.

❏ If there is an allowance for inventory shrinkage, limit the allowance to 2 percent of the consigned inventory and require that any additional shrinkage be accounted for as if the books had been sold.

❏ Require that consigned books be kept separate from the distributor's own books in an area marked to show that the books belong to the self-publisher. This is to protect the books from creditors of the distributor. (Paragraph 12)

❏ State that the distributor shall undertake at its own expense an annual physical inventory of any consigned books in accordance with accepted accounting procedures.

❏ Require the distributor to use best efforts to sell the books, including placing each title in its catalog. (Paragraph 13)

❏ Specify other kinds of promotional activities that the distributor should pay for, such as the preparation and sending of press releases, displaying the books at trade shows, and advertising. If the distributor will advertise, the nature of the advertising and a minimum budget might be specified. The distributor may try to have the self-publisher handle and pay for the sending of press releases and advertising, and it may be that these expenses will be shared in some way between the parties. (Paragraph 13)

❑ Require the distributor to warrant that none of its promotional materials shall either infringe any copyright or violate any other rights (such as rights of privacy).

❑ Decide who should pay for other promotional expenses, such as whether the self-publisher should provide extra copies of each book for review or be responsible for providing extra covers or jackets (or color photocopies of covers) for the sales reps at sales conference. (Paragraph 13)

❑ Specify the information about the distributor to be included in each book, including the placement of this information. By letting the public know how to order the book, orders should be increased. However, the self-publisher may want certain types of orders (such as direct mail) to come to him or her rather than going to the distributor. (Paragraph 13)

❑ The distributor should have a right to remainder books it has purchased. However, this right should not be exercisable until a reasonable effort has been made to sell the book through normal trade channels such as bookstores. So the distributor should have to wait for some period of time, such as eighteen or twenty-four months after publication, before it can remainder books. Also, it should have to offer the books back to the self-publisher at the lesser of either the remainder price or the original price. Often the self-publisher will have a way to dispose of such books and want the inventory. (Paragraph 14)

❑ Agree that the contract and its terms are confidential and will not be disclosed to any other party.

❑ If the distributor insists that the self-publisher agree to a warranty and indemnity clause in which the self-publisher states that he or she has the authority to enter the contract and that the books are not copyright infringements, obscene, or otherwise unlawful, seek to limit this clause to a certain maximum dollar amount (or, perhaps, to no more than 50 percent of the money received under the contract for the particular title at issue) and reserve the right to conduct the defense of any lawsuit.

❑ Do not allow the distributor an option with respect to future titles, since each title requires the best distributor for its particular markets. Unless it is clear that the distributor will successfully handle all of the self-publisher's titles, it is best to proceed one title at a time.

❑ Compare the standard provisions in the introductory pages with Paragraphs 15-20.

Other provisions that can be added to Form 15:

❑ Review by distributor. Especially if the distributor is purchasing the books, it may demand a right to review each book as the manuscript moves from the proposal to the printing press. The self-publisher must consider whether such review by the distributor is unwanted interference or welcome assistance. A crucial issue will be whether the self-publisher must take the suggestions of the distributor. Certainly the self-publisher should seek to keep the power to make final decisions. On the other hand, it can be helpful to have the distributor approve a work-in-progress at a number of stages, because ultimate satisfaction with the finished books is far more likely. If a distributor is forced to purchase books it feels inferior (and these books are not successful sellers), the long-term relationship with the distributor is jeopardized.

Review by Distributor. Publisher shall provide the Distributor with sketches for the front cover design, suggested copy for the front and back of the cover, and a copy of the complete manuscript (prior to copyediting) and shall make such changes as are reasonably requested. Distributor agrees to review these materials and return same to Publisher with comments for changes within _____ weeks of receipt. If any title is to be changed, the new title shall be agreed to by both parties.

❏ Condition of books. If the distributor is purchasing the books, it may demand assurance as to the condition in which the books will be delivered. The self-publisher must be careful that any quality standards or requirements for the condition of the books on delivery are not made unreasonably difficult. In relation to the quality of the books, the distributor may also seek to cover production specifications in the memorandum for each book under Paragraph 1 of the contract.

Condition of Books. The books shall be delivered in mint condition and shall be of the same quality as books previously supplied by the Publisher. The Distributor shall have no obligation to pay for books which are damaged or faulty in printing or binding.

❏ Referral of orders. The distributor will want the self-publisher to refer any orders which fall into the scope of the contract's exclusivity to the distributor. For example, a bookstore might try to order from the self-publisher instead of the distributor. The self-publisher should make certain that none of these orders are of the type that the self-publisher has the right to fulfill (such as a direct mail order when both parties have nonexclusive direct-mail rights).

Referral of Orders. The Publisher shall refer to the Distributor all orders or inquiries that concern the sale of the books in the markets and territory in which the Distributor has exclusive rights.

Contract with Book Distributor

AGREEMENT, entered into as of _____, 20____, between _____ (hereinafter referred to as the "Publisher"), located at _____, and _____ (hereinafter referred to as the "Distributor"), located at _____.

WHEREAS, Publisher has developed and printed a book or books and seeks distribution; and

WHEREAS, Distributor is in the business of book distribution and wishes to distribute books of the Publisher;

NOW, THEREFORE, in consideration of the foregoing premises and the mutual covenants hereinafter set forth and other valuable considerations, the parties hereto agree as follows:

1. **Duties of the Parties and Titles Covered.** This Agreement shall provide the terms under which Distributor and Publisher shall henceforth do business. The Publisher shall perform at its sole expense and be solely responsible for accepting and rejecting works for publication, negotiating author's contracts, copyright registration and renewal, manufacture of books, payments of author's advances and royalties, and the sale or licensing of subsidiary rights. The Distributor shall perform at its sole expense and be solely responsible for soliciting orders pursuant to the grant of rights in Paragraph 2, order processing and billing, maintaining and collecting accounts receivable, shipping and warehousing of books and processing of returns, and listing Publisher's titles in its catalog. The expense of and responsibility for promotion shall be determined pursuant to Paragraph 13 hereof. For each title to be distributed a Distribution Memorandum in the form attached hereto as Schedule A shall be signed by the parties specifying the title, the author, the subject matter, the specifications (including whether the book is hard or softcover, the trim size of the book, and the number of pages), the suggested retail price (which is the price appearing on the book), the quantity to be delivered, the time for delivery of books, and the publication date.

2. **Grant of Rights.** For each title, Publisher grants to Distributor the rights to distribute and sell copies of the books in the following markets: _____ and in the following territories: _____. All rights not granted to Distributor are reserved by Publisher.

3. **Term.** For each title, this Agreement shall have a term ending one year after the publication date, after which it is automatically renewed for periods of one year.

4. **Sale.** ❏ Publisher agrees to sell books to Distributor at a discount of _____ percent off the suggested retail price. All books are purchased on a nonreturnable basis.

5. **Consignment.** ❏ Publisher agrees to consign books to Distributor, which agrees to pay Publisher _____ percent of Distributor's net receipts for each book sold. Net receipts are defined as all proceeds received by the Distributor from sales of the book, except for proceeds received to cover postage or sales tax. In no event shall Distributor sell books at a discount of more than 60 percent from retail price without obtaining the prior written consent of the Publisher.

6. **Delivery.** Publisher agrees to deliver the books by the delivery date set forth in each Distribution Memorandum. Freight and insurance charges for the delivery shall be paid by Distributor.

7. **Payment.** If books are sold pursuant to Paragraph 4, any payment to be made to the Publisher at the time of signing for each title shall be specified in the Distribution Memorandum for that title and the remaining balance shall be payable ____ days after receipt of the books in Distributor's warehouse. If books are consigned pursuant to Paragraph 5, payment shall be due ____ days after the last day of the month in which the books were sold by the Distributor. Any advance for consigned books shall be specified in the Distribution Memorandum for each title, paid at the time of signing that Memorandum, and recouped from first proceeds due Publisher hereunder. Time is of the essence with respect to payment. Consigned books shall be deemed sold in the accounting period in which the order is received; returns of consigned books shall be deducted from sales for the accounting period in which the books are returned. The Distributor shall bear the risk of any accounts which have purchased books

consigned hereunder and prove to be uncollectible. Without limitation on any other rights or remedies available to Publisher, if Distributor does not pay on time Publisher may add a late payment charge of _____ percent per month on the unpaid balance.

8. Statements of Account. Distributor shall provide Publisher with a monthly statement of account including, for each title, sales and returns for the month and sales to date. If the books are consigned pursuant to Paragraph 5, the statement of account shall also show for each title the net receipts for the month and the amount due Publisher. Each statement of account shall be provided within _____ days after the last day of the month for which the accounting is given.

9. Inspection of Books. The Distributor shall maintain accurate books and documentation with respect to all transactions entered into for the Publisher. Within two weeks of receipt of the Publisher's written request, the Distributor shall permit the Publisher or the Publisher's authorized representative to examine these books and documentation during the normal business hours of the Distributor. If such inspection causes errors which are found to be to the Publisher's disadvantage and represent more than 5 percent of the paymet due the Publisher pursuant to a statement of account, the cost of that inspection shall be paid for by the Distributor.

10. Title and Security Interest. Until such time that Distributor shall fully pay for any book pursuant to Paragraph 7, Publisher retains and is vested with full title and interest to the copies of the books not paid for. For any books not paid for under this Agreement, a security interest in such books or any proceeds of sale therefrom is reserved to the Publisher. In the event of any default by the Distributor, the Publisher shall have the rights of a secured party under the Uniform Commercial Code and the books shall not be subject to claims by the Distributor's creditors. The Distributor agrees to execute and deliver to the Publisher, in the form requested by the Publisher, a financing statement and such other documents which the Publisher may require to perfect its security interest in the books. Distributor agrees not to pledge or encumber any books to which Publisher retains title, nor to incur any charge or obligation in connection therewith for which the Publisher may be liable.

11. Termination. Either party may terminate this Agreement as to any title by giving the other party sixty (60) days written notice prior to the renewal date. In the event the Distributor is in default of any of its obligations hereunder, the Publisher may terminate this Agreement at any time by giving written notice to the Distributor. This Agreement shall automatically terminate in the event of the insolvency or bankruptcy of the Distributor. In the event of termination, Distributor shall at its own expense immediately return to the Publisher all books consigned pursuant to Paragraph 5 and shall have the right to sell off books purchased pursuant to Paragraph 4 for a period of _____ months only. The rights and obligations of the Distributor pursuant to Paragraphs 7, 8, 9, 11, 12, and 14 shall survive termination hereunder.

12. Risk of Loss or Damage and Insurance. In the event the books are consigned pursuant to Paragraph 5, Distributor agrees that such books are the property of the Publisher and shall keep the books insured in the name of the Publisher against all risks for _____ percent of retail value until the books are sold or returned to the Publisher. Distributor shall be liable to Publisher for any damages to the consigned books arising from any cause whatsoever from the time Distributor receives possession of the books through the time the books are sold or returned to the Publisher. Distributor shall keep the consigned books in a warehouse area separate from any area containing books owned by the Distributor, and shall mark said area as containing books which are the property of the Publisher.

13. Promotion. Distributor agrees to use best efforts to sell the books. Distributor shall include all titles in its catalog and, in addition, promote each title as follows: _____

_____

Publisher shall cooperate in promotional matters, providing samples, photos, proofs, and other material whenever possible, including advance information for Distributor's catalogs. Publisher agrees to list on the reverse of the title page and on the jacket of each title the following information regarding the Distributor:_____

_____

14. Remainder Sales. Commencing _____ months after the date of delivery, Distributor shall have the right to remainder books purchased pursuant to Paragraph 4, except that prior to any such remaindering Distributor shall offer to sell the books to Publisher at either the remainder price or Distributor's purchase price, whichever is less. Publisher shall accept or reject such offer within thirty days of receipt.

15. Force Majeure. If either party is unable to perform any of its obligations hereunder by reason of fire or other casualty, strike, act or order of a public authority, act of God, or other cause beyond the control of the party, then such party shall be excused from such performance during the pendency of such cause.

16. Assignment. This Agreement shall not be assignable by either party hereto, provided, however, that the Publisher shall have the right to assign monies due Publisher hereunder and the Distributor shall have the right to employ at its own cost and expense sub-distributors or sales representatives to work for the Distributor in the sale and distribution of the Publisher's books.

17. Relationship of Parties. The parties hereto are independent entities and nothing contained in this Agreement shall be construed to constitute a partnership, joint venture, or similar relationship between them.

18. Arbitration. All disputes arising under this Agreement shall be submitted to binding arbitration before _____ in the following location _____ and the arbitration award may be entered for judgment in any court having jurisdiction thereof.

19. Notices and Changes of Address. All notices shall be sent by registered or certified mail, return receipt requested, postage prepaid, to the Publisher and Distributor at the addresses first given above unless indicated to the contrary here: _____. Each party shall give written notification of any change of address prior to the date of said change.

20. Miscellany. This Agreement contains the entire understanding between the parties hereto and may not be modified, amended, or changed except by an instrument in writing signed by both parties. A waiver of any breach of any of the provisions of this Agreement shall not be construed as a continuing waiver of other breaches of the same or other provisions hereof. This Agreement shall be binding upon the parties and their respective heirs, successors, assigns, and personal representatives. This Agreement shall be governed by the laws of the State of _____.

IN WITNESS WHEREOF, the parties hereto have signed this Agreement as of the date first set forth above.

Distributor_____   Publisher_____
              Company Name   Company Name

By_____   By_____
     Authorized Signatory, Title   Authorized Signatory, Title

Schedule A: Distribution Memorandum

This Memorandum is to confirm that the title listed below is to be distributed pursuant to the contract between the parties dated as of the _____ day of _____, 20____.

Title _____

Author _____

Description of Contents _____

_____

Page Size _____

Number of Pages _____

Binding   ❑ softcover   ❑ hardcover

Additional Specifications _____

_____

_____

_____

_____

Quantity _____

Retail Price _____

Delivery Date _____

Publication Date _____

If this title is consigned to Distributor, an advance of $_____ shall be paid on signing this Memorandum.

If this title is sold to Distributor, a partial payment of $_____ shall be paid on signing this Memorandum.

AGREED TO:

Distributor_____   Publisher_____
               Company Name   Company Name

By_____   By_____
          Authorized Signatory, Title   Authorized Signatory, Title

Copyright Transfer Form

The copyright law defines a transfer of copyright as an assignment "of a copyright or of any of the exclusive rights comprised in a copyright, whether or not it is limited in time or place of effect, but not including a nonexclusive license." A transfer is, in some way, exclusive. The person receiving a transfer has a right to do what no one else can do. For example, the transfer might be of the right to make copies of the work in the form of posters for distribution in the United States for a period of one year. While this transfer is far less than all rights in the copyright, it is nonetheless exclusive within its time and place of effect.

Any transfer of an exclusive right must be in writing, and signed either by the owner of the rights being conveyed or by the owner's authorized agent. While not necessary to make the assignment valid, notarization of the signature is *prima facie* proof that the assignment was signed by the owner or agent.

Form 16 can be used in a variety of situations. If the author wanted to receive back rights which had been transferred in the past, the author could take an all-rights transfer. If the author enters into a contract involving the transfer of an exclusive right, the parties may not want to reveal all the financial data and other terms contained in the contract. Form 16 could then be used as a short form to be executed along with the contract for the purpose of recordation in the Copyright Office. The assignment in Form 16 should conform exactly to the assignment in the contract itself.

Recordation of copyright transfers with the Copyright Office can be quite important. Any transfer should be recorded within thirty days if executed in the United States, or within sixty days if executed outside the United States. Otherwise, a later conflicting transfer, if recorded first and taken in good faith without knowledge of the earlier transfer, will prevail over the earlier transfer. Simply put, if the same exclusive rights are sold twice and the first buyer doesn't record the transfer, it is quite possible that the second buyer who does record the transfer will be found to own the rights.

Any document relating to a copyright, whether a transfer of an exclusive right or only a nonexclusive license, can be recorded with the Copyright Office. Such recordation gives constructive notice to the world about the facts in the document recorded. Constructive notice means that a person will be held to have knowledge of the document even if, in fact, he or she did not know about it. Recordation gives constructive notice only if (1) the document (or supporting materials) identifies the work to which it pertains so that the recorded document would be revealed by a reasonable search under the title or registration number of the work, and (2) registration has been made for the work.

Another good reason to record exclusive transfers is that a nonexclusive license, whether recorded or not, can have priority over a conflicting exclusive transfer. If the nonexclusive license is written and signed and was taken before the execution of the transfer or taken in good faith before recordation of the transfer and without notice of the transfer, it will prevail over the transfer.

A fee must be paid to record documents. Once paid, the Register of Copyrights will record the document and return a certificate of recordation.

Filling in the Form

Give the name and address of the party giving the assignment (the assignor) and the name and address of the party receiving the assignment. Specify the rights transferred. Describe the work or works by title, registration number, and the nature of the work. Date the transfer and have the assignor sign it. If the assignor is a corporation, use a corporate form for the signature.

Negotiation Checklist

❏ Be certain that consideration (something of value, whether a promise or money) is actually given to the assignor.

❏ Have the transfer benefit the successors in interest of the assignee.

❏ If the author is making the transfer, limit the rights transferred as narrowly as possible.

❏ Describe the works as completely as possible, including title, registration number, and the nature of the work.

❏ Have the assignor or the authorized agent of the assignor sign the assignment.

❏ Notarize the assignment so that the signature will be presumed valid.

❏ If the assignment is to the author, such as an assignment back to the author of rights previously conveyed, an all-rights provision can be used. (See other provisions)

Other Provisions that can be added to Form 16:

❏ Rights transferred. When indicating the rights transferred, the following provision could be used if the author is to receive all rights. Obviously, the author should avoid giving such a transfer to another party.

Rights Transferred. All rights, title, and interest, including any statutory copyright together with the right to secure renewals and extensions of such copyright throughout the world, for the full term of said copyright or statutory copyright and any renewal or extension of same that is or may be granted throughout the world.

Copyright Transfer Form

FOR VALUABLE CONSIDERATION, the receipt of which is hereby acknowledged, _____

(hereinafter referred to as the "Assignor"), located at _____,

does hereby transfer and assign to _____, located

at _____, his or her heirs, executors, administrators,

and assigns, the following rights: _____

_____ in the copyrights,

and any renewals or extensions thereof, in the works described as follows:

Title	Registration Number	Nature of Work
_____	_____	_____
_____	_____	_____
_____	_____	_____
_____	_____	_____
_____	_____	_____

IN WITNESS WHEREOF, the Assignor has executed this instrument on the _____ day of _____, 20____.

Assignor_____

Application for Copyright Registration of Writing

To register a written work, the author must send a completed Form TX, a nonrefundable filing fee, and a nonreturnable deposit of the writing to be registered. These three items should be sent together to the Register of Copyrights, Copyright Office, Library of Congress, Washington, D.C. 20559.

The instructions for filling in Form TX are provided by the Copyright Office and are reproduced here with Form TX. A Short Form TX may be used by living authors for work that is new (not previously published or registered), not work for hire, and solely owned by the author. Short Form TX with its instructions appears after Form TX.

The Copyright Office also makes available a free Copyright Information Kit. This includes copies of Form TX and other Copyright Office circulars and is definitely worth requesting. To expedite receiving forms or circulars, the Forms and Circulars Hotline number can be used: (202) 707-9100. Authors can download copyright forms and get information from the Copyright Office Web site at *www.loc.gov/copyright*.

Because of budget constraints, the Copyright Office will accept reproductions of Form TX such as the form on the CD-ROM in this book. If the author wishes to make copies, however, the copies must be clear, legible, on a good grade of white paper, and printed on a single sheet of paper so that when the sheet is turned over the top of page 2 is directly behind the top of page 1.

It is wise to register any work that the author feels may be infringed. Registration has a number of values, the most important of which is to establish proof that the author created a particular work as of a certain date. Both published and unpublished works can be registered. In fact, unpublished works can be registered in groups for a single application fee. Published works which appeared as contributions to periodicals may qualify for group registration, in which case Form GR/CP would be used with Form TX.

For published works, the proper deposit is usually two complete copies of the work. For unpublished works, one complete copy would be correct. Since the purpose of registering is to protect what the author has created, it is important that the material deposited fully show what is copyrightable.

A copyright registration is effective as of the date that the Copyright Office receives the application, fee, and deposit materials in an acceptable form, regardless of how long it takes to send back the certificate of registration. It may take as long as 4–8 months before the certificate of registration is sent to the author. To ensure that the Copyright Office receives the materials, the author should send them by registered or certified mail with a return receipt requested from the post office.

An author can request information as to the status of an application. However, a fee will be charged by the Copyright Office if such a status report must be given within 6 months of the submission of the application.

For a more extensive discussion of copyright, the author can consult *The Writer's Legal Guide* (Allworth Press and the Authors Guild), which offers in-depth coverage.

Form TX

Detach and read these instructions before completing this form.
Make sure all applicable spaces have been filled in before you return this form.

When to Use This Form: Use Form TX for registration of published or unpublished nondramatic literary works, excluding periodicals or serial issues. This class includes a wide variety of works: fiction, nonfiction, poetry, textbooks, reference works, directories, catalogs, advertising copy, compilations of information, and computer programs. For periodicals and serials, use Form SE.

Deposit to Accompany Application: An application for copyright registration must be accompanied by a deposit consisting of copies or phonorecords representing the entire work for which registration is to be made. The following are the general deposit requirements as set forth in the statute:

Unpublished Work: Deposit one complete copy (or phonorecord)

Published Work: Deposit two complete copies (or one phonorecord) of the best edition.

Work First Published Outside the United States: Deposit one complete copy (or phonorecord) of the first foreign edition.

Contribution to a Collective Work: Deposit one complete copy (or phonorecord) of the best edition of the collective work.

The Copyright Notice: Before March 1, 1989, the use of copyright notice was mandatory on all published works, and any work first published before that date should have carried a notice. For works first published on and after March 1, 1989, use of the copyright notice is optional. For more information about copyright notice, see Circular 3, "Copyright Notices."

For Further Information: To speak to an information specialist, call (202) 707-3000 (TTY: (202) 707-6737). Recorded information is available 24 hours a day. Order forms and other publications from the address in space 9 or call the Forms and Publications Hotline at (202) 707-9100. Most circulars (but not forms) are available via fax. Call (202) 707-2600 from a touchtone phone. Access and download circulars, forms, and other information from the Copyright Office Website at *www.copyright.gov*.

Please type or print using black ink. The form is used to produce the certificate.

1 SPACE 1: Title

Title of This Work: Every work submitted for copyright registration must be given a title to identify that particular work. If the copies or phonorecords of the work bear a title or an identifying phrase that could serve as a title, transcribe that wording *completely* and *exactly* on the application. Indexing of the registration and future identification of the work will depend on the information you give here.

Previous or Alternative Titles: Complete this space if there are any additional titles for the work under which someone searching for the registration might be likely to look or under which a document pertaining to the work might be recorded.

Publication as a Contribution: If the work being registered is a contribution to a periodical, serial, or collection, give the title of the contribution in the "Title of This Work" space. Then, in the line headed "Publication as a Contribution," give information about the collective work in which the contribution appeared.

2 SPACE 2: Author(s)

General Instructions: After reading these instructions, decide who are the "authors" of this work for copyright purposes. Then, unless the work is a "collective work," give the requested information about every "author" who contributed any appreciable amount of copyrightable matter to this version of the work. If you need further space, request Continuation Sheets. In the case of a collective work, such as an anthology, collection of essays, or encyclopedia, give information about the author of the collective work as a whole.

Name of Author: The fullest form of the author's name should be given. Unless the work was "made for hire," the individual who actually created the work is its "author." In the case of a work made for hire, the statute provides that "the employer or other person for whom the work was prepared is considered the author."

What is a "Work Made for Hire"? A "work made for hire" is defined as (1) "a work prepared by an employee within the scope of his or her employment"; or (2) "a work specially ordered or commissioned for use as a contribution to a collective work, as a part of a motion picture or other audiovisual work, as a translation, as a supplementary work, as a compilation, as an instructional text, as a test, as answer material for a test, or as an atlas, if the parties expressly agree in a written instrument signed by them that the works shall be considered a work made for hire." If you have checked "Yes" to indicate that the work was "made for hire," you must give the full legal name of the employer (or other person for whom the work was prepared). You may also include the name of the employee along with the name of the employer (for example: "Elster Publishing Co., employer for hire of John Ferguson").

"Anonymous" or "Pseudonymous" Work: An author's contribution to a work is "anonymous" if that author is not identified on the copies or phonorecords of the work. An author's contribution to a work is "pseudonymous" if that author is identified on the copies or phonorecords under a fictitious name. If the work is "anonymous" you may: (1) leave the line blank; or (2) state "anonymous" on the line; or (3) reveal the author's identity. If the work is "pseudonymous" you may: (1) leave the line blank; or (2) give the pseudonym and identify it as such (for example: "Huntley Haverstock, pseudonym"); or (3) reveal the author's name, making clear which is the real name and which is the pseudonym (for example, "Judith Barton, whose pseudonym is Madeline Elster"). However, the citizenship or domicile of the author **must** be given in all cases.

Dates of Birth and Death: If the author is dead, the statute requires that the year of death be included in the application unless the work is anonymous or pseudonymous. The author's birth date is optional but is useful as a form of identification. Leave this space blank if the author's contribution was a "work made for hire."

Author's Nationality or Domicile: Give the country of which the author is a citizen or the country in which the author is domiciled. Nationality or domicile **must** be given in all cases.

Nature of Authorship: After the words "Nature of Authorship," give a brief general statement of the nature of this particular author's contribution to the work. Examples: "Entire text"; "Coauthor of entire text"; "Computer program"; "Editorial revisions"; "Compilation and English translation"; "New text."

3 SPACE 3: Creation and Publication

General Instructions: Do not confuse "creation" with "publication." Every application for copyright registration must state "the year in which creation of the work was completed." Give the date and nation of first publication only if the work has been published.

Creation: Under the statute, a work is "created" when it is fixed in a copy or phonorecord for the first time. Where a work has been prepared over a period of time, the part of the work existing in fixed form on a particular date constitutes the created work on that date. The date you give here should be the year in which the author completed the particular version for which registration is now being sought, even if other versions exist or if further changes or additions are planned.

Publication: The statute defines "publication" as "the distribution of copies or phonorecords of a work to the public by sale or other transfer of ownership, or by rental, lease, or lending." A work is also "published" if there has been an "offering to distribute copies or phonorecords to a group of persons for purposes of further distribution, public performance, or public display." Give the full date (month, day, year) when, and the country where, publication first occurred. If first publication took place simultaneously in the United States and other countries, it is sufficient to state "U.S.A."

4 SPACE 4: Claimant(s)

Name(s) and Address(es) of Copyright Claimant(s): Give the name(s) and address(es) of the copyright claimant(s) in this work even if the claimant is the same as the author. Copyright in a work belongs initially to the author of the work (including, in the case of a work made for hire, the employer or other person for whom the work was prepared). The copyright claimant is either the author of the work or a person or organization to whom the copyright initially belonging to the author has been transferred.

Transfer: The statute provides that, if the copyright claimant is not the author, the application for registration must contain "a brief statement of how the claimant obtained ownership of the copyright." If any copyright claimant named in space 4 is not an author named in space 2, give a brief statement explaining how the claimant(s) obtained ownership of the copyright. Examples: "By written contract"; "Transfer of all rights by author"; "Assignment"; "By will." Do not attach transfer documents or other attachments or riders.

5 SPACE 5: Previous Registration

General Instructions: The questions in space 5 are intended to show whether an earlier registration has been made for this work and, if so, whether there is any basis for a new registration. As a general rule, only one basic copyright registration can be made for the same version of a particular work.

Same Version: If this version is substantially the same as the work covered by a previous registration, a second registration is not generally possible unless: (1) the work has been registered in unpublished form and a second registration is now being sought to cover this first published edition; or (2) someone other than the author is identified as copyright claimant in the earlier registration, and the author is now seeking registration in his or her own name. If either of these two exceptions applies, check the appropriate box and give the earlier registration number and date. Otherwise, do not submit Form TX. Instead, write the Copyright Office for information about supplementary registration or recordation of transfers of copyright ownership.

Changed Version: If the work has been changed and you are now seeking registration to cover the additions or revisions, check the last box in space 5, give the earlier registration number and date, and complete both parts of space 6 in accordance with the instructions below.

Previous Registration Number and Date: If more than one previous registration has been made for the work, give the number and date of the latest registration.

6 SPACE 6: Derivative Work or Compilation

General Instructions: Complete space 6 if this work is a "changed version," "compilation," or "derivative work" and if it incorporates one or more earlier works that have already been published or registered for copyright or that have fallen into the public domain. A "compilation" is defined as "a work formed by the collection and assembling of preexisting materials or of data that are selected, coordinated, or arranged in such a way that the resulting work as a whole constitutes an original work of authorship." A "derivative work" is "a work based on one or more preexisting works." Examples of derivative works include translations, fictionalizations, abridgments, condensations, or "any other form in which a work may be recast, transformed, or adapted." Derivative works also include works "consisting of editorial revisions, annotations, or other modifications" if these changes, as a whole, represent an original work of authorship.

Preexisting Material (space 6a): For derivative works, complete this space **and** space 6b. In space 6a identify the preexisting work that has been recast, transformed, or adapted. The preexisting work may be material that has been previously published, previously registered, or that is in the public domain. An example of preexisting material might be: "Russian version of Goncharov's 'Oblomov.'"

Material Added to This Work (space 6b): Give a brief, general statement of the new material covered by the copyright claim for which registration is sought. **Derivative work** examples include: "Foreword, editing, critical annotations"; "Translation"; "Chapters 11-17." If the work is a **compilation**, describe both the compilation itself and the material that has been compiled. Example: "Compilation of certain 1917 Speeches by Woodrow Wilson." A work may be both a derivative work and compilation, in which case a sample statement might be: "Compilation and additional new material."

SPACE 7, 8, 9: Fee, Correspondence, Certification, Return Address

Deposit Account: If you maintain a Deposit Account in the Copyright Office, identify it in space 7a. Otherwise leave the space blank and send the fee of $30 with your application and deposit.

Correspondence (space 7b): This space should contain the name, address, area code, telephone number, fax number, and email address (if available) of the person to be consulted if correspondence about this application becomes necessary.

Certification (space 8): The application cannot be accepted unless it bears the date and the **handwritten signature** of the author or other copyright claimant, or of the owner of exclusive right(s), or of the duly authorized agent of author, claimant, or owner of exclusive right(s).

Address for Return of Certificate (space 9): The address box must be completed legibly since the certificate will be returned in a window envelope.

Copyright Office fees are subject to change. For current fees, check the Copyright Office website at *www.copyright.gov*, write the Copyright Office, or call (202) 707-3000.

Ⓒ Form TX
For a Nondramatic Literary Work
UNITED STATES COPYRIGHT OFFICE

REGISTRATION NUMBER

_____

TX   TXU

EFFECTIVE DATE OF REGISTRATION

_____

Month   Day   Year

DO NOT WRITE ABOVE THIS LINE. IF YOU NEED MORE SPACE, USE A SEPARATE CONTINUATION SHEET.

1

TITLE OF THIS WORK ▼

PREVIOUS OR ALTERNATIVE TITLES ▼

PUBLICATION AS A CONTRIBUTION If this work was published as a contribution to a periodical, serial, or collection, give information about the collective work in which the contribution appeared.   **Title of Collective Work ▼**

If published in a periodical or serial give: Volume ▼   Number ▼   Issue Date ▼   On Pages ▼

2 **a**

NAME OF AUTHOR ▼

DATES OF BIRTH AND DEATH
Year Born ▼   Year Died ▼

Was this contribution to the work a "work made for hire"?
☐ Yes
☐ No

AUTHOR'S NATIONALITY OR DOMICILE
Name of Country
OR { Citizen of ▶ _____
Domiciled in▶ _____

WAS THIS AUTHOR'S CONTRIBUTION TO THE WORK
Anonymous?   ☐ Yes ☐ No
Pseudonymous?   ☐ Yes ☐ No

If the answer to either of these questions is "Yes," see detailed instructions.

NATURE OF AUTHORSHIP Briefly describe nature of material created by this author in which copyright is claimed. ▼

NOTE

Under the law, the "author" of a "work made for hire" is generally the employer, not the employee (see instructions). For any part of this work that was "made for hire" check "Yes" in the space provided, give the employer (or other person for whom the work was prepared) as "Author" of that part, and leave the space for dates of birth and death blank.

b

NAME OF AUTHOR ▼

DATES OF BIRTH AND DEATH
Year Born ▼   Year Died ▼

Was this contribution to the work a "work made for hire"?
☐ Yes
☐ No

AUTHOR'S NATIONALITY OR DOMICILE
Name of Country
OR { Citizen of ▶ _____
Domiciled in▶ _____

WAS THIS AUTHOR'S CONTRIBUTION TO THE WORK
Anonymous?   ☐ Yes ☐ No
Pseudonymous?   ☐ Yes ☐ No

If the answer to either of these questions is "Yes," see detailed instructions.

NATURE OF AUTHORSHIP Briefly describe nature of material created by this author in which copyright is claimed. ▼

c

NAME OF AUTHOR ▼

DATES OF BIRTH AND DEATH
Year Born ▼   Year Died ▼

Was this contribution to the work a "work made for hire"?
☐ Yes
☐ No

AUTHOR'S NATIONALITY OR DOMICILE
Name of Country
OR { Citizen of ▶ _____
Domiciled in▶ _____

WAS THIS AUTHOR'S CONTRIBUTION TO THE WORK
Anonymous?   ☐ Yes ☐ No
Pseudonymous?   ☐ Yes ☐ No

If the answer to either of these questions is "Yes," see detailed instructions.

NATURE OF AUTHORSHIP Briefly describe nature of material created by this author in which copyright is claimed. ▼

3 **a**

YEAR IN WHICH CREATION OF THIS WORK WAS COMPLETED This information must be given ◀ Year in all cases.

b DATE AND NATION OF FIRST PUBLICATION OF THIS PARTICULAR WORK
Complete this information ONLY if this work has been published.
Month ▶ _____ Day▶ _____ Year▶ _____ ◀ Nation

4

See instructions before completing this space.

COPYRIGHT CLAIMANT(S) Name and address must be given even if the claimant is the same as the author given in space 2. ▼

TRANSFER If the claimant(s) named here in space 4 is (are) different from the author(s) named in space 2, give a brief statement of how the claimant(s) obtained ownership of the copyright. ▼

APPLICATION RECEIVED

ONE DEPOSIT RECEIVED

TWO DEPOSITS RECEIVED

FUNDS RECEIVED

DO NOT WRITE HERE
OFFICE USE ONLY

MORE ON BACK ▶ • Complete all applicable spaces (numbers 5-9) on the reverse side of this page.
• See detailed instructions.   • Sign the form at line 8.

DO NOT WRITE HERE
Page 1 of _____ pages

EXAMINED BY _____ FORM TX

CHECKED BY _____

☐ CORRESPONDENCE
Yes

FOR
COPYRIGHT
OFFICE
USE
ONLY

DO NOT WRITE ABOVE THIS LINE. IF YOU NEED MORE SPACE, USE A SEPARATE CONTINUATION SHEET.

PREVIOUS REGISTRATION Has registration for this work, or for an earlier version of this work, already been made in the Copyright Office?

☐ **Yes** ☐ **No** If your answer is "Yes," why is another registration being sought? (Check appropriate box.) ▼

a. ☐ This is the first published edition of a work previously registered in unpublished form.

b. ☐ This is the first application submitted by this author as copyright claimant.

c. ☐ This is a changed version of the work, as shown by space 6 on this application.

If your answer is "Yes," give: **Previous Registration Number** ▶ _____ **Year of Registration** ▶ _____

5

DERIVATIVE WORK OR COMPILATION

Preexisting Material Identify any preexisting work or works that this work is based on or incorporates. ▼

a

6

See instructions
before completing
this space.

Material Added to This Work Give a brief, general statement of the material that has been added to this work and in which copyright is claimed. ▼

b

DEPOSIT ACCOUNT If the registration fee is to be charged to a Deposit Account established in the Copyright Office, give name and number of Account.

Name ▼ **Account Number** ▼

a

7

CORRESPONDENCE Give name and address to which correspondence about this application should be sent. Name/Address/Apt/City/State/ZIP ▼

b

Area code and daytime telephone number ▶ Fax number ▶

Email ▶

CERTIFICATION* I, the undersigned, hereby certify that I am the

Check only one ▶ {

☐ author
☐ other copyright claimant
☐ owner of exclusive right(s)
☐ authorized agent of _____

of the work identified in this application and that the statements made
by me in this application are correct to the best of my knowledge.

Name of author or other copyright claimant, or owner of exclusive right(s) ▲

8

Typed or printed name and date ▼ If this application gives a date of publication in space 3, do not sign and submit it before that date.

_____ Date ▶ _____

Handwritten signature (X) ▼

X _

**Certificate
will be
mailed in
window
envelope
to this
address:**

Name ▼

Number/Street/Apt ▼

City/State/ZIP ▼

YOU MUST:
• Complete all necessary spaces
• Sign your application in space 8

**SEND ALL 3 ELEMENTS
IN THE SAME PACKAGE:**
1. Application form
2. Nonrefundable filing fee in check or money order payable to *Register of Copyrights*
3. Deposit material

MAIL TO:
Library of Congress
Copyright Office - TX
101 Independence Avenue, S.E.
Washington, D.C. 20559-6222

Fees are subject to change. For current fees, check the Copyright Office website at www.copyright.gov, write the Copyright Office, or call (202) 707-3000.

9

Rev: July 2003—xxx Web Rev: July 2003 ♲ Printed on recycled paper   U.S. Government Printing Office: 2000-461-113/20,021

Instructions for Short Form TX

For nondramatic literary works, including fiction and nonfiction, books, short stories, poems, collections of poetry, essays, articles in serials, and computer programs

USE THIS FORM IF—

1. You are the **only** author and copyright owner of this work, *and*
2. The work was **not** made for hire, *and*
3. The work is completely new (does not contain a substantial amount of material that has been previously published or registered or is in the public domain).

If any of the above does not apply, you must use standard Form TX.
NOTE: *Short Form TX is not appropriate for an anonymous author who does not wish to reveal his or her identity.*

HOW TO COMPLETE SHORT FORM TX

- Type or print in black ink.
- Be clear and legible. (Your certificate of registration will be copied from your form.)
- Give only the information requested.

NOTE: You may use a continuation sheet (Form __/CON) to list individual titles in a collection. Complete Space A and list the individual titles under Space C on the back page. Space B is not applicable to short forms.

1 Title of This Work

You must give a title. If there is no title, state "UNTITLED." If you are registering an unpublished collection, give the collection title you want to appear in our records (for example: "Joan's Poems, Volume 1"). Alternative title: If the work is known by two titles, you also may give the second title. If the work has been published as part of a larger work (including a periodical), give the title of that larger work in addition to the title of the contribution.

2 Name and Address of Author and Owner of the Copyright

Give your name and mailing address. You may include your pseudonym followed by "pseud." Also, give the nation of which you are a citizen or where you have your domicile (i.e., permanent residence).

Please give daytime phone and fax numbers and email address, if available.

3 Year of Creation

Give the latest year in which you completed the work you are registering at this time. A work is "created" when it is written down, stored in a computer, or otherwise "fixed" in a tangible form.

4 Publication

If the work has been published (i.e., if copies have been distributed to the public), give the complete date of publication (month, day, and year) and the nation where the publication first took place.

5 Type of Authorship in This Work

Check the box or boxes that describe your authorship in the copy you are sending with the application. For example, if you are registering a story and are planning to add illustrations later, check only the box for "text."

A "compilation" of terms or of data is a selection, coordination, or arrangement of such information into a chart, directory, or other form. A compilation of previously published or public domain material must be registered using a standard Form TX.

6 Signature of Author

Sign the application in black ink and check the appropriate box. The person signing the application should be the author or his/her authorized agent.

7 Person to Contact for Rights and Permissions

This space is optional. You may give the name and address of the person or organization to contact for permission to use the work. You may also provide phone, fax, or email information.

8 Certificate Will Be Mailed

This space must be completed. Your certificate of registration will be mailed in a window envelope to this address. Also, if the Copyright Office needs to contact you, we will write to this address.

9 Deposit Account

Complete this space only if you currently maintain a deposit account in the Copyright Office.

 MAIL WITH THE FORM

- A $30 filing fee in the form of a check or money order (*no cash*) payable to "Register of Copyrights,"
  and
- One or two copies of the work. If the work is unpublished, send one copy. If published, send two copies of the best published edition. (If first published outside the U.S., send one copy either as first published or of the best edition.) **Note:** Inquire about special requirements for works first published before 1978. Copies submitted become the property of the U.S. Government.

Mail everything (**application form, copy or copies, and fee**) *in one package* to:

> Library of Congress
> Copyright Office
> 101 Independence Avenue, S.E.
> Washington, D.C. 20559-6000

QUESTIONS? Call (202) 707-3000 [TTY: (202) 707-6737] between 8:30 a.m. and 5:00 p.m. eastern time, Monday through Friday. For forms and informational circulars, call (202) 707-9100 24 hours a day, 7 days a week, or download them from the Copyright Office website at *www.copyright.gov*. Selected informational circulars but not forms are available from Fax-on-Demand at (202) 707-2600.

Copyright Office fees are subject to change. For current fees, check the Copyright Office website at *www.copyright.gov*, write the Copyright Office, or call (202) 707-3000.

Short Form TX
For a Nondramatic Literary Work
UNITED STATES COPYRIGHT OFFICE

REGISTRATION NUMBER

TX _____ TXU _____

Effective Date of Registration

Application Received

Deposit Received
One _____ | Two _____

Examined By _____

Correspondence ☐

Fee Received

TYPE OR PRINT IN BLACK INK. DO NOT WRITE ABOVE THIS LINE.

1. Title of This Work:

Alternative title or title of larger work in which this work was published:

2. Name and Address of Author and Owner of the Copyright:

Nationality or domicile:
Phone, fax, and email:

Phone ( ) Fax ( )

Email

3. Year of Creation:

4. If work has been published, Date and Nation of Publication:

a. Date _____ _____ _____ *(Month, day, and year all required)*
Month Day Year

b. Nation

5. Type of Authorship in This Work:

Check all that this author created.

☐ Text (includes fiction, nonfiction, poetry, computer programs, etc.)
☐ Illustrations
☐ Photographs
☐ Compilation of terms or data

6. Signature:

Registration cannot be completed without a signature.

*I certify that the statements made by me in this application are correct to the best of my knowledge.** Check one:

☐ Author ☐ Authorized agent

X _____

7. Name and Address of Person to Contact for Rights and Permissions:

OPTIONAL

Phone, fax, and email:

☐ Check here if same as #2 above.

Phone ( ) Fax ( )

Email

8. Certificate will be mailed in window envelope to this address:

Name ▼

Number/Street/Apt ▼

City/State/ZIP ▼

Complete this space only if you currently hold a Deposit Account in the Copyright Office.

9. Deposit Account # _____

Name _____

DO NOT WRITE HERE Page 1 of _____ pages

*17 U.S.C. § 506(e): Any person who knowingly makes a false representation of a material fact in the application for copyright registration provided for by section 409, or in any written statement filed in connection with the application, shall be fined not more than $2,500.

Rev: August 2003—30,000 Web Rev: August 2003 ♲ Printed on recycled paper

U.S. Government Printing Office: 2003-496-605/60,027

Contract with an Independent Contractor

Authors and especially self-publishers often hire independent contractors, such as a researcher, copyeditor, substantive editor, proof reader, photographer, illustrator, or indexer. Independent contractors run their own businesses and hire out on a job by job basis. They are not employees, which saves the author in terms of employee benefits, payroll taxes, and paperwork. By not being an employee, the independent contractor does not have to have taxes withheld and is able to deduct all business expenses directly against income.

A contract with an independent contractor serves two purposes. First, it shows the intention of the parties to have the services performed by an independent contractor. Second, it shows the terms on which the parties will do business.

As to the first purpose of the contract—showing the intention to hire an independent contractor, not an employee—the contract can be helpful if the Internal Revenue Service (IRS) decides to argue that the independent contractor was an employee. The tax law automatically classifies as independent contractors physicians, lawyers, general building contractors, and others who follow an independent trade, business, or profession, in which they offer their services to the public on a regular basis. However, many people don't fall clearly into this group. Since IRS reclassification from independent contractor to employee can have harsh consequences for the hiring party, including payment of back employment taxes, penalties, and jeopardy to qualified pension plans, the IRS has promulgated guidelines for who is an employee.

Basically, an employee is someone who is under the control and direction of the employer to accomplish work. The employee is not only told what to do, but how to do it. On the other hand, an independent contractor is controlled or directed only as to the final result, not as to the means and method to accomplish that result. Some twenty factors enumerated by the IRS dictate the conclusion as to whether someone is an employee or an independent contractor, and no single factor is controlling. Factors suggesting someone is an independent contractor would include that the person supplies his or her own equipment and facilities; that the person works for more than one party (and perhaps employs others at the same time); that the person can choose the location to perform the work; that the person is not supervised during the assignment; that the person receives a fee or commission rather than an hourly or weekly wage; that the person can make a loss or a profit; and that the person can be forced to terminate the job for poor performance but cannot be dismissed like an employee. The author should consult his or her accountant to resolve any doubts about someone's status.

The second purpose of the contract is to specify the terms agreed to between the parties. What services will the contractor provide and when will the services be performed? On what basis and when will payment be made by the author? Will there be an advance, perhaps to help defray expenses?

Independent contractors can perform large jobs or render a day's services. Form 19 is designed to help authors deal with small independent contractors who are performing a limited amount of work. The negotiation checklist is also directed toward this situation, such as hiring a researcher, editor, or indexer.

Filling in the Form

In the Preamble fill in the date and the names and addresses of the parties. In Paragraph 1 show in detail what services are to be performed. Attach another sheet of description or a list of procedures, diagram, or a plan to the contract, if needed. In Paragraph 2 give a schedule. In Paragraph 3 deal with the fee and expenses. In Paragraph 4 specify a time for payment. In Paragraph 5 indicate how cancellations will be handled. In Paragraph 6(E) fill in any special criteria that the contractor should warrant as true. In Paragraph 7 fill in regarding rights in any copyrightable work made by the contractor. In Paragraph 10 specify who will arbitrate, where the arbitration will take place, and, if local small claims court would be better than arbitration, give amounts under the small claims court dollar limit as an exclusion from arbitration. In Paragraph 11 give the state whose laws will govern the contract. Have both parties sign the contract.

Negotiation Checklist

❏ Carefully detail the services to be performed. If necessary, attach an additional sheet of description, a list of procedures, or a plan or diagram. (Paragraph 1)

❏ Give a schedule for performance. (Paragraph 2)

❏ State the method for computing the fee. (Paragraph 3)

❏ If the contractor is to bill for expenses, limit which expenses may be charged. (Paragraph 3)

❏ Require full documentation of expenses in the form of receipts and invoices. (Paragraph 3)

❏ Place a maximum amount on the expenses that can be incurred. (Paragraph 3)

❏ Pay an advance against expenses, if the amount of the expenses are too much for the contractor to wait to receive back at the time of payment for the entire job. (Paragraph 3)

❏ State a time for payment. (Paragraph 4)

❏ Deal with payment for cancellations. (Paragraph 5)

❏ If expenses are billed for, consider whether any markup should be allowed.

❏ Require warranties that the contractor is legally able to perform the contract, that all services will be done in a professional manner, that any subcontractor or employee hired by the contractor will be professional, that the contractor will pay all taxes for the contractor and his or her employees, and any other criteria for the proper performance of the services. (Paragraph 6)

❏ If a photographer, illustrator, or writer is to create a copyrightable work, make certain any needed rights of usage are obtained. (Paragraph 7)

❏ State that the parties are independent contractors and not employer–employee. (Paragraph 8)

❏ Do not allow assignment of rights or obligations under the contract. (Paragraph 9)

❏ The author should check with his or her attorney as to whether arbitration is better than suing in the local courts, and whether small claims court might be better than arbitration. (Paragraph 10)

❏ Allow for an oral modification of either the fee or expense agreement, if such oral change is necessary to move the project forward quickly. (Paragraph 11)

❏ Compare Paragraph 11 with the standard provisions in the introduction.

Contract with an Independent Contractor

AGREEMENT, entered into as of the_____day of _____, 20____, between _____

located at _____ (hereinafter referred to as the "Client") and

_____, located at _____

(hereinafter referred to as the "Contractor").

The Parties hereto agree as follows:

1. Services to be Rendered.   The Contractor agrees to perform the following services for the Client

_____

_____

_____

_____

_____

_____

_____

If needed, a list of procedures, diagram, or plan for the services shall be attached to and made part of this Agreement.

2. Schedule. The Contractor shall complete the services pursuant to the following schedule_____

_____

_____

3. Fee and Expenses. The Client shall pay the Contractor as follows:

❑ Hourly rate $_____/ hour

❑ Project rate $_____

❑ Day rate $_____/ day

❑ Other _____ $_____

The Client shall reimburse the Contractor only for the expenses listed here_____
_____.

Expenses shall not exceed $_____. The Contractor shall provide full documentation for any expenses to be reimbursed, including receipts and invoices. An advance of $_____ against expenses shall be paid to the Contractor and recouped when payment is made pursuant to Paragraph 4.

4. Payment. Payment shall be made: ❑ at the end of each day ❑ upon completion of the project ❑ within thirty (30) days of Client's receipt of Contractor's invoice.

5. Cancellation. In the event of cancellation, Client shall pay a cancellation fee under the following circumstances and in the amount specified _____
_____.

6. Warranties. The Contractor warrants as follows:

(A) Contractor is fully able to enter into and perform its obligations pursuant to this Agreement.

(B) All services shall be performed in a professional manner.

(C) If employees or subcontractors are to be hired by Contractor they shall be competent professionals.

(D) Contractor shall pay all necessary local, state, or federal taxes, including but not limited to withholding taxes, workers' compensation, F.I.C.A., and unemployment taxes for Contractor and its employees.

(E) Any other criteria for performance are as follows:

_____
_____.

7. **Rights.** If the services rendered by the Contractor result in copyrightable work(s), the Client shall have the following usage rights in that work(s) _____

_____
_____.

8. **Relationship of Parties.** Both parties agree that the Contractor is an independent contractor. This Agreement is not an employment agreement, nor does it constitute a joint venture or partnership between the Client and Contractor. Nothing contained herein shall be construed to be inconsistent with this independent contractor relationship.

9. **Assignment.** This Agreement may not be assigned by either party without the written consent of the other party hereto.

10. **Arbitration.** All disputes shall be submitted to binding arbitration before _____ in the following location _____ and settled in accordance with the rules of the American Arbitration Association. Judgment upon the arbitration award may be entered in any court having jurisdiction thereof. Disputes in which the amount at issue is less than $_____ shall not be subject to this arbitration provision.

11. **Miscellany.** This Agreement constitutes the entire agreement between the parties. Its terms can be modified only by an instrument in writing signed by both parties, except that oral authorizations of additional fees and expenses shall be permitted if necessary to speed the progress of work. This Agreement shall be binding on the parties, their heirs, successors, assigns, and personal representatives. A waiver of a breach of any of the provisions of this Agreement shall not be construed as a continuing waiver of other breaches of the same or other provisions hereof. This Agreement shall be governed by the laws of the State of _____.

IN WITNESS WHEREOF, the parties hereto have signed this as of the date first set forth above.

Client_____   Contractor_____
                                                                    Company Name

                                                        By_____
                                                                    Authorized Signatory

License of Rights
License of Electronic Rights

If there is one striking change in the world of publishing since *Business and Legal Forms for Authors and Self-Publishers* first appeared in 1990, it is the advent of electronic rights (electronic works being digitized versions that can be stored or retrieved from such media as computer disks, CD-ROM, computer databases, and network servers). Authors have always stood to profit by not giving up all rights when dealing with publishers and other clients. This has been the reason that the battle over work-for-hire contracts has been fought with such ferocity in contractual negotiations, legislative proposals, and litigation. The desire of users for extensive rights must constantly clash with the desire of creators to give only limited rights. As work for hire offered the most potent path for users to gain all rights (including rights which such users had no intention or ability to exercise), so electronic rights have become the latest frontier where users seek to extend their domains at the expense of creators.

Unlike Form 2, the Confirmation of Assignment, and Form 5, the Book Publishing Contract, which refer to works to be created in the future, Forms 20 and 21 are for works which already exist. These forms seek to maximize the opportunities of the author for residual income. To use these forms, of course, the author must first limit the rights which he or she grants to the first users of work. Assuming the author of a magazine article, book, or other work has retained all usage rights that the publisher did not actually need, that author then becomes the potential beneficiary of income from further sales of the work to other users.

Forms 20 and 21 are almost identical. However, for both didactic and practical reasons, the distinction between electronic and nonelectronic rights is important enough to justify two forms. Just as traditional rights have come to have generally accepted definitions and familiar divisions between creators and users as to control and

sharing of income, so electronic rights may someday find similar clarification and customary allocation. Today that crystallization is far from a reality. In addition, the constant evolution of new storage and delivery media for electronic works (most recently the Internet) means that definitions must also be adaptable and constantly scrutinized to ascertain accuracy.

An electronic work might first be a computer file, then be transmitted as e-mail, then incorporated into a multi-media product (along with art and a sound track), then uploaded to a site on the World Wide Web, and finally downloaded into the computer of someone cruising in cyberspace. Such digital potential for shape-shifting makes contractual restrictions both more challenging to engineer and absolutely essential to negotiate.

The Authors Guild (212-563-5904), The National Writers Union (212-254-0279), and a number of other organizations have recognized the importance of capturing residual income streams for authors. These organizations have facilitated registries to benefit authors willing to have their works marketed in electronic form. Information about these helpful and pioneering efforts can be obtained from the Guild or the Union. Forms 20 and 21 are designed for when a potential user approaches the author directly to use work that has been previously distributed. That previous distribution might have been in traditional media or, as is becoming ever more likely, in electronic media.

Because many of the concerns with both Forms 20 and 21 are the same as for commissioned works, the negotiation checklist refers to the checklists for Form 2 and Form 5. One key point addressed in both forms is the narrow specification of the nature of the usage as well as the retention of all other rights. When electronic rights are being granted, it is important if possible to try to limit the form of the final use (such as CD-ROM) and whether consumers can make copies (as is possible with material on the World Wide Web).

Another problem addressed by Forms 20 and 21 has been the widely publicized inability of publishers to determine who should receive payments that are sent to the publishers by licensees. This may seem a bizarre problem to the author or self-publisher who only has one or a few works to license, but for large publishing houses with hundreds or thousands of licensed works the problem is of a different magnitude.

Authors and agents have complained that many publishers simply can't keep track of income from licensing. The effect of this failure is that the publishers enrich themselves at the expense of authors. Paragraph 9 requires that licensees provide certain information that will avoid this problem. The required information is similar to that in the "Subsidiary Rights Payment Advice Form" promulgated by the Book Industry Study Group, Inc. (646-336-7141) in the hope that widespread adoption of the form by publishers will

Subsidiary Rights Payment Advice Form

This form must be completed and attached to your check or faxed to this number:_____ when you send payment pursuant to licenses granted by us to you.

Failure to do so may result in our inability to record your payments and prevent us from determining that you are in compliance with the terms of your license(s).

❑ Amount remitted: _____

❑ Check or wire transfer number: _____

❑ Check or wire transfer date: _____

❑ Bank and account number to which moneys were deposited (for wire transfers): _____

❑ Publisher/agent payor's name: _____

❑ Title of the work for which payment is being made: _____

_____

❑ Author(s) of the work: _____

❑ Our Unique Identifying Number for the work, as it appears in the Appendix to the relevant contract. If none, the

original publisher's ISBN number of the work: _____

❑ The period covered by the payment: _____

The following information will be very helpful, so we ask that you also provide it:

❑ Reason for payment (guarantee, earned royalty, fee, etc.): _____

_____

❑ Payment's currency: _____

❑ Type of right (book club, reprint, translation, etc.): _____

_____

❑ Summary justification of your payment:

Gross amount due: _____

Taxes: _____

Commissions: _____

Bank charges: _____

Net amount paid: _____

cause licensees to give the needed information for proper accounting. Paragraph 9 could be modified to refer to the Subsidiary Rights Payment Advice Form, which would then be attached to the licensing contract. The form is reproduced by permission of BISAC, a committee of the Book Industry Study Group, Inc., 19 West 21st Street, New York, NY 10010.

Filling in the Forms

Fill in the date and the names and addresses for the client and the author. In Paragraph 1 describe the work in detail and indicate the form in which it will be delivered. In Paragraph 2 give the delivery date. In Paragraph 3 specify the limitations as to which rights are granted, including the nature of the use (magazine, book, advertising, CD-ROM, etc.), the language, the name of the product or publication, the territory, and the time period of use. In an unusual case, the usage might be specified to be exclusive. Also, give an outside date for the usage to take place, after which the right will terminate. For an ongoing use, fill in a minimum amount which must be paid in order for the license not to terminate. For Form 21 indicate whether consumers may copy the work, or whether the electronic rights granted are for display (viewing but not copying) use only. In Paragraph 5 give the fee or the amount of the advance against a royalty (in which case the calculation of the royalty must be included). If alteration of the work is permitted, give guidelines for this in Paragraph 7. In Paragraph 8 give a monthly interest charge for late payments. Show in Paragraph 10 whether copyright notice must appear in the author's name and in Paragraph 11 whether authorship credit will be given. In Paragraph 13 specify who will arbitrate disputes, where this will be done, and give the maximum amount which can be sued for in small claims court. In Paragraph 14 give the state whose laws will govern the contract. Both parties should then sign the contract.

Negotiation Checklist

❏ Review the negotiation checklist for Form 2 on pages 17–20.

❏ To limit the grant of rights, carefully specify the type of use, language, name of the product or publication, territory, and time period for the use.

❏ Since rights are being licensed in pre-existing work, do not grant exclusive rights or limit the exclusivity to very narrow and precisely described uses. (Paragraph 3)

❏ If electronic rights are licensed, try to limit the form of final use (such as a particularly named CD-ROM or site on the World Wide Web). (Paragraph 3)

❏ For electronic rights indicate whether consumers or end users may only see a display of the work or will actually have a right to download a copy of the work. (Paragraph 3)

❏ Limit the time period for the use and specify a date by which all usage must be completed and all rights automatically revert to the author. (Paragraph 3)

❏ Specify that all rights will revert if the income stream falls below a certain level. (Paragraph 3)

❏ For Form 20, reserve all electronic rights to the author.

❏ For Form 21, reserve all traditional (nonelectronic rights) to the author.

❏ If royalties are agreed to for Paragraph 5, review pages 35–37 with respect to the computation of royalties in the negotiation checklist for Form 5.

❏ For electronic rights especially, negotiate the right of the client to enlarge, reduce, or combine the work with other works (whether literary, artistic, or musical). (Paragraph 7)

❏ For Form 21, require the client to use the best available technology to prevent infringements. (Paragraph 10)

❏ Review the standard provisions in the introductory pages and compare to Paragraph 14.

License of Rights

AGREEMENT, entered into as of the _____ day of _____, 20 _____, between _____, located at _____ (hereinafter referred to as the "Client") and _____, located at _____ (hereinafter referred to as the "Author") with respect to the licensing of certain rights in the Author's writing (hereinafter referred to as the "Work").

1. **Description of Work.** The Client wishes to license certain rights in the Work which the Author has created and which is described as follows:

    Title_____Number of Words_____

    Subject matter_____

    _____.

    Other materials to be provided_____

    _____.

    Form in which work shall be delivered   ❏ double-spaced manuscript

        ❏ computer file (specify format _____)

2. **Delivery Date.** The Author agrees to deliver the Work within _____ days after the signing of this Agreement.

3. **Grant of Rights.** Upon receipt of full payment, Author grants to the Client the following rights in the Work:

    For use as_____in the_____language

    For the product or publication named_____

    In the following territory_____

    For the following time period_____

    With respect to the usage shown above, the Client shall have nonexclusive rights unless specified to the contrary here_____

    Other limitations:_____

    If the Work is for use as a contribution to a magazine, the grant of rights shall be for one-time North American serial rights only unless specified to the contrary above.

    If the Client does not complete its usage under this Paragraph 3 by the following date_____ or if payments to be made hereunder fall to less than $____ every ____ months, all rights granted shall without further notice revert to the Author without prejudice to the Author's right to retain sums previously paid and collect additional sums due.

4. **Reservation of Rights.** All rights not expressly granted hereunder are reserved to the Author, including but not limited to all rights in preliminary materials and all electronic rights. For purposes of this agreement, electronic rights are defined as rights in the digitized form of works that can be encoded, stored, and retrieved from such media as computer disks, CD-ROM, computer databases, and network servers.

5. **Fee.** Client agrees to pay the following for the usage rights granted: ❏ $_____
    ❏ an advance of $_____ to be recouped against royalties to be computed as follows_____
    _____
    _____.

6. Additional Usage. If Client wishes to make any additional uses of the Work, Client agrees to seek permission from the Author and make such payments as are agreed to between the parties at that time.

7. Alteration. Client shall not make or permit any alterations, whether by adding or removing material from the Work, without the permission of the Author. Alterations shall be deemed to include the addition of any illustrations, photographs, sound, text, or computerized effects, unless specified to the contrary here_____

8. Payment. Client agrees to pay the Author within thirty days of the date of Author's billing, which shall be dated as of the date of delivery of the Work. Overdue payments shall be subject to interest charges of _____ percent monthly.

9. Statements of Account. The payments due pursuant to Paragraph 8 shall be made by Client to Author whose receipt of same shall be a full and valid discharge of the Clients' obligations hereunder only if accompanied by the following information: **(a)** amount remitted; **(b)** check or wire transfer number and date, as well as the bank and account number to which funds were deposited by wire transfer; **(c)** Client's name as payor; **(d)** title of the work for which payment is being made; **(e)** author(s) of the work; **(f)** the identifying number, if any, for the work, or the ISBN, if any; **(g)** the period which the payment covers; **(h)** the reason for the payment, the payment's currency, and the details of any withholdings from the payment (such as for taxes, commissions, or bank charges).

10. Copyright Notice. Copyright notice in the name of the Author ❏ shall ❏ shall not accompany the Work when it is reproduced.

11. Authorship Credit. Authorship credit in the name of the Author ❏ shall ❏ shall not accompany the Work when it is reproduced. If the work is used as a contribution to a magazine or for a book, authorship credit shall be given unless specified to the contrary in the preceding sentence.

12. Releases. The Client agrees to indemnify and hold harmless the Author against any and all claims, costs, and expenses, including attorney's fees, due to uses for which no release was requested, uses which exceed the uses allowed pursuant to a release, or uses based on alterations not allowed pursuant to Paragraph 7.

13. Arbitration. All disputes arising under this Agreement shall be submitted to binding arbitration before _____ in the following location _____ and settled in accordance with the rules of the American Arbitration Association. Judgment upon the arbitration award may be entered in any court having jurisdiction thereof. Disputes in which the amount at issue is less than $_____ shall not be subject to this arbitration provision.

14. Miscellany. This Agreement shall be binding upon the parties hereto, their heirs, successors, assigns, and personal representatives. This Agreement constitutes the entire understanding between the parties. Its terms can be modified only by an instrument in writing signed by both parties, except that the Client may authorize expenses or revisions orally. A waiver of a breach of any of the provisions of this Agreement shall not be construed as a continuing waiver of other breaches of the same or other provisions hereof. This Agreement shall be governed by the laws of the State of _____.

IN WITNESS WHEREOF, the parties hereto have signed this Agreement as of the date first set forth above.

Author_____   Client_____
                                                                       Company Name

                                             By:_____
                                                          Authorized Signatory, Title

License of Electronic Rights

AGREEMENT, entered into as of the _____ day of _____, 20 _____, between _____,
located at _____ (hereinafter referred to as the "Client")
and _____, located at _____
(hereinafter referred to as the "Author") with respect to the licensing of certain electronic rights in the Author's writing
(hereinafter referred to as the "Work").

1. **Description of Work.** The Client wishes to license certain electronic rights in the Work which the Author has created and which is described as follows:

    Title_____Number of Words_____

    Subject matter_____
    _____.

    Other materials to be provided_____
    _____.

    Form in which work shall be delivered   ❏ double-spaced manuscript
      ❏ computer file (specify format _____)

2. **Delivery Date.** The Author agrees to deliver the Work within _____ days after the signing of this Agreement.

3. **Grant of Rights.** Upon receipt of full payment, Author grants to the Client the following electronic rights in the Work:

    For use as_____in the_____language

    For the product or publication named_____

    In the following territory_____

    For the following time period_____

    For display purposes only without permission for digital copying by users of the product or publication unless specified to the contrary here_____

    With respect to the usage shown above, the Client shall have nonexclusive rights unless specified to the contrary here_____
    Other limitations:_____

    If the Client does not complete its usage under this Paragraph 3 by the following date_____,
    all rights granted but not exercised shall without further notice revert to the Author without prejudice to the Author's right to retain sums previously paid and collect additional sums due.

4. **Reservation of Rights.** All rights not expressly granted hereunder are reserved to the Author, including but not limited to all rights in preliminary materials and all nonelectronic rights. For purposes of this agreement, electronic rights are defined as rights in the digitized form of works that can be encoded, stored, and retrieved from such media as computer disks, CD-ROM, computer databases, and network servers.

5. **Fee.** Client agrees to pay the following: ❏ $_____ for the usage rights granted.
    ❏ an advance of $_____ to be recouped against royalties to be computed as follows_____
    _____
    _____.

6. Additional Usage. If Client wishes to make any additional uses of the Work, Client agrees to seek permission from the Author and make such payments as are agreed to between the parties at that time.

7. Alteration. Client shall not make or permit any alterations, whether by adding or removing material from the Work, without the permission of the Author. Alterations shall be deemed to include the addition of any illustrations, photographs, sound, text, or computerized effects, unless specified to the contrary here_____

8. Payment. Client agrees to pay the Author within thirty days of the date of Author's billing, which shall be dated as of the date of delivery of the Work. Overdue payments shall be subject to interest charges of _____ percent monthly.

9. Statements of Account. The payments due pursuant to Paragraph 8 shall be made by Client to Author whose receipt of same shall be a full and valid discharge of the Clients' obligations hereunder only if accompanied by the following information: **(a)** amount remitted; **(b)** check or wire transfer number and date, as well as the bank and account number to which funds were deposited by wire transfer; **(c)** Client's name as payor; **(d)** title of the work for which payment is being made; **(e)** author(s) of the work; **(f)** the identifying number, if any, for the work, or the ISBN, if any; **(g)** the period which the payment covers; **(h)** the reason for the payment, the payment's currency, and the details of any withholdings from the payment (such as for taxes, commissions, or bank charges).

10. Copyright Notice. Copyright notice in the name of the Author ❑ shall ❑ shall not accompany the Work when it is reproduced.

11. Authorship Credit. Authorship credit in the name of the Author ❑ shall ❑ shall not accompany the Work when it is reproduced. If the work is used as a contribution to a magazine or for a book, authorship credit shall be given unless specified to the contrary in the preceding sentence.

12. Releases. The Client agrees to indemnify and hold harmless the Author against any and all claims, costs, and expenses, including attorney's fees, due to uses for which no release was requested, uses which exceed the uses allowed pursuant to a release, or uses based on alterations not allowed pursuant to Paragraph 7.

13. Arbitration. All disputes arising under this Agreement shall be submitted to binding arbitration before _____ in the following location _____ and settled in accordance with the rules of the American Arbitration Association. Judgment upon the arbitration award may be entered in any court having jurisdiction thereof. Disputes in which the amount at issue is less than $_____ shall not be subject to this arbitration provision.

14. Miscellany. This Agreement shall be binding upon the parties hereto, their heirs, successors, assigns, and personal representatives. This Agreement constitutes the entire understanding between the parties. Its terms can be modified only by an instrument in writing signed by both parties, except that the Client may authorize expenses or revisions orally. A waiver of a breach of any of the provisions of this Agreement shall not be construed as a continuing waiver of other breaches of the same or other provisions hereof. This Agreement shall be governed by the laws of the State of _____.

IN WITNESS WHEREOF, the parties hereto have signed this Agreement as of the date first set forth above.

Author_____   Client_____
                                                                    Company Name

                                            By:_____
                                                          Authorized Signatory, Title

Translation Contract

Translation offers an opportunity for the self-publisher to benefit by publication in many languages and countries. Once a book is published in English, foreign publishers may take notice and want to license rights to publish a translation in their respective languages. Books may be translated into innumerable languages, from French, Italian, German, Japanese, Chinese, and Korean, to Bulgarian, Indonesian, Iranian, Romanian, Thai, and many more. This Tower of Babel represents potential subsidiary income for the self-publisher.

In a translation deal, the English language publisher is the "licensor" and the foreign publisher is the "publisher". The contract is much like Form 5, Book Publishing Contract, with a number of modifications and simplifications. The key point is to limit the rights to a specific language in a specified territory. In some cases, a language may be spoken in more than one country and the territory may cover several countries or the world. For example, a Spanish translation might be for Mexico only, or it might be for the world (to cover Spain and the many other countries south of Mexico where Spanish is spoken). If a Mexican publisher obtained a license to do a Spanish translation for Mexico, a Spanish publisher might license the rights for Spain, an Argentine publisher might license the rights for Argentina, and so on.

The term of the license is also significant. Unlike book publishing contracts that an author might sign, the term for a translation license will usually be five or seven years. Then the success of the book can be evaluated and an extension negotiated if warranted.

The amount of the advance is especially important, because many or perhaps most translations fail to earn out the advance. Part of the reason for this is the strength of the dollar against many foreign currencies. If it is likely the only money the self-publisher will earn is the advance, then the highest possible advance should be a goal of the negotiation. A related problem is the failure of many foreign publishers to give accountings and the difficulty of enforcing the accounting and payment terms of a contract against a party in a foreign country.

For certain smaller countries, it may actually be better for the foreign publisher to pay the licensor in the advance for a specific number of copies to be printed. If more than the anticipated number of copies are printed or the price of the book is higher than projected, the foreign publisher would make an additional payment upon publication. If the foreign publisher wishes to print more copies beyond the first print run, they would have to negotiate again with the licensor.

Agents who handle foreign rights establish a network of subagents in the main foreign markets. While a self-publisher might be able to contact foreign publishers directly by using industry directories (such as *International Marketplace* published by R. R. Bowker) and going to book fairs (such as those held in Frankfurt and London), it might be best to find an agent able to handle translation sales and give the agent an exclusive right to do so with respect to certain titles. The agent would charge 10 percent and the subagents in the various countries would also charge 10 percent, so the net proceeds to the self-publisher would be 80 percent (which may be reduced further by tax withholding in the foreign country and the agent's various expenses for submitting abroad).

Filling in the Form

In the Preamble fill in the date and the names and addresses of the parties as well as the title of the book. In Paragraph 1 indicate the language, whether the book will be hardcover or softcover, the territory, and the term. In Paragraph 3 give the amount of the advance. If there is an agent, fill in Paragraph 11 and indicate to whom the checks should be payable. If there is no agent, Paragraph 11 can be deleted. In Paragraph 12 indicate which state's laws will govern the contract. Both parties should then sign.

Negotiation Checklist

❏ Specify the title and edition of the work to be licensed. (Preamble)

❏ Indicate the language to be licensed. (Paragraph 1)

❏ Limit the territory in which the translation may be sold. (Paragraph 1)

❏ If the translation is only to be sold in a specified country or countries, do not include any provision making an "open market" of the rest of the world.

❏ Limit the term of the license. (Paragraph 1)

❏ Retain all rights not explicitly transferred.

❏ Retain all electronic rights. (Paragraph 1)

❏ Require that publication take place within a specified time period. (Paragraph 2)

❏ Keep any advances paid if publication does not take place. (Paragraph 2)

❏ Seek maximum royalties. (Paragraph 3)

❏ Require accountings every six months. (Paragraph 3)

❏ Negotiate the highest possible advance. (Paragraph 3)

❏ For certain smaller countries, consider having the foreign publisher pay an advance based on the projected print run and retail price, after which the foreign publisher would have to negotiate again to do additional print runs.

❏ Allow termination of the license if the translation goes out of print. (Paragraph 4)

❏ Require that the name of the author appear with appropriate placement on the book. (Paragraph 5)

❏ Require that the original title of the work and copyright notice appear on the book. (Paragraphs 5 and 7)

❏ Indicate that the foreign publisher will provide a certain number of copies, usually six, to the licensor. (Paragraph 6)

❏ If any changes are to be made to the text, require the licensor's permission. (Paragraph 7)

❏ Make appropriate warranties. (Paragraph 8)

❏ Allow the licensor to assign monies due under the contract. (Paragraph 9)

❏ Require the licensor to give some copies of the English language work to the foreign publisher. (Paragraph 10)

❏ Specify the licensor's agent, if any, by name and address and indicate if checks should be payable to the agent. (Paragraph 11)

❏ Compare the standard provisions in the introductory pages with Paragraph 12.

❏ Review the checklist for Form 5, since many of the points covered there could also apply to a translation contract.

Translation Contract

AGREEMENT dated as of the _____ day of _____, 20_____ between _____ _____with offices at _____ (hereinafter referred to as the "Licensor"), and _____ with offices at _____ (hereinafter referred to as the "Publisher"), with respect to the licensing of a book titled _____ (hereinafter referred to as the "work").

1. Subject to the provisions of Paragraph 4, Licensor agrees to grant Publisher the exclusive right to publish and sell the work in the _____ language in ❑ hardcover or ❑ quality paperback book form in the following territory _____. The term of this Agreement shall be for _____ years from the date of the Publisher's first publication of the work. This agreement shall thereafter continue automatically in full force and effect until the Licensor gives written notice of termination to the Publisher. Upon termination of the Agreement, the Publisher shall retain the right to sell or otherwise dispose of copies of the work then on hand or in process of manufacture subject to the terms of this Agreement. This license does not include any electronic rights to the work. For purposes of this agreement, electronic rights are defined as rights in the digitized form of works that can be encoded, stored, and retrieved from such media as computer disks, CD-ROM, computer databases, and network servers, including but not limited to the Internet.

2. Publisher agrees to publish the work within eighteen (18) months of the date of this Agreement. If Publisher does not publish the work within the specified time, it shall revert all rights to the Licensor which shall retain any advances paid to the date of the reversion, but the Publisher shall have no further liability.

3. Publisher shall pay the Licensor the following royalties: (A) For sales of hardcover edition, ten (10%) percent of the suggested retail list price on all copies sold up to five thousand copies; twelve-and-a-half (12½%) percent of the suggested retail list price on all copies sold from five thousand copies up to ten thousand copies; and fifteen (15%) percent on all sales thereafter; (B) for sales of a quality paperback edition, eight (8%) percent of the suggested retail list price on all copies sold up to a total of ten thousand copies and ten (10%) percent of the suggested retail list price on all sales thereafter; (C) for sales under (A) or (B) which take place by direct mail or direct response advertising, the royalty shall be five (5%) percent of suggested retail list price; (D) for remainder sales of overstock, the royalty shall be ten (10%) percent of the net receipts minus the unit printing cost of the books sold; and (E) for all sales not covered by (A), (B), (C), or (D), the royalty shall be ten (10%) percent of net receipts. Net receipts are defined as all sums received by the Publisher from the sale of the book, exclusive of reimbursements for shipping and related expenses. No royalty shall be payable on complimentary copies, copies sold to the Licensor, copies damaged or lost, or copies otherwise disposed of without sale. All computations hereunder shall be net of returns.

Publisher shall pay any sums due on April 15 (for the prior July–December period) and October 15 (for the prior January–June period). Each payment shall be accompanied by a statement of account. Publisher agrees that the Licensor shall have the right to inspect the underlying journals and documentation with respect to the accountings upon giving Publisher reasonable notice in writing.

Upon the signing of this Agreement, the Publisher shall pay Licensor an advance of _____ (   ) dollars. All payments under this Agreement shall be in United States dollars and drawn on a United States bank.

4. All rights to publish the work shall revert to the Licensor if the work shall remain out-of-print for more than nine (9) consecutive months after a written request by the Licensor that the work be reprinted. Out-of-print shall mean that the work is not available for sale in any form from any of the Publisher's distributors.

5. The Publisher shall place the name of the author with due prominence on the binding, front cover, and title page of every copy produced. The original title of the work shall appear on the back of the title page of every copy produced along with an English language copyright notice as follows: Copyright © (Author's Name) (Date of Original Publication).

6. The Licensor shall receive six (6) copies of the work free of charge.

7. Publisher agrees not to change the title or text of the work or abridge the text thereof without written consent of the Licensor, which consent shall not be unreasonably withheld or delayed, except that the Publisher may at its option use or not use the design, subtitle, illustration, index or introductory material from the jacket or text of the hardcover edition, and Publisher may also make other reasonable modifications for its special market with the consent of the Licensor, which consent shall not be unreasonably withheld. The Publisher agrees to print on the copyright page of the work the copyright notices contained in the said hardcover edition or any other copyright notices furnished in writing by the Licensor.

8. The Licensor represents and warrants that: (a) the Licensor is able to grant the rights herein granted and that such rights are not limited by any outstanding encumbrance or lien; (b) the Licensor shall not permit any other publisher to publish the Book in the territories during the term of this Agreement; (c) the Book does not infringe any copyright; (d) copyright in the book validly exists in the territories covered by this Agreement and shall continue to exist during the term hereof; (e) the work contains no plagiarized passages or statements or any violation of any right of privacy or any libelous or obscene matter or any other matter contrary to law. The Licensor hereby agrees to indemnify and hold harmless the Publisher and such wholesalers, jobbers and retailers who may traffic in the work against any loss or expense, including counsel fees incurred, arising from any breach or alleged breach by the Licensor of this Agreement or any of Licensor's covenants, warranties and representations hereunder. The foregoing covenants, warranties and indemnities shall survive the termination of this Agreement.

9. The Licensor shall have the right to assign monies due under this agreement and Publisher shall have the right to assign all its rights and obligations under this agreement.

10. Licensor shall provide Publisher with five (5) copies or photocopies of the English language work immediately upon signing of this Agreement.

11. All statements of account and monies payable hereunder shall be sent to the Licensor's agent, whose name and address are as follows _____ .
All checks shall be made payable to _____ .

12. This Agreement contains the entire understanding between the parties and may only be modified or amended by a written instrument signed by both parties. A waiver or default under any provision of this Agreement shall not permit future waivers or defaults under that or other provisions of this Agreement. Written notice can be given to the parties at the addresses shown for them. This Agreement shall be binding on the parties' heirs, legal representatives, successors-in-interest, and assigns. This Agreement can only be modified in writing and shall be governed by the laws of the State of _____ .

IN WITNESS WHEREOF, the parties have signed this agreement as of the date first set forth above to constitute it a binding agreement between them.

Licensor _____   Publisher _____

Commercial Lease
Sublease
Lease Assignment

FORM 23 FORM 24 FORM 25

Every business, whether small or large, must find suitable space for its activities. For the sole proprietor, the studio may be in the home. For a larger enterprise, the studio or office is likely to be in an office building. While some businesses may own their offices, most will rent space from a landlord. The terms of the rental lease may benefit or harm the business. Large sums of money are likely to be paid not only for rent, but also for security, escalators, and other charges. In addition, the tenant is likely to spend additional money to customize the space by building in offices, darkrooms, reception areas, and the like. Form 23 and the accompanying analysis of how to negotiate a lease are designed to protect the tenant from a variety of troublesome issues that may arise.

The old saw about real estate is, "Location, location, location." Location builds value, but the intended use of the rented premises must be legal if value is to accrue. For example, sole proprietors often work from home. In many places, zoning laws govern the uses that can be made of property. It may be that an office at home violates zoning restrictions against commercial activity. What is fine in one town—a studio in an extra room, for example—may violate the zoning in the next town. Before renting or buying a residential property with the intention of also doing business there, it's important to check with an attorney and find out whether the business activity will be legal.

In fact, it's a good idea to retain a knowledgeable real estate attorney to negotiate a lease, especially if the rent is substantial and the term is long. That attorney can also give advice as to questions of legality. For example, what if the premises are in a commercial zone, but the entrepreneur wants to live and work there? This can be illegal and raise the specter of eviction by either the landlord or the local authorities.

In addition, the lease contains what is called the "use" clause. This specifies the purpose for which the premises are being rented. Often the lease will state that the premises can be used for the specified purpose and no other use is permitted. This limitation has to be observed or the tenant will run the risk of losing the premises. The tenant therefore has to seek the widest possible scope of use, certainly a scope sufficient to permit all of the intended business activities.

Another risk in terms of legality involves waste products or emissions that may not be legal in certain areas. Again, an attorney should be able to give advice about whether a planned activity might violate environmental protection as well as zoning laws.

The premises must lend themselves to the intended use. Loading ramps and elevators must be large enough to accommodate whatever must be moved in to set up the office (unless the tenant is willing and able to use a crane to move large pieces of equipment in through windows) and any products that need to be shipped once business is underway. Electric service must be adequate for air conditioning, computers, and other machinery. It must be possible to obtain telephone service and high-speed Internet connections. If the building is commercial and the tenant intends to work on weekends and evenings, then it will be necessary to ascertain whether the building is open and heated on weekends and evenings. If clients may come during off hours, it is even more important to make sure the building is open and elevator service is available.

Who will pay for bringing in electric lines, installing air conditioners, building any needed offices, installing fixtures, painting, or making other improvements? This will depend on the rental market, which dictates the relative bargaining strengths of the landlord and tenant. The lease (or an attached rider) must specify who will pay for each such improvement. It must also specify that the landlord gives the tenant permission to build what the tenant needs.

A related issue is who will own structures and equipment affixed to the premises when the lease term ends. Since the standard lease gives ownership to the landlord of anything affixed to the premises, the tenant must have this provision amended if anything of this nature is to be removed from the premises or sold to a new incoming tenant at the end of the lease term.

If the tenant has to make a significant investment in the costs of moving into and improving the premises, the tenant will want to be able to stay long enough to amortize this investment. One way to do this is to seek a long lease term, such as ten years. However, the landlord will inevitably want the rent to increase during the lease term. This leads to a dilemma for the tenant who can't be certain about the needs of the business or the rental market so far into the future.

One approach is to seek the longest possible lease, but negotiate for a right to terminate the lease. Another strategy would be to seek a shorter initial term, but have options to extend the lease for additional terms at agreed-upon rents. So, instead of asking for a ten-year lease, the tenant might ask for a four-year lease with two options for additional extensions of three years each.

Yet another tactic, and probably a wise provision to insist on in any event, is to have a right to sublet all or part of the premises or to assign the lease. The lease typically forbids this, so the tenant will have to demand such rights. Having the ability to sublet or assign offers another way to take a long lease while keeping the option to exit the premises if more space is needed, the rent becomes too high, or other circumstances necessitate a move. However, the right to sublet or assign will be of little use if the real estate market turns down, so it should probably be a supplement to a right to terminate or an option to renew.

Part of the problem with making a long-term commitment is that the stated rent is likely not going to be all of the rent. In other words, the lease may say that the rent is $2,400 per month for the first two years and then escalates to $3,000 per month for the next two years. But the tenant may have to pay for other increases or services. It is common for leases to provide for escalators based on increases in real estate taxes, increases in inflation, or increases in indexes designed to measure labor or operating costs. In fact, the standard lease will make the tenant responsible for all nonstructural repairs that are needed. The tenant has to evaluate all of these charges not only for reasonableness but for the impact on what will truly be paid each month. There may also be charges for refuse removal, cleaning (if the landlord provides this), window washing, water, and other services or supplies. If the landlord has installed submeters for electricity, this may result in paying far more to the landlord than would have been paid to the utility company. It may be possible to lessen the markup, obtain direct metering, or, at the least, factor this cost into considerations for the budget.

Faced with costs that may increase, the tenant should try to determine what is realistically likely to occur. Then, as a safeguard, the tenant might ask for ceilings on the amounts that can be charged in the various potential cost categories.

Leases are usually written documents. Whenever a written agreement exists between two parties, all amendments and modifications should also be in writing and signed by both parties. For example, the lease will probably require one or two months' rent as security. The tenant will want this rent to be kept in an interest-bearing account in the tenant's name. But if the parties agree to use part of the security to pay the rent at some point, this should be documented in a signed, written agreement.

The tenant should also seek to avoid having personal liability for the lease. Of course, if the tenant is doing business as a sole proprietor, the tenant, by signing the lease, will assume personal liability for payments. But if the tenant is a corporation, it would certainly be best not to have any officers or owners give personal guarantees that would place their personal assets at risk.

Leases can grow to become thick sheaves of paper filled with innumerable clauses of legalese. Since the lease agreement can be such an important one for a business, it is ideal to have a knowledgeable attorney as a companion when entering its maze of provisions. If an attorney is too expensive and the lease is short-term and at an affordable rent, then this discussion may give a clue that will help the tenant emerge from lease negotiations with success.

Form 23 is an educational tool. It has been drafted more favorably to the tenant than would usually be the case. Because it would be unlikely for the tenant to present a lease to the landlord, form 23 shows what the tenant might hope to obtain from the negotiations that begin with a lease form presented to the tenant by the landlord.

Forms 24 and 25 relate to a transformation of the role of the tenant. Whether to move to superior space, lessen cash outflow, or make a profit, the tenant may want to assign the lease or sublet all or a portion of the premises. Form 24 is for a sublease in which the tenant essentially becomes a landlord to a subtenant. Here the tenant must negotiate the same issues that were negotiated with the landlord, but from the other point of view. So, for example, while a corporate tenant would resist having its officers or owners give personal guarantees for a lease, when subletting, the same corporate tenant might demand such personal guarantees from a corporate subtenant. Form 25 for the assignment of a lease is less complicated than the sublease form. It essentially replaces the tenant with an assignee who becomes the new tenant and is fully responsible to comply with the lease. A key issue in such an assignment is whether the original tenant will remain liable to the landlord if the assignee fails to perform. A related issue

with a corporate assignee would be whether the assignee would give a personal guarantee of its performance. In any event, both the sublease and the assignment will usually require the written consent of the landlord. This consent can take the form of a letter signed by both the tenant and the landlord. In the case of an assignment, the letter of consent could also clarify whether the original tenant would have continuing liability pursuant to the lease.

Filling in Form 23 (Lease)

In the Preamble fill in the date and the names and addresses of the parties. In Paragraph 1 give the suite number, the approximate square footage, and floor for the premises as well as the address for the building. In Paragraph 2 give the number of years as well as the commencement and termination dates for the lease. In Paragraph 3 give a renewal term, if any, and indicate what modifications of the lease would take effect for the renewal term. In Paragraph 5 indicate the annual rent. In Paragraph 6 specify the number of months' rent that will be given as a security deposit. In Paragraph 7 indicate any work to be performed by the landlord and the completion date for that work. In Paragraph 8 specify the use that the tenant will make of the premises. In Paragraph 9 give the details as to alterations and installations to be done by the tenant and also indicate ownership and right to remove or sell these alterations and installations at the termination of the term. In Paragraph 10 indicate any repairs for which the tenant shall be responsible. In Paragraph 13 check the appropriate box with respect to air conditioning, fill in the blanks if the tenant is not paying for electricity or the landlord is not paying for water, and indicate who will be responsible for the cost of refuse removal. In Paragraph 14 state whether or not the landlord will have a key for access to the premises. In Paragraph 15 indicate the amount of liability insurance the tenant will be expected to carry as well as any limitation in terms of the landlord's liability for tenant's losses due to fire or other casualty affecting the building. In Paragraph 18 indicate which state's laws shall govern the agreement. Have both parties sign and append a rider, if necessary. Leases frequently have riders, which are attachments to the lease. This gives the space to add additional provisions or amplify details that require more space such as how construction or installations will be done. If there is such a rider, it should be signed by both parties.

Negotiation Checklist for Form 23

❏ If the tenant is a corporation, do not agree that any owner or officer of the corporation will have personal liability with respect to the lease.

❏ Consider whether, in view of the rental market, it may be possible to negotiate for a number of months rent-free at the start of the lease (in part, perhaps, to allow time for construction to be done by the tenant).

❏ In addition to rent-free months, determine what construction must be done and whether the landlord will do the construction or pay for all or part of the construction. (Paragraph 7)

❏ Since landlords generally rent based on gross square footage (which may be 15–20 percent more than net or usable square footage), carefully measure the net square footage to make certain it is adequate. (Paragraph 1)

❏ Specify the location and approximate square footage of the rented premises as well as the location of the building. (Paragraph 1)

❏ Indicate the duration of the term, including starting and ending dates. (Paragraph 2)

❏ Determine what will happen, including whether damages will be payable to the tenant, if the landlord is unable to deliver possession of the premises at the starting date of the lease.

❏ Especially if the lease gives the tenant the right to terminate, seek the longest possible lease term. (Paragraphs 2 and 4)

❏ Specify that the lease shall become month-to-month after the term expires. (Paragraph 2)

❏ If the landlord has the right to terminate the lease because the building is to be demolished or taken by eminent domain (i.e., acquired by a governmental body), consider whether damages should be payable by the landlord based on the remaining term of the lease.

❏ If the tenant is going to move out, consider whether it would be acceptable for the landlord to show the space prior to the tenant's departure and, if so, for how long prior to the departure and under what circumstances.

❏ Seek an option to renew for a specified term, such as three or five years, or perhaps several options to renew, such as for three years and then for another three years. (Paragraph 3)

❏ Seek the right to terminate the lease on written notice to the landlord. (Paragraph 4)

❏ Although the bankruptcy laws will affect what happens to the lease in the event of the tenant's bankruptcy, do not agree in the lease that the tenant's bankruptcy or insolvency will be grounds for termination of the lease.

❏ Specify the rent and indicate when it should be paid. (Paragraph 5)

❏ Carefully review any proposed increases in rent during the term of the lease. Try to resist adjustments for inflation. In any case, if an inflation index or a porter's wage index is to be used to increase the rent, study the particular index to see if the result is likely to be acceptable in terms of budgeting.

❏ Resist being responsible for additional rent based on a prorated share of increases in real estate taxes and, if such a provision is included, make certain how it is calculated and that it applies only to increases and not the entire tax.

❏ Resist having any of the landlord's cost treated as additional rent.

❏ Indicate the amount of the security deposit and require that it be kept in a separate, interest-bearing account. (Paragraph 6)

❏ Specify when the security deposit will be returned to the tenant. (Paragraph 6)

❏ If the tenant is not going to accept the premises "as is," indicate what work must be performed by the landlord and give a completion date for that work. (Paragraph 7)

❏ If the landlord is to do work, consider what the consequences should be in the event that the landlord is unable to complete the work on time.

❏ Agree to return the premises in broom-clean condition and good order except for normal wear and tear. (Paragraph 7)

❏ Seek the widest possible latitude with respect to what type of businesses the tenant may operate in the premises. (Paragraph 8)

❏ Consider asking that "for no other purpose" be stricken from the use clause.

❏ If the use may involve residential as well as business use, determine whether this is legal. If it is, the use clause might be widened to include the residential use.

❏ Obtain whatever permissions are needed for tenant's alterations or installation of equipment in the lease, rather than asking for permission after the lease has been signed. (Paragraph 9)

❏ If the tenant wants to own any installations or equipment affixed to the premises (such as an air conditioning system), this should be specified in the lease. (Paragraph 9)

❏ If the tenant owns certain improvements pursuant to the lease and might sell these to an incoming tenant, the mechanics of such a sale would have to be detailed because the new tenant might not take possession of the premises immediately and the value of what is to be sold will depend to some extent on the nature of the lease negotiated by the new tenant. (Paragraph 9)

❏ Nothing should prevent the tenant from removing its furniture and equipment that is not affixed to the premises. (Paragraph 9)

❏ Make landlord responsible for repairs in general and limit the responsibility of the tenant to specified types of repairs only. (Paragraph 10)

❏ Obtain the right to sublet all or part of the premises. (Paragraph 11)

❏ Obtain the right to assign the lease. (Paragraph 11)

❏ If the landlord has the right to approve a sublease or assignment, specify the basis on which approval will be determined (such as "good character and sound finances") and indicate that approval may not be withheld unreasonably. (Paragraph 11)

❏ If the tenant has paid for extensive improvements to the premises, a sublessee or assignee might be charged for a "fixture" fee.

❏ If a fixture fee is to be charged, or if the lease is being assigned pursuant to the sale of a business, do not give the landlord the right to share in the proceeds of the fixture fee or sale of the business.

❏ Guarantee the tenant's right to quiet enjoyment of the premises. (Paragraph 12)

❏ Make certain that tenant will be able to use the office seven days a week, twenty-four hours a day. (Paragraph 12)

❏ Review the certificate of occupancy as well as the lease before agreeing to occupy the premises in accordance with the lease, the building's certificate of occupancy, and all relevant laws. (Paragraph 12)

❏ Determine who will provide and pay for utilities and services, such as air conditioning, heat, water, electricity, cleaning, window cleaning, and refuse removal. (Paragraph 13)

❏ The landlord will want the right to gain access to the premises, especially for repairs or in the event of an emergency. (Paragraph 14)

❏ Decide whether the landlord and its employees are trustworthy enough to be given keys to the premises, which has the advantage of avoiding a forced entry in the event of an emergency. (Paragraph 14)

❏ Make the landlord an additional named insured for the tenant's liability insurance policy. (Paragraph 15)

❏ Fix the amount of liability insurance that the tenant must maintain at a reasonable level. (Paragraph 15)

❏ Specify that the landlord will carry casualty and fire insurance for the building. (Paragraph 15)

❏ Indicate what limit of liability, if any, the landlord is willing to accept for interruption or harm to tenant's business. (Paragraph 15)

❏ Agree that the lease is subordinate to any mortgage or underlying lease on the building. (Paragraph 16)

❏ If the lease requires waiver of the right to trial by jury, consider whether this is acceptable.

❏ If the lease provides for payment of the legal fees of the landlord in the event of litigation, seek to have this either stricken or changed so that the legal fees of the winning party are paid.

❏ Indicate that any rider, which is an attachment to the lease to add clauses or explain the details of certain aspects of the lease such as those relating to construction, is made part of the lease.

❏ Review the standard provisions in the introductory pages and compare them with Paragraph 18.

Filling in Form 24 (Sublease)

In the Preamble fill in the date and the names and addresses of the parties. In Paragraph 1 give the information about the lease between the landlord and tenant and attach a copy of that lease as Exhibit A of the sublease. In Paragraph 2 give the suite number, the approximate square footage, and floor for the premises as well as the address for the building. If only part of the space is to be subleased, indicate which part. In Paragraph 3 give the number of years as well as the commencement and termination dates for the lease. In Paragraph 4 indicate the annual rent. In Paragraph 5 specify the number of months' rent that will be given as a security deposit. In Paragraph 7 specify the use that the subtenant will make of the premises. In Paragraph 8 indicate whether the subtenant will be excused from compliance with any of the provisions of the lease or whether some provisions will be modified with respect to the subtenant. For Paragraph 10, attach the landlord's consent as Exhibit B if that is needed. For Paragraph 11, if the tenant is leaving property for the use of the subtenant, attach Exhibit C detailing that property. If the lease has been recorded, perhaps with the county clerk, indicate where the recordation can be found in Paragraph 14. Add any additional provisions in Paragraph 15. In Paragraph 16 indicate which state's laws shall govern the agreement. Both parties should then sign the sublease.

Negotiation Checklist for Form 24

❏ If the subtenant is a corporation, consider whether to insist that owners or officers of the corporation will have personal liability with respect to the sublease. (See Other Provisions.)

❏ If possible, do not agree to rent-free months at the start of the sublease or to paying for construction for the subtenant.

❏ Specify the location and approximate square footage of the rented premises as well as the location of the building. (Paragraphs 1 and 2)

❏ Indicate the duration of the term, including starting and ending dates. (Paragraph 3)

❏ Specify that the lease shall become month-to-month after the term expires. (Paragraph 3)

❏ Disclaim any liability if, for some reason, the tenant is unable to deliver possession of the premises at the starting date of the sublease.

❏ Do not give the subtenant a right to terminate.

❏ Do not give the subtenant an option to renew.

❏ Have a right to show the space for three or six months prior to the end of the sublease.

❏ State in the sublease that the subtenant's bankruptcy or insolvency will be grounds for termination of the lease.

❏ Specify the rent and indicate when it should be paid. (Paragraph 4)

❏ Require that rent be paid to the tenant (which allows the tenant to monitor payments), unless the tenant believes that it would be safe to allow the subtenant to pay the landlord directly. (Paragraph 4)

❏ Carefully review any proposed increases in rent during the term of the lease and make certain that the sublease will at least match such increases.

❏ Indicate the amount of the security deposit (Paragraph 5)

❏ Specify that reductions may be made to the security deposit for sums owed the tenant before the balance is returned to the subtenant. (Paragraph 5)

❏ Require the subtenant to return the premises in broom-clean condition and good order except for normal wear and tear. (Paragraph 6)

❏ Specify very specifically what type of businesses the tenant may operate in the premises. (Paragraph 7)

❏ Do not allow "for no other purpose" to be stricken from the use clause.

❏ Nothing should prevent the subtenant from removing furniture and equipment that is not affixed to the premises.

❏ Require the subtenant to occupy the premises in accordance with the sublease, the lease, the building's certificate of occupancy, and all relevant laws. (Paragraph 8)

❏ Indicate if any of the lease's provisions will not be binding on the subtenant or have been modified. (Paragraph 8)

❏ State clearly that the tenant is not obligated to perform the landlord's duties and that the subtenant must look to the landlord for such performance. (Paragraph 9)

❏ Agree to cooperate with the subtenant in requiring the landlord to meet its obligations, subject to a right of reimbursement from subtenant for any costs or attorney's fees the tenant must pay in the course of cooperating. (Paragraph 9)

❏ If the landlord's consent must be obtained for the sublet, attach a copy of the consent to the sublease as Exhibit B. (Paragraph 10)

❏ If tenant is going to let its property be used by the subtenant, attach an inventory of this property as Exhibit C and require that the property be returned in good condition. (Paragraph 11)

❏ Have the subtenant indemnify the tenant against any claims with respect to the premises that arise after the effective date of the sublease.

❏ Do not give the subtenant the right to subsublet all or part of the premises.

❏ Do not give the subtenant the right to assign the sublease.

❏ If the lease has been recorded with a government office, indicate how it can be located. (Paragraph 14)

❏ Add any additional provisions that may be necessary. (Paragraph 15)

❏ Review the standard provisions in the introductory pages and compare them with Paragraph 16.

Filling in Form 25 (Lease Assignment)

In the Preamble fill in the date and the names and addresses of the parties. In Paragraph 1 give the information about the lease between the landlord and tenant and attach a copy of that lease as Exhibit A of the lease assignment. In Paragraph 3 enter an amount, even a small amount such as $10, as cash consideration. For Paragraph 8, attach the landlord's consent as Exhibit B if that is needed. If the lease has been recorded, perhaps with the county clerk, indicate where the recordation can be found in Paragraph 9. Add any additional provisions in Paragraph 10. In Paragraph 11 indicate which state's laws shall govern the agreement. Both parties should then sign the assignment.

Checklist for Form 25

❏ In obtaining the landlord's consent in a simple letter, demand that the tenant not be liable for the lease and that the landlord look only to the assignee for performance. (See Other Provisions.)

❏ It would be wise to specify the amount of security deposits or any other money held in escrow by the landlord for the tenant/assignor.

❏ Consideration should exchange hands and, if the lease has extra value because of tenant's improvements or an upturn in the rental market, the consideration may be substantial. (Paragraph 3)

❏ Require the assignee to perform as if it were the original tenant in the lease. (Paragraph 4)

❏ Have the assignee indemnify the tenant/assignor with respect to any claims and costs that may arise from the lease after the date of the assignment. (Paragraph 5)

❏ Make the assignee's obligations run to the benefit of the landlord as well as the tenant. (Paragraph 6)

❏ Indicate that the assignor has the right to assign and the premises are not encumbered in any way.

❏ If the landlord's consent must be obtained for the assignment, attach a copy of the consent to the sublease as Exhibit B. (Paragraph 8)

❏ If the lease has been recorded with a government office, indicate how it can be located. (Paragraph 9)

❏ Add any additional provisions that may be necessary. (Paragraph 10)

❏ Review the standard provisions in the introductory pages and compare them with Paragraph 11.

Other Provisions That Can Be Used with Forms 24 or 25

❏ Personal Guaranty. The tenant who sublets or assigns is bringing in another party to help carry the weight of the tenant's responsibilities pursuant to the lease. If the sublessee or assignee is a corporation, the tenant will only be able to go after the corporate assets if the other party fails to meet its obligations. The tenant may, therefore, want to have officers or owners agree to personal liability if the corporation breaches the lease. One or more principals could sign a guaranty, which would be attached to and made a part of the sublease or assignment. The guaranty that follows is for a sublease but could easily be altered to be for an assignment:

Personal Guaranty. This guaranty by the Undersigned is given to induce _____ _____ (hereinafter referred to as the "Tenant") to enter into the sublease dated as of the _____ day of _____, 20____, between the Tenant and _____ (hereinafter referred to as the "Sublessee"). That sublease would not be entered into by the Tenant without this guaranty, which is made part of the sublease agreement. The relationship of the Undersigned to the Sublessee is as follows_____ _____. Undersigned fully and unconditionally guarantees to Tenant the full payment of all rent due and other amounts payable pursuant to the Sublease. The Undersigned shall remain fully bound on this guaranty regardless of any extension, modification, waiver, release, discharge, or substitution of any party with respect to the Sublease. The Undersigned waives any requirement of notice and, in the event of default, may be sued directly without any requirement that the Tenant

first sue the Sublessee. In addition, the Undersigned guarantees the payment of all attorney's fees and costs incurred in the enforcement of this guaranty. This guaranty is unlimited as to amount or duration and may only be modified or terminated by a written instrument signed by all parties to the Sublease and Guaranty. This guaranty shall be binding and inure to the benefit of the parties hereto, their heirs, successors, assigns, and personal representatives.

❏ Assignor's Obligations. In the case of an assignment, the tenant/assignor may ask the landlord for a release from its obligations pursuant to the lease. If the landlord gives such a release, perhaps in return for some consideration or because the new tenant has excellent credentials, the tenant would want this to be included in a written instrument. This would probably be the letter of consent that the landlord would have to give to permit the assignment to take place. Shown here are options to release the tenant and also to do the opposite and affirm the tenant's continuing obligations.

Assignor's Obligations. Check the applicable provision: ❏ This Agreement relieves and discharges the Assignor from any continuing liability or obligation with respect to the Lease after the effective date of the lease assignment. ❏ This Agreement does not relieve, modify, discharge, or otherwise affect the obligations of the Assignor under the Lease and the direct and primary nature thereof.

Commercial Lease

AGREEMENT, dated the _____ day of _____, 20 _____, between_____
_____ (hereinafter referred to as the "Tenant"),
whose address is _____
_____ and
_____(hereinafter referred to as the
"Landlord"), whose address is _____
_____

WHEREAS, the Tenant wishes to rent premises for office use;

WHEREAS, the Landlord has premises for rental for such office use;

NOW, THEREFORE, in consideration of the foregoing premises and the mutual covenants hereinafter set forth and other valuable considerations, the parties hereto agree as follows:

1. Demised premises. The premises rented hereunder are Suite # _____, comprising approximately _____ square feet, on the _____ floor of the building located at the following address _____ in the city or town of _____ in the state of _____.

2. Term. The term shall be for a period of _____ years (unless the term shall sooner cease and expire pursuant to the terms of this Lease), commencing on the _____ day of _____, 20__, and ending on the _____ day of _____, 20__. At the expiration of the term and any renewals thereof pursuant to Paragraph 3, the Lease shall become a month-to-month tenancy with all other provisions of the Lease in full force and effect.

3. Option to Renew. The Tenant shall have an option to renew the lease for a period of _____ years. Such option must be exercised in writing prior to the expiration of the term specified in Paragraph 2. During such renewal term, all other provisions of the Lease shall remain in full force and effect except for the following modifications _____.

4. Termination. The Tenant shall retain the right to terminate this Lease at the end of any month by giving the Landlord thirty (30) days written notice.

5. Rent. The annual rent shall be $_____, payable in equal monthly installments on the first day of each month to the Landlord at Landlord's address or such other address as Landlord may specify. The first month's rent shall be paid on signing this Lease.

6. Security Deposit. The security deposit shall be in the amount of ___ month(s) rent and shall be paid by check at the time of signing this Lease. The security deposit shall be increased at such times as the monthly rent increases, so as to maintain the security deposit at the level of ___ month(s) rent. The security deposit shall be kept in a separate interest-bearing account with interest payable to the Tenant. The security deposit, after reduction for any sums owed to Landlord, shall be returned to the Tenant within ten (10) days of the Tenant's vacating the premises.

7. Condition of Premises. Tenant has inspected the premises and accepts them in "as is" condition except for the following work to be performed by Landlord _____ _____ and completed by _____, 20___. At the termination of the Lease, Tenant shall remove all its property and return possession of the premises broom-clean and in good order and condition, normal wear and tear excepted, to the Landlord.

8. Use. The Tenant shall use and occupy the premises for _____ and for no other purpose.

9. Alterations. Tenant shall obtain Landlord's written approval to make any alterations that are structural or affect utility services, plumbing, or electric lines, except that Landlord consents to the following alterations _____ _____. In addition, Landlord consents to the installation by the Tenant of the following equipment and fixtures _____ _____ _____. Landlord shall own all improvements affixed to the premises, except that the Tenant shall own the following improvements _____ _____ and have the right to either remove them or sell them to a new incoming tenant. If Landlord consents to the ownership and sale of improvements by the Tenant, such sale shall be conducted in the following way _____ _____. If Landlord consents to Tenant's ownership and right to remove certain improvements, Tenant shall repair any damages caused by such removal. Nothing contained herein shall prevent Tenant from removing its trade fixtures, moveable office furniture and equipment, and other items not affixed to the premises.

10. Repairs. Repairs to the building and common areas shall be the responsibility of the Landlord. In addition, repairs to the premises shall be the responsibility of the Landlord except for the following_____ _____.

11. Assignment and Subletting. Tenant shall have the right to assign this Lease to an assignee of good character and sound finances subject to obtaining the written approval of the Landlord, which approval shall not be unreasonably withheld. In addition, Tenant shall have the right to sublet all or a portion of the premises on giving written notice to the Landlord.

12. Quiet Enjoyment. Tenant may quietly and peaceably enjoy occupancy of the premises. Tenant shall have access to the premises at all times and, if necessary, shall be given a key to enter the building. Tenant shall use and occupy the premises in accordance with this Lease, the building's certificate of occupancy, and all relevant laws.

13. Utilities and Services. During the heating season the Landlord at its own expense shall supply heat to the premises at all times on business days and on Saturdays and Sundays. The Landlord ❏ shall ❏ shall not supply air conditioning for the premises at its own expense. The Tenant shall pay the electric bills for the meter for the premises, unless another arrangement exists as follows _____.
The Landlord shall provide and pay for water for the premises, unless another arrangement exists as follows _____. Tenant shall be responsible for and pay for having its own premises cleaned, including the securing of licensed window cleaners. ❏ Tenant ❏ Landlord shall be responsible to pay for the removal of refuse from the premises. If Landlord is responsible to pay for such removal, the Tenant shall comply with Landlord's reasonable regulations regarding the manner, time, and location of refuse pickups.

14. Access to Premises. Landlord and its agents shall have the right, upon reasonable notice to the Tenant, to enter the premises to make repairs, improvements, or replacements. In the event of emergency, the Landlord and its agents may enter the premises without notice to the Tenant. Tenant ❏ shall ❏ shall not provide the Landlord with keys for the premises.

15. Insurance. Tenant agrees to carry liability insurance and name Landlord as an additional named insured under its policy and furnish to Landlord certificates showing liability coverage of not less than $_____ for the premises. Such company shall give the Landlord ten (10) days notice prior to cancellation of any such policy. Failure to obtain or keep in force such liability insurance shall allow Landlord to obtain such coverage and charge the amount of premiums as additional rent payable by the Tenant. Landlord agrees to carry casualty and fire insurance on the building, but shall not have any liability in excess of $_____ with respect to the operation of the Tenant's business.

16. Subordination. This Lease is subordinate and subject to all ground or underlying leases and any mortgages that may now or hereafter affect such leases or the building of which the premises are a part. The operation of this provision shall be automatic and not require any further consent from Tenant. To confirm this subordination, Tenant shall promptly execute any documentation that Landlord may request.

17. Rider. Additional terms may be contained in a Rider attached to and made part of this Lease.

18. Miscellany. This Lease shall be binding upon the parties hereto, their heirs, successors, assigns, and personal representatives. This Agreement constitutes the entire understanding between the parties. Its terms can be modified only by an instrument in writing signed by both parties unless specified to the contrary herein. A waiver of a breach of any of the provisions of this Agreement shall not be construed as a continuing waiver of other breaches of the same or other provisions hereof. This Agreement shall be governed by the laws of the State of _____.

IN WITNESS WHEREOF, the parties hereto have signed this Agreement as of the date first set forth above.

Tenant _____   Landlord _____
           Company Name   Company Name

By_____   By_____
        Authorized Signatory, Title   Authorized Signatory, Title

Sublease

AGREEMENT, dated the _____ day of _____, 20 ____, between _____ (hereinafter referred to as the "Tenant"), whose address is _____ _____ and _____(hereinafter referred to as the "Subtenant"), whose address is _____.

WHEREAS, the Tenant wishes to sublet certain rental premises for office use;

WHEREAS, the Subtenant wishes to occupy such rental premises for such office use;

NOW, THEREFORE, in consideration of the foregoing premises and the mutual covenants hereinafter set forth and other valuable considerations, the parties hereto agree as follows:

1. **The Lease.** The premises are subject to a Lease dated as of the ____ day of _____, 20__, between _____ (referred to therein as the "Tenant") and _____ (referred to therein as the "Landlord") for the premises described as _____ and located at _____ _____. A copy of the Lease is attached hereto as Exhibit A and made part hereof. Subtenant shall have no right to negotiate with the Landlord with respect to the Lease.

2. **Demised premises.** The premises rented hereunder are Suite # _____, comprising approximately _____ square feet, on the _____ floor of the building located at the following address _____ in the city or town of _____ in the state of _____. If only a portion of the premises subject to the Lease are to be sublet, the sublet portion is specified as follows _____.

3. **Term.** The term shall be for a period of _____ years (unless the term shall sooner cease and expire pursuant to the terms of this Sublease), commencing on the ____ day of _____, 20__, and ending on the ____ day of _____, 20__. At the expiration of the term and any renewals thereof pursuant to Paragraph 3, the Sublease shall become a month-to-month tenancy with all other provisions of the Sublease in full force and effect.

4. **Rent.** The annual rent shall be $_____, payable in equal monthly installments on the first day of each month to the Tenant at Tenant's address or such other address as Tenant may specify. The Subtenant shall also pay as additional rent any other charges that the Tenant must pay to the Landlord pursuant to the lease. Subtenant shall make payments of rent and other charges to the Tenant only and not to Landlord. The first month's rent shall be paid to the Tenant on signing this Sublease.

5. **Security Deposit.** The security deposit shall be in the amount of ___ month(s) rent and shall be paid by check at the time of signing this Sublease. The security deposit shall be increased at such times as the monthly rent increases, so as to maintain the security deposit at the level of ___ month(s) rent. The security deposit, after reduction for any sums owed to Tenant, shall be returned to the Subtenant within ten (10) days of the Subtenant's vacating the premises.

6. **Condition of Premises.** Subtenant has inspected the premises and accepts them in "as is" condition. At the termination of the Sublease, Subtenant shall remove all its property and return possession of the premises broom-clean and in good order and condition, normal wear and tear excepted, to the Tenant.

7. **Use.** The Subtenant shall use and occupy the premises for _____ and for no other purpose.

8. **Compliance.** Subtenant shall use and occupy the premises in accordance with this Sublease. In addition, the Subtenant shall obey the terms of the Lease (and any agreements to which the Lease, by its terms, is subject), the building's certificate of occupancy, and all relevant laws. If the Subtenant is not to be subject to certain terms of the Lease or if any terms of the Lease are to be modified for purposes of this Sublease, the specifics are as follows _____ _____.

9. Landlord's Duties. The Tenant is not obligated to perform the duties of the Landlord pursuant to the Lease. Any failure of the Landlord to perform its duties shall be subject to the Subtenant dealing directly with the Landlord until Landlord fulfills its obligations. Copies of any notices sent to the Landlord by the Subtenant shall also be provided to the Tenant. Tenant shall cooperate with Subtenant in the enforcement of Subtenant's rights against the Landlord, but any costs or fees incurred by the Tenant in the course of such cooperation shall be reimbursed by the Subtenant pursuant to Paragraph 12.

10. Landlord's Consent. If the Landlord's consent must be obtained for this Sublease, that consent has been obtained by the Tenant and is attached hereto as Exhibit B and made part hereof.

11. Inventory. An inventory of Tenant's fixtures, furnishings, equipment, and other property to be left in the premises is attached hereto as Exhibit C and made part hereof. Subtenant agrees to maintain these items in good condition and repair and to replace or reimburse the Tenant for any of these items that are missing or damaged at the termination of the subtenancy.

12. Indemnification. The Subtenant shall indemnify and hold harmless the Tenant from any and all claims, suits, costs, damages, judgments, settlements, attorney's fees, court costs, or any other expenses arising with respect to the Lease subsequent to the date of this Agreement. The Tenant shall indemnify and hold harmless the Subtenant from any and all claims, suits, costs, damages, judgments, settlements, attorney's fees, court costs, or any other expenses arising with respect to the Lease prior to the date of this Agreement.

13. Assignment and Subletting. Subtenant shall not have the right to assign this Lease or to sublet all or a portion of the premises without the written approval of the Landlord.

14. Recordation. The Lease has been recorded in the office of _____ on the ____ day of _____, 20___, and is located at _____.

15. Additional provisions: _____
_____
_____.

16. Miscellany. This Lease shall be binding upon the parties hereto, their heirs, successors, assigns, and personal representatives. This Agreement constitutes the entire understanding between the parties. Its terms can be modified only by an instrument in writing signed by both parties unless specified to the contrary herein. A waiver of a breach of any of the provisions of this Agreement shall not be construed as a continuing waiver of other breaches of the same or other provisions hereof. This Agreement shall be governed by the laws of the State of _____.

IN WITNESS WHEREOF, the parties hereto have signed this Agreement as of the date first set forth above.

Subtenant _____   Tenant _____
                 Company Name   Company Name

By_____   By_____
       Authorized Signatory, Title   Authorized Signatory, Title

Lease Assignment

AGREEMENT, dated the _____ day of _____, 20 _____, between _____ _____ (hereinafter referred to as the "Assignor"), whose address is _____ _____ and (hereinafter referred to as the "Assignee"), whose address is_____ _____.

WHEREAS, the Assignor wishes to assign its Lease to certain rental premises for office use;

WHEREAS, the Assignee wishes to accept the Lease assignment of such rental premises for such office use;

NOW, THEREFORE, in consideration of the foregoing premises and the mutual covenants hereinafter set forth and other valuable considerations, the parties hereto agree as follows:

1. **The Lease.** The Lease assigned is dated as of the _____ day of _____, 20___, between _____ (referred to therein as the "Tenant") and _____ (referred to therein as the "Landlord") for the premises described as _____ and located at _____. A copy of the Lease is attached hereto as Exhibit A and made part hereof.

2. **Assignment.** The Assignor hereby assigns to the Assignee all the Assignor's right, title, and interest in the Lease and any security deposits held by the Landlord pursuant to the Lease.

3. **Consideration.** The Assignee has been paid $_____ and other good and valuable consideration for entering into this Agreement.

4. **Performance.** As of the date of this Agreement the Assignee shall promptly perform all of the Tenant's obligations pursuant to the Lease, including but not limited to the payment of rent, and shall assume full responsibility as if the Assignee had been the Tenant who entered into the Lease.

5. **Indemnification.** The Assignor shall indemnify and hold harmless the Assignee from any and all claims, suits, costs, damages, judgments, settlements, attorney's fees, court costs, or any other expenses arising with respect to the Lease subsequent to the date of this Agreement. The Assignee shall indemnify and hold harmless the Assignor from any and all claims, suits, costs, damages, judgments, settlements, attorney's fees, court costs, or any other expenses arising with respect to the Lease prior to the date of this Agreement.

6. **Benefitted Parties.** The Assignee's obligations assumed under this Agreement shall be for the benefit of the Landlord as well as the benefit of the Assignor.

7. **Right to Assign.** The Assignor warrants that the premises are unencumbered by any judgments, liens, executions, taxes, assessments, or other charges; that the Lease has not been modified from the version shown as Exhibit A; and that Assignor has the right to assign the Lease.

8. **Landlord's Consent.** If the Landlord's consent must be obtained prior to assignment of the Lease, that consent has been obtained by the Assignor and is attached hereto as Exhibit B and made part hereof.

9. **Recordation.** The Lease has been recorded in the office of _____ on the ____ day of _____, 20___, and is located at _____.

10. Additional provisions: _____

_____

_____.

11. Miscellany. This Agreement shall be binding upon the parties hereto, their heirs, successors, assigns, and personal representatives. This Agreement constitutes the entire understanding between the parties. Its terms can be modified only by an instrument in writing signed by both parties unless specified to the contrary herein. A waiver of a breach of any of the provisions of this Agreement shall not be construed as a continuing waiver of other breaches of the same or other provisions hereof. This Agreement shall be governed by the laws of the State of _____.

IN WITNESS WHEREOF, the parties hereto have signed this Agreement as of the date first set forth above.

Assignee _____   Assignor _____
                    Company Name   Company Name

By_____   By_____
            Authorized Signatory, Title   Authorized Signatory, Title

Index

About the Author

Tad Crawford, president and publisher of Allworth Press in New York City, studied economics at Tufts University, graduated from Columbia Law School, clerked on New York State's highest court, and represented many artists and arts organizations when he actively practiced as an attorney. Author or coauthor of twelve books on business and the creative professions, he is Legal Affairs editor for *Communication Arts* magazine and has also written articles for magazines such as *Art in America, Family Circle, Glamour, The Nation, The Writer,* and *Writer's Digest.* He served as Chairman of the Board of the Foundation for the Community of Artists, General Counsel for the Graphic Artists Guild, and Legislative Counsel for the Coalition of Visual Artists' Organizations. For the Coalition, he lobbied for state and federal artists' rights legislation. He has addressed most of the national arts organizations and served as a faculty member at the School of Visual Arts in New York City. The recipient of the Graphic Artists Guild's first Walter Hortens Memorial Award for service to artists, he has also been a grant recipient from the National Endowment for the Arts for his writing on behalf of artists.

Books by Tad Crawford

AIGA Professional Practices in Graphic Design (editor)
The Artist-Gallery Partnership (with Susan Mellon)
Business and Legal Forms for Fine Artists
Business and Legal Forms for Graphic Designers (with Eva Doman Bruck)
Business and Legal Forms for Illustrators
Business and Legal Forms for Interior Designers (with Eva Doman Bruck)
Business and Legal Forms for Industrial Designers (with Eva Doman Bruck and Carl W. Battle)
Business and Legal Forms for Photographers
The Money Mentor
The Secret Life of Money
Selling Your Photography (with Arie Kopelman)
Selling Your Graphic Design and Illustration (with Arie Kopelman)
Starting Your Career as a Freelance Photographer
The Writer's Legal Guide (with Kay Murray)

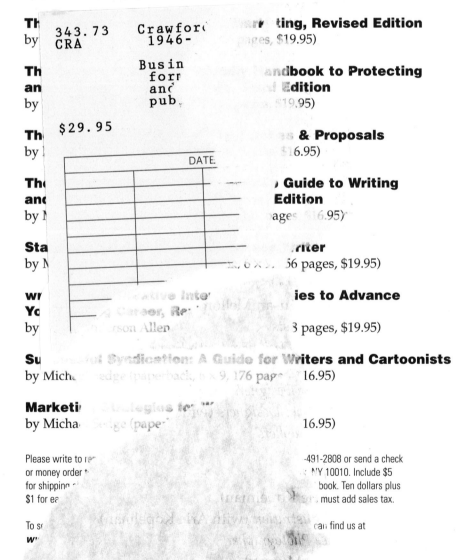